KING
DECISIONS

A MULTIDISCIPLINARY INTRODUCTION

D1298688

DATE LOANED

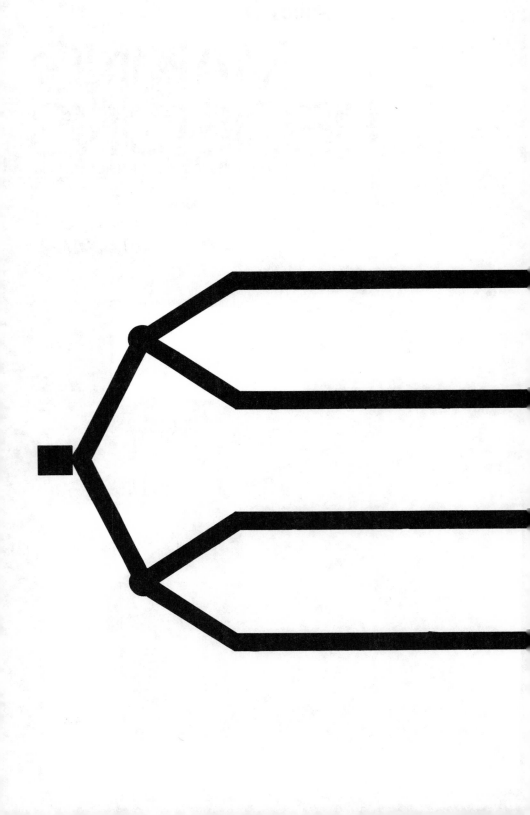

MAKING DECISIONS

A MULTIDISCIPLINARY INTRODUCTION

Foreword by
JEAN MAYER, *President, Tufts University*

PERCY H. HILL
S.M., *Engineering Design*

HUGO A. BEDAU
Ph.D., *Philosophy*

RICHARD A. CHECHILE
Ph.D., *Psychology*

WILLIAM J. CROCHETIERE
Ph.D., *Engineering Design*

BARBARA L. KELLERMAN
Ph.D. *Political Science*

DANIEL OUNJIAN
Ph.D., *Economics*

STEPHEN G. PAUKER
M.D., *Medicine*

SUSAN P. PAUKER
M.D., *Pediatrics*

JEFFREY Z. RUBIN
Ph.D., *Psychology*

UNIVERSITY
PRESS OF
AMERICA

LANHAM • NEW YORK • LONDON

Library of Congress Cataloging in Publication Data

Making decisions.

   Includes bibliographies and index.
   1. Decision-making—Mathematical models.
2. Decision-making—Case studies.   I. Hill, Percy H.
HD30.23.M34   1986   658.4'03   86-9057
ISBN 0-8191-5388-5 (pbk. : alk. paper)

Contents

Biographical Data

THE CONTRIBUTORS

Percy H. Hill holds a bachelor's degree in mechanical engineering from Rensselaer Polytechnic Institute and a master of science degree from Harvard University. He has been an instructor at Virginia Polytechnic Institute and a lecturer at the Lincoln Institute of Northeastern University, as well as a consultant for industrial and governmental organizations. Since 1948 he has been on the faculty at Tufts University, where he holds the titles of university professor and chairman of the Department of Engineering Design. Hill is a registered professional engineer in Massachusetts and New Hampshire and holds a patent on Johnson and Johnson's "Reach" toothbrush. The author of many publications involving engineering, mathematics, and design, Hill is a member of the American Association of University Professors, the American Society for Engineering Education, the American Society for Mechanical Engineers, the national honor societies Tau Beta Pi and Sigma Xi, the Creative Education Foundation, and the Human Factors Society. The recipient of the Frank Oppenheimer Award for 1968 and the Distinguished

The Contributors
(continued)

Service Award from the American Society for Engineering Education, Engineering Design, Graphics Division in 1977, Hill is listed in *Engineers of Distinction, Who's Who in American Education,* and *Who's Who in Massachusetts.*

Hugo A. Bedau

holds a bachelor of arts degree from the University of Redlands, master's degrees from Boston University and Harvard University, and a doctorate from Harvard. He has taught at Dartmouth College, Princeton University, and Reed College. Since 1966 he has been on the faculty at Tufts University, where he holds the title of Austin Fletcher Professor of Philosophy. He is the author of *The Courts, The Constitution, and Capital Punishment,* co-author of *Victimless Crimes: Two Views,* and the editor of several other volumes. He is also the author of numerous articles and reviews in philosophical, legal, and political journals and magazines. Bedau has received research grants from the Russell Sage Foundation and the Social Science Research Council, travel grants from the Foundation for Research in Philosophy of Science and the American Council of Learned Societies, and fellowships from Harvard Law School and the Danforth Foundation. He is a member of the American Philosophical Association, the American Society for Political and Legal Philosophy, the Society for Philosophy and Public Affairs, the American Association of University Professors, and the American Civil Liberties Union, and is listed in *Who's Who.*

Richard A. Chechile

holds a B.S. and M.S. in physics from Case-Western Reserve University and an M.S. and Ph.D. in experimental psychology from the University of Pittsburgh. He has been a teaching fellow at Case-Western University and the University of Pittsburgh and a National Science Foundation pre-doctoral trainee psychology at

The Contributors
(continued)

the University of Pittsburgh. Chechile has worked in research and development for the General Electric Company, Rockwell International, and Philco Ford. Since 1973, he has been assistant professor of psychology at Tufts University. Chechile received a grant from the National Aeronautics and Space Administration to study psychometric modeling of the human information processing demands of interactions with avionic computers. The author of many publications in the areas of physics and psychology, Chechile is a member of the American Psychological Association, the American Statistical Association, the Eastern Psychological Association, the Mathematical Psychological Association, the Psychonomic Society, the national science honor society, Sigma Xi, and the Scientific Research Society of North America.

William J. Crochetiere

received a B.S. in electrical engineering from Tufts University and M.S. and Ph.D. degrees in engineering from Case Institute of Technology in 1964 and 1967. He has been an industrial apprentice at General Electric Company, a lecturer at Ohio State University, and a research assistant, project engineer, and research associate at Case Institute. Since 1967, he has been on the faculty at Tufts University, where he is associate professor of engineering design and assistant professor of physical and rehabilitation medicine. Crochetiere received the Oppenheimer Award for "Excellence in Presentation" at a national meeting of the Engineering Design Graphics Division of the American Society for Engineering Education (ASEE) in 1970, and the National Aeronautics and Space Administration-ASEE Fellowship in Systems Design in 1969. He is a full member of the national honor societies, Sigma Xi and Tau Beta Pi. A registered engineer in Massachusetts and Maine, Crochetiere is the author of many publications concerning physical

The Contributors
(continued)

rehabilitation, electricity, and electronics. He is a member of the Institute of Electrical and Electronic Engineers, the American Association of University Professors, and the American Society for Engineering Education.

Barbara L. Kellerman

holds a B.A. from Sarah Lawrence College, a master's degree in Russian and East European studies from Yale University, and a master of philosophy and doctorate in political science from Yale. The recipient of a Fulbright certificate in political science from the University of Bonn, she is the author of *Willy Brandt: Portrait of the Leader as a Young Politician* and several political science publications. Since 1976, she has been an assistant professor of political science at Tufts University. Kellerman held a Danforth graduate fellowship in 1969-75 and Fulbright fellowships in 1972 and 1973. A member of the American Political Science Association, the Women's Caucus for Political Science, the American Council on Germany and the Society for Values in Higher Education, she is currently involved in research concerning the political functions of the presidential family and the democratic executive in comparative perspective.

Daniel Ounjian

holds an A.B. in economics from Tufts University and a doctorate in economics from Harvard University. He has been a research economist for the Federal Reserve Bank of Boston and a consultant for the U.S. Agency for International Development in Ethiopia and Sudan. Since 1962, he has been on the faculty at Tufts University, where he holds the titles of university professor and department chairman. He has also been a consultant to the Massachusetts Board of Higher Education, participated in panel discussions with industrial and governmental organizations, and lectured at

The Contributors
(continued)

Simmons College and Northeastern University. Ounjian received the Outstanding Educator of America Award for 1974-75, the National Science Foundation Summer Institute Awards for 1972 and 1973, and the Dissertation Research Award of the Federal Reserve Bank of Boston in 1960. He was also one of several recipients of a grant from the National Science Foundation Industrial Undergraduate Participation Project in 1977, 1978, and 1979. He is the author of *Long Term Public Financing of Small Corporations — The Reg A Market* and co-author of *A History of Investment Banking in New England.*

Stephen G. Pauker, M.D.
and
Susan P. Pauker, M.D.

are co-authors of many genetic counseling medical publications. Dr. Stephen Pauker holds a bachelor of arts degree from Harvard College and an M.D. from Harvard Medical School. An associate professor of medicine at Tufts University School of Medicine and a physician at the New England Medical Center Hospital, he received the Bausch and Lomb Science Award in 1960, the Massachusetts Medical Society Award in 1968, and the Research Career Development Award from the General Medical Sciences Institute of the National Institutes of Health in 1977. He is a fellow of the American College of Physicians, the American College of Cardiology, and the American Heart Association's Council on Clinical Cardiology.

Dr. Susan Pauker holds a B.S. from Jackson College and an M.D. from Tufts University School of Medicine. A fellow of the American Academy of Pediatrics, she is presently chief of pediatrics and clinical geneticist for the Harvard Community Health Plan.

Jeffrey Z. Rubin

holds a B.A. in biology form Antioch College and a doctorate in psychology from Teachers College, Columbia University. He has been a research and teaching assistant at Teachers College and a National Institute of Mental Health postdoctoral research fellow at the University of North Carolina. Since 1969 he has been on the faculty at Tufts University, where he currently holds the title of associate professor of psychology. Rubin received the American Psychological Association's Young Psychologists Award in 1969 and the John Simon Guggenheim Memorial Foundation Fellowship for 1977-78. He is co-author of the books *Social Psychology: People in Groups* and *The Social Psychology of Bargaining and Negotiation,* as well as many experimental papers on psychology and the behavioral sciences. Rubin is a member of the American Psychological Association, the Society for the Psychological Study of Social Issues, the Eastern Psychological Association, the New England Psychological Association, the New England Social Psychological Association, and the International Studies Association.

Foreword

In this tense, ever more crowded, ever more interdependent world, wise decision making is becoming more and more crucial. At present, we are not very good at it. Our candidates for office, middle-aged and young, daily confuse attractive, facile slogans with the goals of national policy. There is a total absence of a systematic approach to our many complex problems. Rather, what we call "solutions" consist of isolated actions, usually involving throwing money at social misfortunes. We bus children to remedy what is, in fact, an error in metropolitan planning and housing. We jail more and more youthful offenders to remedy teenage and minority unemployment. We raise municipal parking rates to deal with a total absence of a transportation policy.

We have endless debates on whether we are number one or number two in national defense when we should be examining our international commitments and their consequences. Obviously we will have totally different military needs and budgets, if we are content to defend "fortress America," or if we want to guarantee the independence of our friends and allies in some areas of the world, or if we want to be able to deter major wars everywhere.

We do not have an energy policy, we have slogans. We are against the loss of national control over our major energy sources. We are against black lung for coal miners. We are against damage to our western landscapes and to our coastal waters. We are against radioactive risks for our population. On the other hand, we are for cheap electricity, for plentiful gasoline, for bringing the comforts of life to our poorer citizens, and we are for full employment. We cannot have all these, completely, at the same time, right

xv

away. We must learn to make the complex and difficult decisions that a
rational energy policy will entail. We must learn to weigh political,
economic, ethical, and even esthetic factors.

There are always costs to decisions, financial and human. There are
always alternative uses for money. There are always ripple effects, good and
bad, to any decision. And there are always risks. Some can be estimated;
some can only be guessed. Whether we are dealing with land use, health care
delivery, transportation policy, international security, education, a national
policy on the arts, or with scientific research, we need to assemble a variety
of data in a number of fields, assess their significance and interdependence,
weigh them to determine a course of action, assess costs and estimate remote
consequences, and set criteria to estimate relative success.

Finally, but perhaps most important, in examining the various options
we need also to assess the ethical consequences. It is crucial that, in making
far-reaching social decisions, we devise ethically-acceptable compromises
among values where they are in conflict. I firmly believe that the future of
our civilization and of the human race will depend on whether we, citizens
of the greatest democracy on earth, members of the most highly developed
technological society in the world, have the wisdom and the courage to
make and to carry out the right decisions. Individual achievements and the
successful pursuit of happiness will continue to be dependent, obviously, on
individuals making the right decisions for themselves.

Decision making as a discipline is a very recent phenomenon. Thus far,
its methods have been used primarily and successfully in graduate schools of
business administration and in advanced courses in strategy for members of
our armed services. This book, so far as I am aware, represents the first
attempt to apply the basic tenets of this developing science to the study of
general decision making for college undergraduates. It is the outgrowth of
courses developed two years ago at Tufts and received with enthusiasm by
our students. A rational understanding of the ways in which decisions are
made and of the ways in which decision-making techniques can be applied
can do much to create an informed and active citizenry. We offer this text in
the hope that it will make a contribution toward that end.

Jean Mayer, President
Tufts University

Preface

A growing body of knowledge deals with the analysis of alternatives and related problems in the theory and practice of decision making. Much of this information results from research in economics, business, systems analysis, forecasting, and operations research. Some universities have even begun to offer programs in decision making. Many of these are highly technical and sophisticated courses for graduate students; others are designed primarily for undergraduates in professional studies, such as business or engineering. So far, however, there is very little information on the subject accessible to the nonspecialist or interested lay readers.

Students in the sciences, social sciences, and engineering are often trained to the point of making a decision and are then left to their own devices. The process of good decision making as such is not taught. Yet, inevitably, the student is a decision maker — as a member of a family, as a citizen, in his profession, and on the job. Quality of life is affected in multiple ways by an ability to make timely, efficient, and reasonable decisions.

This text has been written to fill an apparent void in the literature by providing the nonspecialist with several decision-making techniques, methods, and points of view. The volume is intended to teach skill in decision making to an interdisciplinary audience with no prior background in the discipline.

The materials presented in the following chapters grew out of a general course in decision making at Tufts University involving students from different fields of study. The course was designed for undergraduates from all departments in liberal arts and engineering, and was open to all without prerequisite. The case study method of teaching was used to introduce concepts dealing with all aspects of the decision-making process. In this way, the material presented in class could be directly applied to real life situations with which the student could readily identify. A number of these case studies are included in the Appendix.

In order to preserve the interdisciplinary approach imposed upon the material presented, the course was team-taught by six faculty members from four departments: economics, engineering design, political science, and psychology. Special lectures by members of the departments of English and philosophy and from the School of Medicine were also included. The writings of this six-member faculty team and invited guest lecturers comprise the major portions of the text.

In reading and studying this book, it may be of interest to know the identity and discipline of each author in relation to his or her specific contribution. Even though the authors worked very closely with one another in the development of cases and materials — reading, editing, and commenting upon each of the chapters — the original thoughts and primary responsibility for drafting chapters are as follows:

Chapters 1, 3, 8	Percy H. Hill	Engineering Design
Chapters 5, 7, 11	Daniel Ounjian	Economics
Chapter 4	Hugo A. Bedau	Philosophy
Chapter 5	Jeffrey Z. Rubin	Psychology
Chapters 2, 6	Barbara L. Kellerman	Political Science
Chapters 1, 9	Richard A. Chechile	Psychology
Chapter 10	Stephen G. Pauker	Medicine
	Susan P. Pauker	Pediatrics
Chapter 12	William J. Crochetiere	Engineering Design

We wish to express our appreciation to the Administration at Tufts University for its moral and financial support of our teaching and writing efforts, to our students who patiently tested in class a preliminary edition of this book and helped teach us about the decision-making process, to Professor Howard Kunreuther of the Wharton School, University of Pennsylvania, for his critical review of the original edition, and to Margaret Vilaine for her careful typing of the final manuscript.

Percy H. Hill

MAKING
DECISIONS

A MULTIDISCIPLINARY INTRODUCTION

Chapter 1
Introduction

Consider for a moment the following set of situations:

☐   A design engineer works for a small company that manufactures and sells machine tools and equipment. One of the company's draftsmen has developed an idea for a revolutionary new grinding process, together with the machinery and apparatus for implementing it. As a result of several unpleasant incidents, the two employees are not on speaking terms. The draftsman has presented his ideas to company management and has obtained approval to spend up to $500,000 of company funds on the further development of the process. If the product is successful, he will receive a substantial promotion to become chief engineer of the development program. The design engineer has seen the basic description of the proposed process and is convinced that it is fundamentally flawed. Considering his responsibility to the company as well as his associate, he must decide upon a course of action. If he points out the weakness in the proposed process to management, he will probably save the company a great deal of money, but in turn destroy his associate. If he remains silent, the company may suffer an embarrassing loss both of funds and reputation, and his associate may not survive the program.

Percy H. Hill et al., Making Decisions: A Multidisciplinary Introduction

☐   A husband and wife are in graduate school and each is studying for the Ph.D. Her field is physics and his is biology. They have been married for six years and are in their mid-thirties. Both wish to continue in their chosen fields of research when they have completed their degrees. Their immediate problem is to determine whether to have any children. They both would like to have a small family but believe that it may interfere with their professional development.

☐   The manager of a division of a large company has employed a university-based consulting group to develop and patent a new product which, if successful, would have large sales potential. After three years of research and testing, the product has been use-tested and shows every possibility of being a success against its competition. The product would enter a market with $100,000,000 sales per year, and the advertising division predicts 10% of this market in the first year. This estimate assumes that a budget of $6,000,000 would be available to launch the product in its first year. All indicators point to a successful product, but this division of the company has had a bad "track record" with products of this type in the past. In fact, the division has lost money on three new product ventures in the past two years. The manager must make a decision regarding this product that the division now owns. Should she approve the advertising budget, on the assumption that the product will return over 100 times this amount, and thereby risk losing millions of dollars? Or should she try to interest another company, one with a better sales record, in purchasing the product and patents outright?

☐   A student at a university must decide on his field of major concentration by the end of his freshman year. He feels that this decision will establish certain constraints that may affect his well-being for the rest of his life. Such a decision could eventually affect his social status, limit his perspective, determine his profession, income, habitat, and perhaps lifestyle. If his interests were limited to one body of knowledge, the choice would be simple. His interests, however, are equally divided between the sciences and the humanities. In fact, he has both a strong interest in chemistry as well as the study of classical Greek literature. Majoring in either field would require him to eventually pursue a Ph.D. degree in order to reach a professional level of competence. Chemistry would probably lead to a position in a research laboratory, while Greek literature might lead to a university faculty position.

☐   The owner of a major league baseball team is faced with the choice of censuring (or perhaps firing) his $85,000-a-year manager or suspending his $175,000-a-year superstar, because of friction between them that is destroying team morale.

☐ A physician must decide whether to operate or to treat the patient with a new wonder drug.

☐ A mayor is confronted with a large deficit and must propose a sizable increase in the city budget. Should he raise property taxes and face a property owners' revolt or levy an across-the-board sales tax and take the chance of losing reelection?

The protagonists in the above situations have something in common. Each wants to select the best possible course of action, the decision that will have the most favorable possible outcome.

Without a doubt, you too will be called upon in the months and years ahead to make a number of important decisions that will affect your well-being and that of others. Obviously you can also count on being involved in decisions of a minor nature, whose outcome will be less important.

This book has been written in the belief that if a person can better understand the thought process involved in making decisions, the personal values placed upon decision outcomes, and possibly one or two relevant mathematical techniques or tools, it should be possible for the individual to make better decisions. The chapters to follow have been prepared in the hope that some portion of this understanding can be successfully conveyed.

The book is concerned throughout both with the *descriptive* and the *prescriptive* aspects of decision making. Descriptive decision analysis refers to the way in which decisions are *actually* made, regardless of their efficiency, wisdom, or practicality. Thus, we are interested in identifying those individual, interpersonal, group, institutional, and societal factors that may affect the outcome of the decision process — and that best describe how decisions are usually made. Descriptive decision analysis is concerned not with rational or ideal behavior but rather with actual behavior, and it is assumed here that some measure of understanding of actual conduct is necessary in order to prescribe how decisions ought to be made.

Prescriptive decision analysis is concerned with the art and science of *optimal* decision making. It is often, although not always, the case that prescriptive recommendations differ from the choice behavior that would actually occur in the absence of decision aids. In such cases, the insights afforded through prescriptive analysis may result in an improvement in decision-making quality.

Obviously, both description and prescription are essential in decision analysis. Suppose, for example, that we wish to improve traffic safety, by upgrading the quality of the decisions typically made by drivers about whether to tailgate, speed, wear seat belts, and so forth. Before we could make appropriate recommendations about how the individual driver should behave so as to improve traffic safety, it would clearly be necessary to understand first what drivers are actually doing, and why. A series of simulation experiments and driver attitude surveys might first be conducted in order to reveal valuable background information that would facilitate an understanding of driver habits. Following this descriptive phase, a set of prescriptions might then have a far greater chance of being wisely adopted from among the available alternatives that could improve driving quality. In Chapter 3, a process is outlined by which both prescriptive and descriptive procedures are brought to bear on the decision problem in a step-by-step manner. Although few decisions lend themselves completely to the ramifications of this methodical approach, careful attention to this procedure may help discipline the decision maker to proceed with logic and care.

Decision analysis, whether approached descriptively or prescriptively, is not, as are some other bodies of knowledge and techniques, the subject matter of one academic or professional discipline to the exclusion of others. On the contrary, engineers, physicians, counsellors, economists, psychologists, lawyers, political scientists, and many others have developed their own distinctive approaches to decision problems in their fields. There is, of course, some overlap in the methods and assumptions with which persons trained in one of these disciplines approach a given problem. But there is also a growing body of knowledge more or less unique to each discipline's approach to the study of decision making. In Chapters 2 and 3, we give an illustration of these divergences and convergences in approach.

Chapters 4 through 6 present relatively discursive, rather than mathematical, discussions of the subject of decision making as seen from the view points of ethical theory, social psychology, and political science. Most of the emphasis in these chapters is also on describing how people actually do make decisions, rather than on prescribing for the reader how they should be made.

Chapters 7 through 12 are more rigorous and contain material that requires attention to mathematical and computational techniques. Here, the reader will receive an introduction to a variety of standard and widely-used techniques of decision analysis. Throughout these chapters, there is an implicit prescriptive stance: since these methods and techniques, as best as can be ascertained at present, constitute the way in which a rational person (or group) would analyze and resolve its decision problems, then these methods are what anyone *ought* to use who wants to be rational (and who does not?).

The Appendix contains a series of case studies presented in a sequence parallel to the sequence in which Chapters 4 through 12 present problems and the techniques for their solution.

Thus, by the time you have worked your way through this volume from cover to cover, read each of the chapters, and struggled with the case studies, you should have a general grasp of the three major themes around which this book has been written. First, you will have been exposed to decision making in both its descriptive (how-it-is-done) and prescriptive (how-it-ought-to-be-done) phases. Second, you will have confronted hypothetical situations that require decisions to be made that present a great diversity of considerations and factors, illustrating the range and complexity of decision-making problems to be faced in real life. Third, you will have been introduced to the basic techniques that have been developed with considerable rigor and detail in more advanced treatises on decision theory.

A final word of caution. This book is not meant to be a decision-making primer, a "how to make the right decision" handbook, one more contribution to the endless flow of self-help manuals. This volume does not pretend to offer a set of infallible techniques to bring order to the confusion of your private life, family relations, education, or career. No mere book could do that! Our hope, rather, has been more modest, and your expectations should be scaled accordingly. The methods and techniques of decision analysis to which you will be introduced do have application to real problems that you face; but these techniques have their limits, too. Their results are no better than the data on which their use relies in each instance. There is no rule or guideline to tell you when to use one rather than another decision method in any given situation. The science of decision analysis is still relatively young, and the future will no doubt see great advances both in theory and practical applications. Meanwhile, in this book we have tried to be aware of these and other difficulties and obstacles to understanding, and we have tried to stimulate thought and open up new vistas, even at the risk of overstimulating the careful and inquisitive reader.

Chapter 2
The Case of
Dear Aunt Sarah

1 INTRODUCTION

Among other things, this book is intended to teach the skill of *case analysis*. This skill allows you to examine many different kinds of decision-making situations; to take them apart and consider each of their components; and, on the basis of the information given in the case and one's own creative inferences, to generate solutions for constructive decision making. Here and there throughout this book, actual and hypothetical cases are examined from several different points of view. The Appendix contains a collection of seventeen different cases, each designed to highlight a different facet of the decision-making process. You might turn to that part of the book for a moment, especially to read the short introductory statement on how to study a case.

Case analysis is fun. Rarely does a case have one right answer, one correct way to make the decision, one right outcome that is mutually agreed on by all who look at the available evidence. As a result, cases are provocative; they stimulate discussion and disagreement, often among those who seem to be on equally firm ground in advocating their own particular approaches. But, there is a more basic reason that case analysis leads to such lively exchanges — very simply, people see the same materials differently. Each of us views a fixed set of materials in light of our own particular

Percy H. Hill et al., Making Decisions: A Multidisciplinary Introduction

history and body of knowledge. We bring to the analysis our own idiosyncratic cognitive lens, and therefore, we end up filtering and focusing the same evidence in different ways.

Nothing has taught us this truism as well as our shared experience with "Aunt Sarah." It all began when we decided to use the case about lonely, old Aunt Sarah as a way to begin the interdisciplinary class in decision making that we teach together each semester. Our plan was to acquaint the class with the facts of the case, and then to have each of us speak for five minutes or so about our interpretation of the facts through the cognitive lenses of our respective disciplines. As our presentations unfolded, what struck us was the startling *dissimilarity* in the ways that the six or seven of us responded to the identical material. There was virtually no overlap in what each of us had to say in our allotted five minutes. The disciplines in which each of us has been trained taught us to stress different aspects of the case as those most relevant to the decision to be made. The results of our several independent commentaries vividly illustrate the importance of who you are in what you see.

2 DEAR AUNT SARAH*

Connie Arnold looked at her husband Jim as she handed him the third letter in two weeks from Aunt Sarah. They both knew they had to respond in the next couple of days to Sarah Dawson's request to come and live with their family.

Connie and Jim sat down in the living room with the three letters and tried to think through the situation. Aunt Sarah was Connie's mother's older sister. Her husband, George, had died four years ago. George and Sarah Dawson had no children. Now that Connie's parents were both dead, the Arnolds were Sarah's only living relatives. Two years after George died, Sarah had sold their house and had rented a little apartment in the same neighborhood. Jim and Connie knew that Aunt Sarah had a small but livable income from George's pension plan and that interest on the investment of the proceeds from the sale of the house just covered her rent.

Connie read aloud two paragraphs from Aunt Sarah's first letter:

> It is always my greatest joy to see you, Jim, and those three beautiful children of yours. I know what a long drive it is out here to Appleton — almost three hours. Though I remember when I was a girl the trip took over seven hours on the train. I know how busy you are, but with George and all

---

*By permission from the Case-Study Institute; case prepared by Alice Frazer Evans as a basis for class discussion rather than to illustrate either effective or ineffective handling of the situation; copyright ©1977.

of our friends gone now, the weeks seem so long between your visits.

Even though I am 78, I'm still a spry old girl. Connie, I know you have talked about getting a job. I do not approve of a mother being out of her home, but if you're set on it, I would be glad to come and live with you to take care of little Joel when he comes home from school. A seven-year-old still needs a lot of loving.

Connie later told Jim she was a bit surprised by Aunt Sarah's offer. She had thought that "absolutely nothing" would pull Sarah Dawson away from Appleton. Rather, Connie assumed this was really Aunt Sarah's way of showing her unhappiness over the job issue. Connie had responded to the letter by writing that she hadn't yet decided on going back to work and that if she did, it would only be part-time and that Anne, their 14-year-old, would also be at home when Joel got out of school.

Aunt Sarah's second letter came by return mail:

I've been thinking about all the work you and Jim have done on your house. I remember you had wanted to fix up that top floor for a long time. The two bedrooms for Anne and Susan sound very nice and I know how glad they are to finally have their own separate den and a bathroom. With Susan going away to college this year, you'll have a lot of extra room. It doesn't make much sense to me to pay rent for this apartment when I could be giving you and Jim all that money for Susan's empty room. Anne will be lonely up there by herself.

Before Connie could answer this letter, a third one from Aunt Sarah arrived in the mail two days later.

I've been thinking that it might be hard for us all to manage in your little kitchen. I still have most of the money from the sale of our house. I'll be glad to pay to convert a section of the new den into a nice little kitchen for Anne and myself.

Though I have been so well, I think I had another little heart spell last night. You remember my George died of a heart attack. I told Fluffy and Meow that we will be moving soon, so they need not be afraid of anything happening to me all alone.

After rereading the last line, Jim burst out, "Connie, as dearly as I love Aunt Sarah, I don't see how we could survive with those two obnoxious cats of hers. Our old beagle Sam would turn this house into a combat zone."

"Now, Jim," Connie responded quickly, "You and I both know we don't want to make a decision like this based on two cats. We're the only ones Aunt Sarah has left. I think of all the beautiful summers I spent as a child with Uncle George and Aunt Sarah. And it was Uncle George who really supported my last two years of college. Now I feel it's my turn to be on the giving end."

Jim answered slowly, "Connie, I don't know how we can ask Susan to give up her room after she waited seven years to have a place of her own.

And even if she agrees, I don't want her to feel that because she's going away to college, she no longer has a place in our home. And, do you really believe that an active 14-year-old is going to thrive with Sarah pouring vitamins down her throat, telling her to turn down — or off — the stereo, and wanting to go to bed at 8 o'clock? We've expanded this house as much as possible, and on my salary a bigger one is out of the question."

"I know the kids love Sarah, but they run to the car when it's time to come back home after visits. You told me yourself that on our last trip home Susan whispered to you that she thought Aunt Sarah was 'really neat' but her 'remembering the old days' was enough to drive Susan 'up the wall'."

"Connie, I'm not trying to be so negative. I do agree that we have some responsibility for Sarah and she has a folksy wisdom that I respect. I just want us to be clear about the pressures Sarah would introduce. In a few years she may not be able to get around at all. This would dramatically change all our lives if she is living here with us."

Connie nodded her head. "Jim, I'm not naive about the problems. Aunt Sarah lives in another era. It is particularly hard for me to deal with her strong and constant disapproval of my decision to get a job, and I'm sure that would carry over into other areas of our lifestyle. But what other options are there? I don't see how she could afford any decent apartment here in the city without cutting into the principal of her savings. You and I both know that's her only emergency resource beyond Medicare. There is no way we could afford a nursing home and I don't think she would even consider that. On our last visit she told me with real anger about old Mrs. Robbins who moved into the home in Appleton. Aunt Sarah said Eulie Robbins' children had 'committed her to the grave'."

"Jim, I've already mentioned the idea of Aunt Sarah living here to each of the children, but I'm not clear what we're really asking them. I feel a deep love and responsibility for Sarah. I think we all do. But I also feel it's a decision the whole family has to make and not just the two of us."

Connie Arnold looked down at the almost blank sheet of stationery in her hands. So far the only words were "Dear Aunt Sarah, . . . "

3 DISCUSSION

The case of "Dear Aunt Sarah" is not designed to illustrate either effective or ineffective handling of the decision-making process. It is intended to generate discussion, and to this end, each of the authors of this book was asked to write a few pages analyzing the Aunt Sarah case. As you will see in the following commentaries, true to form, each of us has used our space to focus on different aspects of the problem. Indeed, even the two engineering designers and the two psychologists wrote distinctly different analyses, a fact which suggests strongly that even those from within the same discipline cannot be counted on to mirror each other's perceptions. Within this sample, in fact, the bedfellows could not be predicted. As it happened, the social psychologist and the political scientist focused their primary attentions on an analysis of the situation in which Connie and Jim Arnold quite suddenly found themselves playing a very reluctant role.

The Social Psychologist:

When Jim and Connie first hear from Aunt Sarah, they discover that the spry old girl is lonely, and much in need of love and affection. The implicit influence message in her first letter is, "Take me in, and do what I ask, because I need and depend on you."

Connie's response to Aunt Sarah's first letter is quite ambivalent. Despite this, Aunt Sarah remains undaunted. In her second letter, Jim and Connie discover that Aunt Sarah has a proposal in mind: if they will let her move into their daughter's empty room, nice old Aunt Sarah will be happy to pay rent — and keep their other daughter company to boot. Notice that in this second letter, the implicit influence message has been transformed from "let me do X because I need you" to "let me do X because you need me."

Before Connie can respond to this letter, a third arrives. In it Jim and Connie find that Aunt Sarah will "pay to convert a section of the new den into a nice little kitchen" . . . for herself! Aunt Sarah is rather clearly planning to move in; it's a matter, not of "if," but of "when" this event will occur — "I told Fluffy and Meow that we will be moving soon." Notice that the implicit influence message has been further transformed from "let me do X because you need me" to "I'm glad to hear that we're going to do X — when do we get started?"

Two observations seem particularly germane regarding this sequence of influence attempts. First, it is clear that Aunt Sarah has managed quite skillfully to shift the locus of control from Jim and Connie's shoulders ("you can do something for me") to her own ("I can do something for you"); at the same time, a conditional event (her move) has been transformed into a certainty. Second, these shifts have occurred almost without notice; although the stakes have changed, they have done so with great subtlety, a bit at a time. One can picture poor Connie and Jim sitting together late at night, scratching their collective head, wondering how this miserable situation ever came to pass. Somehow, without Jim and Connie ever actually having made a conscious choice, the decision to invite in poor old Aunt Sarah seems to have been just about made!

More generally, it appears that decision makers all too often find themselves in the uncomfortable situation of having made a decision without any clear sense of having done so. The decision maker begins to behave in a particular way — perhaps in an attempt to explore that behavior, perhaps out of idle curiosity or some other motive — only to turn around subsequently, acknowledge this behavior, and come to the conclusion that since one behaved in a particular way, a decision must have been made. This "decision," moreover, may lead the decision maker to justify the wisdom of his behavior by further committing himself to some course of action.

We would all like to believe that decisions are made as a consequence of some rational process in which alternatives are first canvassed, information about their relative virtues and liabilities is then obtained, and finally — based on full understanding of all available information — a wise decision is rendered. Unfortunately, the decision-making process is not always so neat, clearcut, and sensible. All too often, decisions are rationalizing rather than rational, "psycho-logical" rather than logical. This is particularly likely to be the case when commitment to behave in some way, to pursue one alternative rather than another, occurs in the absence of the decision maker's full awareness and ken. Jim and Connie are in serious danger of making their own decision on the basis of these sorts of social psychological considerations.

The Political Scientist:

Consider first of all, as one would want to in any analysis of a political choice, who is participating in this decision, and in what kind of a setting. The decision about what to do with Aunt Sarah appears, on the surface at least, to be for Connie and Jim to make. But think — it was Aunt Sarah who forced the issue in the first place, and her behavior, even at this stage, will contribute to the outcome. And what about the three children? Are they completely powerless here? What if, per chance, little Joel were to object fiercely to the idea of Aunt Sarah permanently residing in the next bedroom? Would that give him a louder voice than his presumably lowly status in the family would otherwise suggest? Is there an analogue here to what happens in politics? And what are the settings? Aunt Sarah's apartment, the Arnolds' house, Appleton, the Arnolds' community, the particular state, and the United States (which has its own sociopolitical culture and, therefore, its own laws and attitudes pertaining to the elderly) — how do all of these influence the decision making?

We would also want to evaluate the central actors in terms of personality and position. Who has the primary influence in this situation? Do Connie and Jim, for example, have the same stake in this decision? Is it not the case that Connie's special ties to Aunt Sarah make her utility with regard to Sarah's welfare different from that of her husband? What are the dynamics of how they all get along? How significant is the fact that so far it has been Aunt Sarah who has been the mover and shaker? Does Jim have more power than Connie in this family? Does Connie really call the shots? Can we tell how they reached decisions of some magnitude in the past?

Clearly, the Arnolds are not behaving very rationally. They let the situation sweep over them without taking action at an early stage, and now Aunt Sarah has pushed them into a corner. Had they moved more quickly, other alternatives could more easily have been proposed. And even at this stage, it does not seem that Connie and Jim are sorting out their overall goals or exploring the options that are really open to them. As the case is presented to us, there is a startling lack of imagination in evidence. Not one creative solution has been generated. Might Aunt Sarah not possibly be satisfied with the idea of an interesting companion, for example, or her own small apartment five minutes instead of three hours away from the Arnolds?

The physician, the economist, and one each of the engineers and psychologists had in common the fact that they focused on the question of what could be done with the materials of the case to generate solutions more creative than any Connie and Jim Arnold seem likely to propose.

The Physician:

Sarah Dawson is a 78-year-old widow who has lived in Appleton her entire life and who now has outlived her husband and friends and has become both lonely and frightened about her future. A woman of her age would have a life expectancy of almost nine years if she were well. However, we are told that she is having "heart spells." These could simply represent anxiety or they could be more serious, either palpitations (irregular heartbeat) or chest pain. In either case, they may well be a marker for serious heart disease and could imply a far shorter life expectancy. If they in fact denote such disease and if this elderly widow is subject to sudden cardiac problems, it would be best for her not to live alone.

The options available include leaving Aunt Sarah in Appleton, moving her to the Arnolds' home, and moving her to a nursing home. Nursing homes are not happy places, and many elderly people indeed do die soon after entering such facilities. Of course, this could be an illusion of selection — only the weakest and sickest elderly members of our society enter such homes; relatively healthy patients could do quite well. What may contribute to the poor prognosis of the elderly in nursing homes is a feeling of being abandoned and cast out by their families. Often they just give up.

A less drastic alternative might be for Aunt Sarah to move into a retirement community where she could meet and make friends with other elderly people. Of course, there is no reason to believe that elderly people will become friends just because they have "being old" in common. In fact, the elderly are often quite rigid and set in their ways and adapt rather poorly to new situations. Such inability to adapt would be an argument against any change, however. Undoubtedly, Aunt Sarah has some friends and support mechanisms in Appleton which she would lose if she moved. The counter argument is, of course, that most of her peers have died.

From the case description, we can see that Aunt Sarah is not only rigid, but also quite aggressive. She might well begin to take over the Arnolds' home and become a family matriarch. She already disapproves of Connie's plan to work part-time and is speaking of "managing in your little kitchen" and of bringing her two pet cats. Certainly, such relocation would be disruptive to the Arnolds, but the effects would not be all bad. Our current society offers children little in the way of an extended family and provides few models of family responsibilities. If the Arnolds take in Aunt Sarah, they provide a model for their own children to care for them in their own sunset years.

Connie expresses some feeling of obligation to Aunt Sarah and Uncle George, and she would undoubtedly feel considerable guilt in turning away her aunt. When Aunt Sarah gets sick, as she undoubtedly will, Jim and Connie will scarcely be able to avoid the impact on their lives. If she is not living with them, she may then require relocation which might then be even more difficult. As is true of many of our elderly, when she becomes sick she will rapidly consume her meager savings and, in the end, will become destitute and a financial burden to her family. Thus, attempting to protect her savings as an emergency resource may well be folly. It might be better to consume those savings while she is still in a position to appreciate the benefits.

Clearly, Sarah Dawson is crying out for help, and clearly, the Arnolds must respond. In the short run, at least, one solution might be to move this lady to an apartment in the city where she could be near her family but not in their laps. One might generate some expectations of her future financial needs and duration of survival, and plan to consume the principal of her savings in an orderly way over her remaining years. No choice will be entirely satisfactory and all future complications cannot be anticipated. One can only hope that the Arnolds carefully think of all the alternatives and try to reach a decision which considers the needs of the entire family unit. One final resource not yet mentioned is for both the Arnolds and Sarah Dawson to speak to other people who have faced this common problem so that at least some unforeseen problems might be anticipated.

The Engineer:

The first step in analyzing this case is to define the problem. After a careful reading and re-reading of the case, the following problem definition emerges: Aunt Sarah is lonely, wants desperately to come and live with her niece and family, and has clearly made this fact known to them. Connie and Jim must respond to Aunt Sarah's request in a way that will satisfy her expectations as well as preserve their own family lifestyle.

We should now begin to gather background information that will have a bearing on the decision. The following facts are readily identified:

1. Connie feels an obligation to Aunt Sarah, since Uncle George supported her during her last two years of college.
2. Jim is not very receptive to the idea of Aunt Sarah moving in, since it would probably affect his lifestyle adversely.
3. Both Connie and Jim have negative feelings about accepting responsibility for the care of an elderly relative moving in with them.
4. Certain financial gains could result to the Arnolds from accepting Aunt Sarah's offer:
   a. The chance of having a new kitchen plus other possible remodeling to their house.
   b. Aunt Sarah is 78 and would be lucky to live another ten years; in the event of her death, her estate would probably be left to Connie and Jim.
5. The children, if asked to cast a vote for or against Aunt Sarah's moving in, would probably vote in favor of it. This decision from a practical view would probably be short-sighted, for they cannot look as far into the future as their parents.

Connie and Jim should now begin to list a number of alternatives, each offering a different possible solution to the problem. The following are offered from an engineer's view:

A. Accept Aunt Sarah's request.
B. Reject Aunt Sarah's request.
C. Suggest that Aunt Sarah move in for six months, while the children are in school, and return to her own home during the remaining time.
D. Try to locate a senior citizen center nearby, and arrange for Aunt Sarah to visit on a weekly basis.
E. Try to find a live-in companion for Aunt Sarah.

It is suggested that the next step in the process might be to construct a Decision Matrix* in which each of the five alternatives would be scored

*The Decision Matrix is discussed in detail in Chapter 8.

against overriding selection criteria. The highest score among alternatives would be the best course of action for Connie and Jim to take. Selection criteria that would have a bearing on each of the alternatives might include the following: preserve present lifestyle, family obligations, Aunt Sarah's peace of mind, financial gain, happiness of children, Connie's daily schedule, and responsibility.

Engineers are interested in analyzing a problem so that is is solved to the best advantage of all parties concerned. This involves understanding all of the variables included as well as making tradeoffs, since all goals are rarely satisfied when making a decision.

The Economist:

Sarah is 78 years old and apparently in good health. A quick check with a local insurance firm reveals that her life expectancy is 7.6 years, i.e., 50% of the people of her age and of her state of health will live for at least another 7.6 years. The probabilities of her living any given number of years are just as easily obtainable.

Without directly asking her, it would also be possible to estimate the amount of capital that Aunt Sarah would bring into the Arnold household. We know that she has the money from the sale of her old home, that she has invested it, and that the interest on it covers her rent. If we assume that she is paying $200 a month in rent for a small apartment, and that her money is earning a modest yet safe return of 6%, we merely have to answer the question: What sum of money invested at 6% will generate an annual flow of income equal to $2400 (i.e., 12 × $200)? This procedure, called capitalizing, gives an answer of $40,000. The formula is:

$$\text{Principal} = \frac{\text{Annual Income}}{\text{Interest Rate}}$$

Different assumptions about rent and rate of interest would give other answers. We assume here that Aunt Sarah, badly in need of this income, has not invested in other higher-interest-yielding assets since they invariably carry a greater risk.

In addition to that lump sum, Aunt Sarah is also receiving a "small but livable income" from her husband's pension plan. Again it would be easy to estimate this amount, possibly $70 to $80 per week. One important aspect of the pension plan that cannot be estimated, however, is whether the benefits will continue until the time of her death. There are many different forms of pension benefit payments and it could be that her particular benefits may soon run out. It is a direct question that eventually should be asked.

At first blush it appears that Aunt Sarah will not impose any particular financial hardships on the Arnolds. To the contrary, it seems that they could use her capital to enlarge or even buy a bigger home. The only major financial risk that they would be taking centers around her health and the possibility that Aunt Sarah would have a prolonged illness that would become extraordinarily costly. Medicare would not cover all of the expenses; and, if left in her own name, the $40,000 could diminish rapidly. Legal advice should be sought on whether giving her $40,000 to the Arnolds would make her eligible for Medicaid. In the latter event all such expenses would be paid by the government.

The Psychologist:

The first step would be to identify the alternatives. Certainly two obvious alternatives immediately come to mind, namely, to accept or to reject Aunt Sarah's plan. To some (e.g., Connie), these are the only alternatives. However, on closer examination, several other actions are also possible. Why not also consider suggesting to Aunt Sarah that she find an apartment nearby? Connie believes that this is not a realistic possibility because it will require Aunt Sarah to spend a part of the principal from the sale of her house. However, Aunt Sarah's principal is not a small sum of money, and at her age she could possibly spend a small part of it to pay for the increase in rent. Perhaps other alternatives could be considered as well, such as offering to help Aunt Sarah find a compatible roommate to share her present apartment. The point is that creative decision making should not restrict the alternatives prematurely.

Once the alternatives have been identified, it is often wise to evaluate the consequences of each action as well as evaluate the probabilities of these consequences. For example, if Aunt Sarah were to live with the Arnolds, how probable is it that the entire family would live in peace and enjoy each other's company? If Aunt Sarah's plan were to be refused, how probable is it that she can be made to understand the Arnolds' decision? How likely is it that she would become embittered and the Arnolds depressed by feelings of guilt? If the option of trying to find Aunt Sarah an apartment were to be selected, how likely is it that she would agree to spend the increase in rent? How probable is it that she would need this money to pay for medical expenses? If the option of suggesting a roommate for Aunt Sarah were pursued, how likely is it that she could find a suitable person? Conversely, how probable is it that she would feel rejected and hence become embittered? Although it is difficult for us to evaluate these alternatives, the Arnolds obviously have more information than was presented in the case. This information could lead (with a little training) to numerical assignments for the probabilities associated with the consequences of each of the above alternatives.

For each of these possible outcomes, it is also wise to evaluate the outcome's desirability or undesirability. This is not an easy task since there are many dimensions of desirability (e.g., the family's obligation to Aunt Sarah, the family's obligation to itself, money, living space, love). Also, there are several members in the group, thus increasing the probability of differing or conflicting values. However, once the outcomes are identified and discussed by the family, it is possible that a consensus will be reached on an evaluation of each outcome, or at least a rank ordering of the outcomes from most to least desirable.

Once the above steps have been completed, all of the information necessary to make a decision is available. It is often the case, however, that this information is too extensive or too complex to be kept in focus by even the most sophisticated person. Hence, decision aids such as decision trees are used to model and structure the problem.* By applying decision rules to our decision tree, the best alternative can perhaps be selected. Decision trees also can assist us in seeing new possibilities in a case. For example, in working out a decision tree for this problem in class recently we discovered that a chained decision was possible. By "chained decision" we mean a decision rule such that an initial action is selected, but if some undesirable outcome occurs then a new alternative is chosen. In summary, decision trees can illustrate and structure the relevant information of a case, and thereby aid in the selection of an optimal course of action.

One of the engineers took a different tack from the rest of us. He looked not at the present, but into the future.

The Systems Engineer:

One thing Connie and Jim must consider in making this difficult decision is that their home environment will change, whether or not Aunt Sarah moves in with them. They will not always be a nuclear family of five with a dog named Sam. In fact, their home environment has already been changed recently, because their older daugher, Susan, is now in college and does not live with them for most of the year. In three short years, Anne will most likely also leave home to attend college.

As a forecaster, one views a decision, not only in terms of how it will affect the present, but also in light of its likely impact on the future. In this case, certain events can be forecast merely by noting the ages of the actors. Assuming that Connie and Jim are in their early forties, and in good health,

---

*Decision trees are discussed in detail in Chapter 9.

we may list the ages of the actors over the next ten years, together with the events which are likely to occur.

	Time	Aunt Sarah	Jim	Connie	Susan	Anne	Joel
Uncle George dies	−4	74	38	37	13	10	3
Aunt Sarah sells house	−2	76	40	39	15	12	5
Susan enters college	0	78	42	41	17	14	7
Anne enters college	3	81	45	44	20	17	10
Susan graduates	4	82	46	45	21	18	11
Anne graduates	7	85	49	48	24	21	14
Joel enters college	10	88	52	51	27	24	17

The first critical event occurred four years ago when Uncle George died of a heart attack. Two years later, Aunt Sarah sold the house and moved into a nearby apartment. At the time the case is described, she has been living in the apartment for two years. Note that if Aunt Sarah moves in, and Anne enters college at the age of 17, there will be a three-year period that may be stressful. After this critical period, things may get better. In seven years, both girls will have graduated and be on their own (over 21). In only ten years, Joel will enter college leaving Jim, Connie, Aunt Sarah, old Sam, Fluffy, and Meow to rattle around the house. This, of course, assumes that they all live that long.

Not all forecasts are related to the actors. More generally, the forecaster either looks at the past and extrapolates a trend, observes certain lead indicators which are known to precede change, or investigates the cause and effect relations which produce change.

And finally, it is left to the philosopher to pose what are probably the most difficult questions of all. Not every decision-making situation poses an ethical dilemma. The decision as to which kind of a car to purchase involes no moral agony. But in cases such as "Dear Aunt Sarah," in which legitimate rights and needs appear to conflict, the kinds of issues that are addressed in the following paragraphs can be the toughest of all.

The Philosopher:

Aunt Sarah acts as if the Arnolds had *promised* her a place in their household — but they have not. She does not have any *right* to move in with them until they *invite* her to do so. The tone of her letters, therefore, shows how eager she is to join their household, even how anxious and frightened she is lest they not encourage her to do so. Because her letters show her to be both overeager (hence intrusive) and overanxious (hence pitiable), the need for a careful and considerate response from the Arnolds is all the greater.

Do the Arnolds have a *duty* or *obligation* to invite Aunt Sarah to join them? Connie all but says that she thinks they do (". . . now I feel it's my turn to be on the giving end"); this does not trouble her because she seems also to think that this is what her family *wants* to do even apart from obligation. On both points, she may be wrong. Her husband, for one, does not share her view. In an earlier era, most persons would have said that any family did have an obligation to take care of its aging members. Even if this is still true today, however, it is doubtful whether the form that the care must take is inclusion in one's own household.

It is true that Connie, and to that extent the family in which she is wife and mother, is obligated in gratitude to Aunt Sarah (and her deceased husband) for helping finance her college education. Aunt Sarah, whether she chooses to claim it or not, is thus entitled to some reciprocal benefit. Still, moral obligations (except under antiquated codes of honor) are not transitive; even if Connie is under a moral obligation to Aunt Sarah, her husband and daughers do not share or acquire her moral obligation, unless they choose to accept it.

Connie is right, from the moral point of view, that "it's a decision the whole family must make and not just the two of us," i.e., not just Connie and Aunt Sarah, nor Connie and her husband. The two girls deserve the respect of their parents on this matter, and respect can be shown them only by taking them into the discussion. Yet a family decision cannot be reached merely by a vote under majority rule. The two daughters do not have the right to veto their parents' decision. Families cannot live together very effectively where the members' rights against each other dominate their moral relations. If the daughers do not appreciate this, then their parents must use the occasion of Aunt Sarah's hopes and needs to teach this lesson. If the parents do not appreciate this, then they have not got much of a family in the first place.

If the situation is defined in terms of relevant rights and obligations, no clear answer emerges to tell Connie what she should write to Aunt Sarah. Other considerations need to be brought into play, one of which is: what is the *best* thing to do for all concerned? It is possible that the best thing to do is what most of those concerned *want;* but it is also possible that this is not so. What is the best thing for all concerned to do? What do they all want?

From the moral point of view, the right thing to do is whatever each would accept as fair in whatever position or role he or she might occupy in the family (niece, daughter, husband, aunt). The wrong thing to do would be to do something which in your actual situation (e.g., as daughter of Connie) you would *not* accept if you were in someone else's shoes (e.g., Aunt Sarah).

A last word should probably be added about the larger setting within which decision-making situations take place. In some cases, this larger setting can be of special importance. Two of the authors made a brief reference to it with regard to Aunt Sarah.

The political scientist observed:

> There are several public policies that impact directly on the lives of the elderly. Aunt Sarah is just one of an ever increasing number of persons over the age of 65 who are alone, lonely, and very concerned about what will become of them if they need any kind of assistance. This particular woman is not, in fact, destitute. Still, the kinds of material and emotional support generated by the community for the benefit of the aged must affect how this woman lives her life, and how those who love her decide to cope with her situation. As any family who partakes of government programs soon finds out, even in a modified welfare state, (the United States is not nearly as far along in the field of programs for the elderly as, for example, Sweden), the dividing line between the system and the home is often more illusory than real.

The economist noted:

> From a more general point of view, there is the issue of the status of the elderly in our society. Who will care for them and how will their needs be provided for? Unlike private pension plans, whose funds are actually set aside, our Social Security system is one in which current workers pay taxes that go to current beneficiaries. Greater life expectancies and changes in rates of population growth have been putting a heavy strain on our ability to continue financing Social Security in this way. The current rate of taxation is high, and higher rates are forecast to meet expected future payments. The financing of medical expenses and retirement benefits for the elderly will continue to be among the more challenging social issues of the coming decade.

The lack of any apparent cohesion in our various approaches to the case of "Dear Aunt Sarah" should not render us suspect. Rather than create the false impression that this book, or any course on the subject, can describe and advocate a single process that will produce uniform, and uniformly effective decision makers, we prefer to demonstrate the validity of approaching a given problem in different ways. Underlying these manifest differences, however, there is the shared assumption that decisions *do* lend themselves to intelligent analysis. Although the authors of this book may disagree about a thousand particulars, we share the conviction that a measure of vigilance in decision making will, under almost all circumstances, yield better decisions.

Chapter 3
The Decision-Making Process

1 INTRODUCTION

The process of making a decision should be approached carefully, step by step. To ensure a well-planned approach, a series of discrete steps or events are described in the following pages; they provide the decision maker with an ideal model to follow. One often finds situations in reality where this ideal model must be violated, for example, when other variables affecting the decision-making process come into play. Such variables include the personality of the decision maker, ethical norms, psychological considerations, and the decision maker's own subjective utilities. When a decision maker follows the sequence outlined here, his conduct is an instance of *prescriptive* decision making as discussed in Chapter 1. When the decision maker deviates from the ideal model, his conduct may still exhibit certain regularities and patterns of the sort we have called a *descriptive* procedure.

The ideal decision-making process is illustrated in the form of a flowchart in Figure 3-1. Do not consider this to be a formula that guarantees the making of a correct decision; rather, remember it as a logical sequence of events which, if followed, may increase the likelihood of reaching a satisfactory decision. The process begins with *problem definition* and ends with the *implementation* of the decision. Iteration of steps occurs when there is insufficient information to complete a given step. The previous step

Percy H. Hill et al., Making Decisions: A Multidisciplinary Introduction

must then be repeated until the necessary data are in hand. Each step in the sequence will now be discussed in some detail.

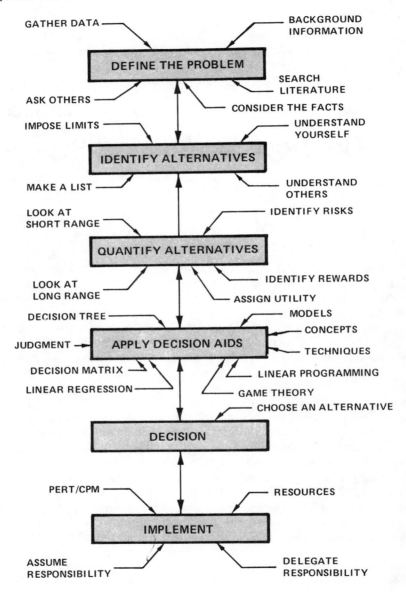

FIGURE 3-1. The Decision-Making Process

2 DEFINE THE PROBLEM

The first step in making any important or worthwhile decision is to define the problem. Too often we address our remedies to what is merely a symptom, rather than to the underlying cause itself. Even as a skilled physician treats a fever he attempts to diagnose the cause. Similarly, an environmentalist who seeks legislation to reduce pollution should know in advance what the pollutant is and what its effects are likely to be. Decisions regarding problems of urban transportation might have been more effective had experts looked more closely into the problem of moving people and goods rather than advocating highway improvements. Whatever the decision, it is precipitated by a problem of one sort or another. An accurate definition of the problem is already a major step toward its eventual solution.

To ensure adequate definition of any problem, one should first gather background information in the general area under consideration (some of this information will later have to be discarded as irrelevant). It often helps to talk to others, for they may have confronted the same problem at one time or another. Depending on the problem, the gathering of information can take the form of a literature search, a patent search, a scrutiny of financial data, a visit to the competition, the advice of paid consultants (experts), or an examination of case histories — there are many ways of becoming informed on a subject. Once the problem has been defined, the definition should be examined in light of the information collected to determine the degree to which it is a true statement of the problem or of the decision to be made.

3 IDENTIFY ALTERNATIVES

Whenever one is confronted with a choice, one must decide which course of action to take. Often the choices are obvious. On the other hand, consider the situation in which a decision maker has identified several choices and used all of his skill to select one of them, yet his choice failed because he overlooked another alternative that was critical to the final outcome. The importance of this second step in the decision-making process, *identifying alternatives,* cannot be stressed too strongly. It is important to write down all possible alternatives to the problem solution, no matter how foolish or far-fetched they may seem at first. Only in this way can one reduce the likelihood that a reasonable alternative was overlooked.

4 QUANTIFY ALTERNATIVES

The list of alternatives generated out of the problem definition must now be quantified in order to rule out those that are not pertinent to the problem solution, and in order to weigh the relative importance of those that are. To restrict the list of alternatives, one must impose limits on what is important to the final decision. For example, when deciding which model of car to drop from next year's line, it may be that color is not a variable one needs to consider, although size of engine, wheel base, and weight are. The quantification or weight one gives to each alternative is usually determined by long- or short-range plans and policies, costs, rewards, facilities, as well as one's own personal preferences.

5 APPLY DECISION AIDS

Unfortunately, many of the critical decisions made by experienced leaders in both business and government are based on a habit, "gut feel," advice from "experts," snap judgment, impulse, or just plain chance (the toss of a coin). In recent years, specialists in business and technology have devised certain mathematical techniques that can assist the decision maker and will help him avoid relying on "gut feel" alone. These techniques are known as *decision aids,* and they are intended to maximize the likelihood that the decision maker reaches the best decision open to him. These aids include *decision matrix, linear programing, game theory, linear regression, mathematical modeling,* and *forecasting.* All are discussed elsewhere in this book.

Since all decision aids rely on the availability of precise information, using these aids may prod the decision maker to understand more fully the scope of his problem, the differences among alternatives, and the relative utility of each. Like any other tool, a decision aid is limited in its usefulness by the skill, resourcefulness, and insight of the decision maker.

6 THE DECISION

The *decision* itself is the culmination of the process. Regardless of the problem, the alternatives, the decision aids, or the consequences to follow, once a decision is made, things begin to happen. Decisions trigger action, movement, and change. Once a decision is made, there is a strong tendency to "stick with it." This is understandable, of course; but it is not necessary and it can be risky. Although the purpose of the stepwise decision-making process is to guide a decision maker to the best choice, there is no reason why this choice cannot be reversed. The consequences of one's decisions, no matter how carefully they were made, should be watched. If these consequences run contrary to the decision maker's analysis and expectations, it may be that the decision itself should be cancelled — if that is still possible. For example, in the winter of 1978-1979, the U.S. Secretary of Energy announced our government's decision not to buy oil from Mexico due to the high competitive price. This decision was abruptly reversed when it was realized that other oil negotiations would possibly fall through, thereby causing a national fuel shortage. The ability, first, to admit that a decision may have been wrong, and second, to reverse it if necessary, may lessen the chances of becoming irrationally overcommitted to a course of action. The consequences of such overcommitment are discussed in detail in Chapter 6.

7 IMPLEMENTATION

Once a decision has been made, appropriate action must be taken to ensure that the decision will be carried out as planned. This is the important last step in the process. All too often even the best decisions fail to be implemented due to lack of resources, such as necessary funds, space, or staff, or some other failure, such as inadequate supervision of subordinates and employees.* In any event, the decision maker should know that his decision will be implemented before he moves on to the next problem. Coupled with an assurance of implementation, it is always a good idea to require some reporting scheme that relates or charts the progress toward the ultimate decision goal. Such a scheme can have as its basis expenditures (in dollars), time (in months), or a series of other increments required to achieve the goal.

8 ITERATION OF STEPS IN THE PROCESS

Finally, remember that the decision is cyclical in nature; although the decision maker may wish to press on in a linear stepwise manner, feedback loops and repetition are often necessary. For example, one may be in the middle of *quantifying alternatives,* only to find that all of the alternatives have not yet been *identified* — a discovery that could possibly result in a *redefinition* of the problem. By iterating the sequence of steps in the basic procedure just described, the chances are good that the best decision will be made.

---

*In a large-scale system, a sophisticated technique of implementing a decision is PERT/CPM (Program Evaluation Review Technique/Critical Path Method) (Hill, 1970).

9 SELECTED BIBLIOGRAPHY

Hill, Percy H. *The Science of Engineering Design.* New York: Holt, Rinehart and Winston, Inc., 1970.

Keen, Peter G.W., and Morton, S. Scott. *Decision Support Systems: An Organizational Perspective.* Reading, Mass.: Addison-Wesley Publishing Co., 1978.

Morris, George E. *Engineering: A Decision-Making Process.* Boston, Mass.: Houghton Mifflin Company, 1977.

Morris, William T. *Decision Analysis.* Columbus, Ohio: Grid, Inc., 1977.

Papps, Ivy, and Henderson, Willie. *Models and Economic Theory.* Philadelphia, Pa.: W.B. Saunders Co., 1977.

Riggs, James L. *Economic Decision Models: For Engineers and Managers.* New York: McGraw-Hill Book Co., 1968.

Rubinstein, Moshe F. *Patterns of Problem Solving.* Englewood Cliffs, N.J.: Prentice-Hall, Inc., 1975.

Chapter 4
Ethical Decision Making

1 INTRODUCTION

Ethical decision making is probably the oldest type of decision making systematically studied and practiced. It originated centuries ago in *casuistry*, the application of ethical principles to particular cases. And it applied especially to *hard cases*, ones in which more than one principle applies but with inconsistent results, so that some exception or qualification to the principle(s) is necessary if the right decision is to be made. Casuistry was widely practiced after the Middle Ages by rabbis and priests. Persons specially trained in this mode of ethical thinking were often consulted when a particularly difficult moral question was faced. Casuistry fell into ill repute when it degenerated into a technique for finding exceptions to ethical principles in order to permit persons to do what they wanted without the appearance of wrong doing.

Like the traditional casuist, our concern throughout this chapter is *within* ethics, and not *about* ethics. When philosophers think *about* ethics, they think mainly about:

1. Explaining the nature of ethical concepts and principles.
2. Constructing and criticizing arguments for (and against) such principles.
3. Analyzing the components and structure of ethical theories.
4. Debating the merits of ethical theories.

Percy H. Hill et al., Making Decisions: A Multidisciplinary Introduction

Since it is applied ethical reasoning, deliberation, and decision making, not theoretical ethics, with which we are concerned, these matters must be ignored here, even though their study would shed much light on our task. Instead, we must work within the framework of those ethical concepts, principles, and judgments that are more or less familiar to us in our own society and are descriptive of how we actually conduct moral reasoning.

2 THE SETTING

Understanding the nature of ethical decision making requires acknowledging three factors that determine how we look at human conduct from the moral or ethical point of view.

2.1 Society

Consider the situation of Robinson Crusoe, castaway alone on a desert island, with no other persons in his environment and with little or no prospect (let us suppose) of returning to civilization. (We are to think of Crusoe's situation *before* Friday and the other natives appear on the scene.) Can we evaluate Crusoe's conduct from the moral point of view? How do issues of ethical decision making look to him in his situation? If we assume that Crusoe is interested in his survival, then he must answer certain questions. How much time and energy, if any, should I spend gathering wood for a bonfire and tending it, on the remote chance of signaling a distant ship for rescue? How much time should I devote to gathering nuts and other edibles, how much to building a safe and strong shelter right where I am, and how much to exploring the island to look for a better place to live? Techniques described elsewhere in this volume (especially Chapters 2 and 7) can be of help to Crusoe in answering these questions.

However Crusoe decides these matters, he can ask later: did I make the best decision under the circumstances? Did I do the right thing? Notice that the correct answers to these questions revolve entirely around Crusoe — *his* interests, preferences, goals, aspirations — and how what *he* did or did not do affects his future circumstances. What can be said of his conduct — good or bad, right or wrong — is entirely a function of its effects upon his future well-being. Such virtues and vices as he can exhibit in his situation — courage or self-pity, enterprise or sloth, patience or impulsiveness, tenacity or pusillanimity — further confirm the point. Right conduct for Crusoe is indistinguishable from acting by reference to goals and standards that have no reference to anyone else's interests or welfare.

The most distinctive features of morality are utterly absent in Crusoe's situation. The reason is clear: there are no other interests — at least no other human interests* — that he has to consider in his deliberations, because (by hypothesis) his conduct affects and is affected by no other persons with interests distinct from his. Similarly, the most familiar kinds of immorality — the use of force or fraud to get one's way, undertaking obligations with no intention of keeping them, evasion or distortion of the truth to the disadvantage of others, neglect or outright repudiation of duties and burdens when no one can enforce them, abuse of privileges — cannot occur in solitude. They are inconceivable except against a background of other persons who can be coerced, defrauded, cheated, lied to, harmed, and so forth. Likewise, the major virtues that we acknowledge — fairness, sincerity, honesty, loyalty — are essentially social in their origin and function. Thus, virtually all the ethical decisions we face, unlike those Crusoe faces, occur in a setting of society — the inescapable, ubiquitous presence of other persons who have their own aims and interests, goals and projects, just as we do.

2.2 Scarcity

Crusoe's situation, both before and after Friday enters his life, is fortunate in that the physical environment is not hostile to his survival. Potable water, ample dry land, tolerable climate, edible plants, game, forests — all these attest to the possibility of survival and of some comfort (if that is what he wants), provided only that he finds or makes some tools, plans sensibly, and works efficiently. He is not, of course, blessed with the prospects of a Garden of Eden, or Elysian fields, where all he must do is reach out and pluck food from the nearest branch, with shelter and other conveniences either miraculously unnecessary or no less miraculously at hand. Crusoe's situation thus lies somewhere between the two extremes of abject scarcity, where even bare survival is impossible, and unlimited abundance, with goods and services free for the taking and endlessly replenished.

Human life typically places us in the same situation. Accordingly, morality is designed primarily for the center portion of the spectrum that lies between scarcity and surfeit. Many of the most distinctive features of morality seem to vanish at the two extremes. What does theft and waste matter if there is no limit to the goods available? What is the point of prudence and honesty, patience and fairness, if we are all doomed to die in the next instant? True, the prospect of imminent death does allow such virtues as courage and patience in adversity to shine forth even though they

*Whether animals, insects, and plants have interests and whether, if they do, ethical decision making must take them into account, are matters that will not be discussed here.

are irrelevant to survival. Even so, honesty and veracity, integrity and charity, fairness and mutual respect, are taught and learned in the assumption that tomorrow is another day and not the end of the world. A species otherwise like us, but doomed to swift extinction and aware of its fate, would have a very different view of right and wrong, good and bad, from ours.

2.3 Inequality

An inescapable consequence of the plurality of persons, with interests in conflict over goods and services that are insufficient to satisfy everyone, is that some will be better off than others. No matter how widespread cooperation may be, there will be room for competition; and no matter how the competition is policed and regulated, not all can win. Some observers will conclude that this is necessarily unfair, and that the only fair arrangement is the equal distribution of goods and services, benefits and burdens. In some situations, e.g., dividing a cake or pie for dessert, "share and share alike" works just fine and probably is fair. With regard to most material goods, however, such strict or radical egalitarianism will not work. It will not work because it is not stable. Even if the division of goods and services is made today with perfect equality, tomorrow or the next day, trades and bargaining, different rates of consumption and waste, will quickly produce unequal remainders in each person's hands. As the Scots philosopher David Hume shrewdly put it, more than two centuries ago, "Render possessions ever so equal, men's different degrees of art, care, and industry will immediately break that equality." No ethical theory can afford to contradict this truth. In addition, some would argue that radical egalitarianism is unfair, because it violates people's rights and ignores differences in desert and merit, which not only permit but require unequal reward.

A better approach, more in tune with human nature, is to accept unequal apportionment of goods and services, benefits and burdens, as unavoidable and possibly even desirable, and to endeavor to make certain that this unequal distribution is not *unfair*. The task then becomes one of searching for principles under which it is known in advance that, once they are applied, some persons will gain and others will lose, but that at least the gains and losses will not be unfair, i.e., disadvantage some in order to advantage others unjustifiably. Equal opportunity to gain advantages, therefore, is a natural provision to seek to build into the principles that govern ethical decision making.* If each person has an equal opportunity to

---

*In this light, consider the basic principles of social justice proposed by John Rawls in his influential treatise, *A Theory of Justice* (1971): "Each person is to have an equal right to the most extensive basic liberty compatible with a similar liberty for others, . . . (and) social and economic inequalities are to be arranged so that they are both reasonably expected to be to everyone's advantage, and attached to positions and offices open to all." (p. 60) It is the last clause in this passage that implicitly refers to equality of opportunity.

win and the game is otherwise fair then, even though it is necessary that most or all but one will lose, the losers have no ground for complaint against the winner(s). They must settle for their lot, without envy for the lucky, because they know they had a fair chance to win. Fair inequalities are specially urgent as the stakes go up. In situations where not all can live, or where some must die if any are to survive, we want assurance that the principles by which the winners and losers are determined are as fair as possible to the persons involved. Examples of such principles can be found in many familiar maxims, the moral clichés of ordinary life, by means of which we justify (however inadequately) the allocation of unequal shares to persons of otherwise equal entitlement: first come, first served; winner take all; you had your turn. Other things being equal, decision making under one or another of these principles is exactly the right thing to do, because these principles reflect the requirements of the moral point of view.

3   ETHICAL DECISION MAKING: First Steps

Imagine that you are a member of a hypothetical primitive society whose ethical outlook is entirely expressed by the Ten Commandments (Exodus 20:3-17). Let us assume that everyone in the society knows and accepts these rules without qualification. How would the problems of ethical decision making look to you in such a society? Given *any* situation in which you find yourself, you could always ask: what is the morally right thing for me to do in this situation? You can find a conclusive answer if you reason as follows.

First, ask yourself whether you are not in a situation covered by one of the ten rules. Either you are, or you are not. If you are not, then there is *no answer* to the quesion: what is the morally right thing to do? Since the ethical rules are silent on your situation (e.g., a neighbor has asked you to trade him some of your sheep for some of his goats), you can conclude that you may do as you please (in this example, you may make the trade or not and on whatever terms, as you wish). How can you tell whether the rules do or do not apply in your situation? Imagine in front of you the list of rules on one side, and all the true descriptions of your situation (and what you want to do) on the other. If there is no fit between anything on either list, then none of the rules applies to the situation.

Suppose you conclude that the situation you are in is covered by one of the rules. The rules either forbid or require you to do something in order to comply; they are a set of ten do's and don't's. Knowing this, you know that the right thing is to do, or refrain from doing, whatever the applicable rule requires or forbids. So, given that the moral point of view in your society is exhaustively expressed by the Ten Commandments, the simple stepwise procedure described above gives a determinate solution to every problem of ethical decision making that you or any member of your society could confront.

It is all too obvious that the moral world of this hypothetical primitive society is both much simpler and very different from the moral world in which we actually live. First, in this primitive society a vast range of conduct is apparently morally indifferent. For example, there seems to be nothing wrong with such acts as turning a cold shoulder on someone in need, stinginess, greed, cowardice, breaking promises, concealing the truth, or dishonesty, as long as you do not break the Eighth, Ninth, and Tenth Commandments. Such conduct is *not* morally indifferent to us. We have far less latitude to do as we please, without being subject to moral criticism, than do the people of this hypothetical society.

Second, all ethical considerations in this hypothetical society are bound up in compliance with rigid general rules of universal application and equal weight that work in an all-or-nothing fashion. The universality of application and generality of scope is a feature of moral rules for us, too. What is right for me in a given situation is right for you, too, except where some morally relevant factor distinguishes us or our situations. What is right for whites is right for blacks, what is right for women is right for men, and so on, except where some morally relevant factor tied to race or sex or whatever applies. For us, however, morality also involves a multitude of maxims and principles (e.g., first come, first served; what's sauce for the goose is sauce for the gander; each tub on its own bottom). These are not simple or rigid rules at all; they have qualifications, contingencies, and exceptions. They are also not of equal weight in every situation to which they apply. They give scope to imagination and make moral conduct far more creative than does mere compliance with rules.

Third, the ethical rules of this society seem to be mutually consistent and apparently never apply with incompatible results to one and the same situation.* For us, ethical decision making frequently, though by no means always, confronts us with conflicts between morally valid considerations. We are pulled toward doing the wrong thing not only by selfishness or other weaknesses but by ethical principles, duties, and obligations of apparently incompatible effect.

---

*Actually, this is not quite true, as the following example shows. Suppose that you lived in this primitive society and thus have a duty both to honor your parents and also not to steal anything of your neighbor's. Suppose further that your mother is deathly ill, but could recover if she could get enough of a new, rare drug, and quickly. She begs you to get it for her. Is so happens that the needed drug, invented a while ago by your neighborhood research biochemist, is available only under the inventor's monopoly, and he refuses to sell you the quantity you need at a price you can pay. No friend or relative or bank will loan you the money you need. You are furious, your mother is dying, but what can you do? If you don't get that drug, then you've failed to care for your sick parent; but surely such care is required (even if only implicitly) by the Fifth Commandment. But the only way you can get the drug, it seems, is to steal it and thus to violate the Eighth Commandment.

Fourth, some of the most distinctive features of our moral landscape are missing in this primitive society. They seem to have no conception of anybody's *rights;* they seem not to understand that people can do things to create *obligations* for themselves; and they have no understanding of trying to do the *best thing for all concerned.* In their view of morality a person is supposed to honor his parents, but not because parents have a right to respect. A person is supposed not to kill anyone, but not because everyone has a right to life. Similarly, although people in this primitive society can make agreements, promises, and give one another their word, there is no moral obligation created by a promise, and so there is nothing wrong in failing to perform on your promise. Finally, the idea that one ought to do the best thing for all concerned, particularly when some conflict of duties or obligations arises, or when there are no duties or obligations and no applicable rules in the situation, is wholly absent. Our moral world, however, is dominated by the structures given to it by our rights, our obligations, and doing the best for all concerned. Our moral world does not consist only of right and wrong conduct, nor is right and wrong conduct determined or required by a small set of rules. The fact that we can disagree over our rights and obligations, and then disagree over whether and how to act upon them, accounts for most of the complexity and perplexity we find in the ethical decision making we face every day.

The common result of these major differences between the problem of ethical decision making in the hypothetical primitive society we have examined and in our natural society is that it is usually easy for them – but often quite difficult for us – to know what is the right thing to do.

4   THE MORAL POINT OF VIEW: Presuppositions

The moral point of view, and thus ethical decision making, have certain basic presuppositions in addition to the pervasive features of society, scarcity, and inequality discussed earlier in this chapter (Section 2). Two of these are especially important to keep in mind throughout our discussion, both because they underlie everything else and because they help contrast ethical decision making with some other kinds of decision making.

4.1 The Moral Agent

In our world, the hallmark of a person who looks at his life from the moral point of view is that he regards himself as morally responsible, a creature able to act (and to refrain from acting), a creature who is responsible for what he does (except when and where something excuses him from responsibility). In the language of traditional moral philosophy, he views himself as a moral agent, an "autonomous" person, as the philosopher Immanuel Kant would have put it.

What this means can be brought out by considering two different and extreme types, each outlandish in its own way. One is to be found in the *nihilist,* someone who abdicates all responsibility on the ground that nothing matters — we're all in the grip of Fate, and we have no control over anything, not even our own conduct. There can be no ethical decision making (nor any kind of decision making!) for such a person. No normal person is likely to be tempted into genuine nihilism, except perhaps briefly in moments of despair or metaphysical confusion. The other extreme type might be called the *bureaucrat,* since he dodges responsibility wherever possible by acting so that someone else, or the role or status he occupies, determines how he acts and his reasons for acting.* "My hands are tied; I have my orders; there's nothing to discuss" expresses this mentality. Such a person does, indeed, make decisions, but he cannot view them as *his* decisions, or as *ethical* decisions, since he never undertakes to evaluate critically his reasons for acting as he does. Unlike nihilism, which is really a form of pathology, bureaucratism tempts us all, because each of us holds one or more "stations," and associated with each station are certain "duties." Moreover, loyalty and fidelity, and the acknowledgement of others' authority over us, are generally regarded as virtues. So it may be difficult to demark the limits of moral autonomy, since it can appear to trespass on the territory protected by these virtues.

4.2 Egoism versus Altruism

The basic problem for ethical decision making is to ensure fair treatment to all concerned, given the fact that there is an irreducible plurality of independent persons to be considered, with distinct and occasionally conflicting and competing interests and rights, situated in a permanent setting somewhere between extreme scarcity (in which no one's needs could be satisfied) and unlimited abundance (in which everyone's whims could be satisfied). On a collision course with this view is *egoism,* or what the popular philosopher, Ayn Rand, defended in her book provocatively titled *The Virtue of Selfishness.* The subject is almost impossible to discuss intelligently, because some simple distinctions are constantly ignored: (a) a person who acts on his interests (which leads to the question of what a person's interests are), (b) a person who acts in (what he believes to be) his self-interests, and (c) a person who acts selfishly. Egoism is

---

*Cf. the "other directed man," made famous a generation ago by David Riesman in his book, *The Lonely Crowd.*

invariably ambiguous as between (b) and (c), so the term is best avoided.

A person's *interests* can be (or be in) anything — his own fame and leisure, the education and welfare of his children, lower taxes for everyone, a pennant for the Red Sox, cleaner sand on the beaches. He may be interested in these things as a means to the satisfaction of some other interests, or he may be interested in them for their own sake — these ends express for him the way he wants the world to be. Something can be an interest (or in the interest) of one person but not another, and something can be an interest of his and an interest of hers but for different reasons. Not all interests of different persons conflict, and not all the interests of a given person are necessarily mutually consistent.

The *self-interests* of a person can be viewed in either of two ways. They can be defined as a subset of that person's interests, i.e., the interests of a given person in his own welfare or advantage, regardless of whether what advantages him also advantages (or disadvantages) others. (We might define a self-centered person as one whose interests are preponderantly self-interests.) Thus, if a person satisfies one of his self-interests, he necessarily satisfied one of his interests. The converse, however, is not true! When you act to benefit another person, and in so doing do what you want, then the *other* person's welfare is something in which *you* are interested. But in satisfying this interest of yours, you do not thereby automatically advance your *own* self-interests; you might easily be acting contrary to them. We could also define a person's self-interests as whatever is to his advantage, whether or not he is interested in it (i.e., whether or not he knows that it is to his advantage and whether or not he cares).

A *selfish* person is anyone who tries to satisfy his self-interests without regard for how his doing so affects the welfare of others. Even though he knows it harms them, he does not care.* We act selfishly whenever we act as a selfish person would act, and each of us at least occasionally acts just like that.

It is most important to notice that a person who has self-interests can pursue them, if not with avidity then up to a certain limit, without being selfish (indifferent to the welfare of others) in the process. Whereas the selfish man is the paradigm of immorality, the self-interested man is Everyman. The selfish man by definition rejects the moral point of view, since that point of view requires that the welfare (and hence the relevant interests) of all persons, not just the agent, be impartially considered and weighed. The moral point of view does not require that persons have no interest in their own welfare, much less that they have no interests at all. On

---

*Sammy Glick, the fictional anti-hero of Budd Schulberg's novel, *What Makes Sammy Run?* is a paradigm of the selfish self-centered person. Some might prefer to say that Sammy Glick is *amoral,* not *immoral,* because he never even recognizes that there are other persons with interests of their own, and therefore he doesn't even understand what an ethical versus an unethical decision would be. It does not much matter for our purposes which way he is classified.

the contrary, it assumes that there is a plurality of persons, each with his or her own interests, some of which are self-interests and others that are not, and that some of the interests of different persons conflict. An ethics without interests is pointless, whereas an "ethics of selfishness" is a contradiction.

Different defects attend the ethic of unlimited altruism or extreme self-sacrifice. Saints and heroes are a bit frightening, because they are so unselfish; they act as if they did not care about their own welfare at all. A person with no self-interests, like a person with no interests at all, is virtually unintelligible to us. If all conduct in society took the ludicrous form of the proverbial pair of friends who, upon entering a doorway together, immediately say, "You first, Gaston" — "No, you first, Alphonse," it would be virtually impossible for anyone to do anything in the vicinity of others. The total suspension of self-interest required by universal altruism is practically as well as theoretically absurd.*

The task of ethical decision making is not to abolish self-interest but to limit it in rational ways, and for rational goals. Right conduct is thus bracketed between the obvious vice of selfishness, which is the pursuit of self-interest to the exclusion of all else, and the imaginary virtue of complete altruism.

5   THE ETHICAL COMPONENT IN DECISION MAKING

What makes ethical decision making different from other kinds of decision making? Does it lie in the *methods* of decision making? In the *conclusions* reached? In the *assumptions* used? In all or none of these? One line of argument that gives an answer to these questions goes like this.

What is distinctive about ethical decision making lies in the role of *ethical priniciples* both in the reasoning that leads up to the decison, and in the fact that the decision maker accepts the principle in question as part of his moral outlook. A person makes an ethical decision, as distinct from some other kind of decision, if an only if he decides what to do by essential reliance upon some ethical rule, principle, standard, or norm. By essential reliance is meant that had he not relied on the rule, he would not have decided to do what he did; or, if he had decided to do what he did then his *reason* for deciding would not have been the same; his reason would not have been an *ethical* principle, but some other sort of principle, perhaps one of business efficiency, class or national self-interest, or even personal advantage.

---

*Perhaps this helps explain why social psychologists find altruism in such short supply (see Chapter 5, Sections 2 and 3).

(It is sometimes said that the path of enlightened self-interest coincides with the path of true morality, even though the motives and principles behind the two are different.) A rule, principle, standard, or norm is ethical if and only if it takes into account the interests and situation of other persons affected by the agent's conduct and treats them impartially along with those of the agent.

The idea of a moral principle, of alternative principles relevant to a given decision, of how a moral principle can be outweighed by competing considerations (and vice versa), and of the circumscribed role that is sometimes granted to ethical principles in foreign policy can all be illustrated by one phase of the famous Cuban missile crisis of 1962. Throughout the Thirteen Days in which our government debated what to do, how to do it, and why, Attorney General Robert Kennedy, we are told,* constantly reminded the others who were advising the President that *everything possible must be done to avoid causing the innocent* (in this case, Cuban civilians) *to suffer even in a just cause* (getting the missiles dismantled or destroyed). This pitted him against those who favored a pre-emptive air strike on the missile sites, no matter how many innocent suffered, as well as against those who opposed any military action in order to get rid of the missiles.

At the risk of oversimplification, it appears that three major positions emerged during the Thirteen Days on the proper role of ethical principles:

a.   In effect, they have no role whatever, because national prestige and self-interest should always prevail.
b.   They have a role, but so have nonethical considerations, and no general rule can be laid down as to which kind of principle should dominate in any situation.
c.   Ethical principles always should have the dominant role in any situation to which they apply, even at the expense of national self-interest.

Because former Secretary of State Dean Acheson seemed to take the position (a), whereas Ambassador Adlai Stevenson seemed to take position (c), Acheson was judged by Robert Kennedy to be needlessly hawkish and Stevenson needlessly dovish. Kennedy's own position was roughly (b).

The situation was compounded by the fact that the parties to the debate relied on competing principles, and each advocate no doubt thought his own preferred principle was the right one to follow. (Whether anyone during the debate ever bothered to formulate these principles in so many words and to compare them from the moral point of view is doubtful; the White House does not have a moral philosopher in residence.) These principles were evident: National self-interest always takes precedence over

---

*See Arthur M. Schlesinger, Jr., *Robert Kennedy and His Times*, Houghton-Mifflin Co., pp. 529-532.

the lives of innocent foreigners; any means to achieve a just end is morally permissible provided that it does so that a favorable cost/benefit ratio; if a pre-emptive military strike (bombing mission, commando raid) in a nation's self-defense can eliminate a dangerous threat, then the strike is justified even if some innocent persons are killed. There was, also, as we have seen, Kennedy's principle that everything possible must be done to avoid causing the innocent to suffer even in a just cause. Let us look more closely at that principle.

It certainly is an ethical principle. First, it is a principle of conduct, because whether or not you accept and rely upon this principle affects what you do. Second, this principle requires those acting in their own interests to keep in mind the interests of others who are vulnerable to severe harm, and to avoid harm if at all possible. In other words, the principle requires the self-judged agents of justice to keep in mind the rights of others who are helpless bystanders (remember, the ordinary Cuban citizen was virtually a hostage of his government's decision to accept the Soviet missiles), because being an agent of justice does not give anyone the right to inflict avoidable harm on the innocent. Third, this principle does not put the interests of the agent ahead of the interests of anyone else; it places the presumed interest of all in justice (self-defense) ahead of any other interest. This can be seen as soon as we challenge Kennedy's principle by asking how *we* would like it if our enemies used this principle in their deliberations, as Kennedy proposed that we use it in ours. Reflection quickly shows our answer must be that we would like that very much; we would want any government about to strike first at our missiles to keep in mind the millions of helpless American citizens who live nearby and who have absolutely no control as individuals over the placement or use of these missiles by their own government. In other words, Kennedy's principle is one that both sides to a controversy can accept, and in this respect is reminiscent of the requirements for moral decision making that are urged on us by the Golden Rule.

Given these considerations, we can say that if our government in the missile crisis acted without *any* regard for the interests of innocent Cuban citizens, then it acted immorally and its decision to act in this way was an immoral one. We can also say that if our government acted in the hawkish fashion described in position (a), then it probably also made an immoral decision, but one that was immoral for a different reason. The hawks did consider the interests of innocent Cubans, but decided that they were outweighed by the incompatible interests of threatened Americans. The problem here is that it is suspect to argue that although the interests of others matter, one's own interests matter more and therefore should prevail; these "others" are unlikely always to see it that way. Such reasoning is functionally equivalent to the position that the interests of others simply do not matter at all, and therefore need not be considered; one hopes that no one in our government during the missile crisis relied on any such immoral "principle." Finally, we should also note that if our government had acted so as to take no account of American interests — if it was prepared to run any risk to this country in order to avoid risking the death of innocent Cubans — then it would have put in unjustifiable jeopardy the very interests whose chief responsibility it was in office to serve: those of the American people.

It is easy to see why a thoughtful person, skeptical of military solutions to political problems, capable of sensing the devastation of even the most "surgical" military strike, unwilling to sacrifice the national interest, and unwilling to act on principles that one would hate to have one's adversary act upon, would find that he had to reject both dovish and hawkish positions.

6   ETHICAL DELIBERATION: Initiatives

Like other decision making, ethical decision making often presents itself to us in a nested or layered structure. Careful deliberation among the open alternatives requires analysis of the *sequence* in which alternative courses of action present themselves, identification of the *range* of alternatives at each stage, and comparative evaluation in order to make the right decison. Sometimes it is possible to construct something like a decision tree (recall Chapter 9) that represents all these alternatives (if not their relative merits) in their proper sequence. In real life we rarely bother to set this out so patiently and sequentially, but it might be useful if we did.*

Let us consider a situation in which you take the initiative to solve a problem. Suppose you are the father of a high school senior, and you attach great weight to your daughter's going to a "good" college. To give her both assurance and incentive, you are willing to *promise* that if she is admitted to a good college you'll undertake to provide all her tuition and expenses, provided she is willing to save for this purpose all she can earn during summers, vacations, and a job at college. There are no other conditions — just that she must be admitted to a good college and must be willing to do her share (as defined) of paying the costs. Let's examine step by step the successive decision-making situations involved, and the ethical factors that are likely to enter at each stage.

☐   **Situation 1: Whether or promise or not.** What are the alternatives to your making her this promise? There are several. You could simply avow your intention ("I can't promise to pay for all four years, but I'll

---

*Whether it is always possible to do this is a question we need not consider; it is enough to know that we often can. Likewise, whether it is more useful as a device to criticize decisions already made, rather than as a method to use to reach a decision in the first place, we can also set aside.

certainly try."). You could declare your preference ("I can't promise, but I'd certainly like to be able to pay your expenses."). Or you could do neither and merely predict your behavior ("I won't promise but you know me, I'll probably pay the bills."). Any of these options may be ethically permissible, in that none violates your daughter's rights, but not all options will be equally desirable given the factual situation. Your primary ethical concern in situation 1 is whether the undertaking in question is best arranged by fixing it with a promise, with all its ethical consequences, rather than making no promise at all. The chief ethical consequences of making a promise are that one comes under an obligation to the other person to perform as promised, and that the other person acquires the right to the promised performance. The best reason for you to hesitate to promise, therefore, is doubt whether you can perform on your word.

In situation 1, the alternatives can be reduced to two: (a) to promise, or (b) not to promise, and to do something else, such as declare one's intention. Let us henceforth ignore alternative (b), with all its variations, and assume that you decide on alternative (a). Having decided to *promise* your daughter, you are now in situation 2.

☐ **Situation 2: What to promise?** For the sake of illustration, we have already specified the content of what you propose to promise her. Obviously, there is a wide range of alternatives here. From an ethical point of view, the content of your promise must take into account (a) how much you can afford to spend on her education, consistent with your other financial obligations (not your preferred standard of living while she is in college, but your *obligations,* e.g., house mortgage), and (b) what incentive if any you want to give her for finishing high school with a good record and motivating her to do well in college once she gets there. The ethical considerations that enter into situation 2 are thus your obligations to others and what is best for your daughter's future welfare. (Other, nonethical considerations will enter too, of course, but we can ignore them here.) Suppose you can foresee heavy expenses for your aging parents, with no one to help them out but you. You then must weigh whether in situation 1 it would be better to promise your daughter nothing and content yourself with some other arrangement; or having decided to promise her something, to make adjustments in situation 2 that (a) specify the contingencies on your promise, and (b) shift onto her shoulders a greater fraction of her total college expenses.

☐ **Situation 3: Whether or not to promise with the intention of keeping your word.** To tell your daughter that you *promise* to pay her college expenses, but with secret reservations (remember how as children we would sometimes promise, but hide our fingers and keep them crossed?) or with no intention at all to keep your word, is to act insincerely and in a morally outrageous manner that wrongs the person to whom you say "I promise." (What might be defended in special circumstances, e.g., when your promise is extracted by force, or given hastily and on some utterly trivial matter, is indefensible here.) This is a solemn promise, carefully weighed, and crucially affects the well-being and expectations of the other person, someone, moreover, who is dependent on you and whom you presumably love. There is no ethical alternative in situation 2 except to promise with the intention of doing as you promise. Let us assume that this is what you do. Having done that, you soon will be in situation 4.

☐ **Situation 4: Whether or not to keep your word.** Here there are, again, two main alternatives.

> Alternative A: Keep your word. Normally, in situation 4, there is really nothing more to decide, after making a sincere promise to do x. One accepts the tacit obligation to do as one promised, and in due course one proceeds to do x. It is usually the case that the right thing to do is to do what one promised, though this is not always true. Suppose that circumstances arise that were not anticipated. If they had been, the sensible thing to do would have been to make a contingent promise and say, "I promise I will, but not if . . . ." You now judge that the best thing to do is to get out of the promise – cancel it and break your word. In such exceptional cases, we are ready to act on the other major alternative here, alternative B.

> Alternative B: Do not keep your word. This alternative itself has three main versions:

>> *Alternative B₁ : Do not apologize and do not explain.* How could you really accept this alternative? Either you don't recognize the obligation created by your promise, or you choose to ignore it. If the former, then you are simply out of touch with the moral world that the rest of us inhabit. If the latter, then you must know you have flagrantly disregarded the rights of your daughter who, on the strength of your promise, has expected you to conform to your word. A decision in favor of alternative B_1, therefore, is simply ethically wrong. You have no right to behave in this way. How grave a wrong you have done to the other person will obviously depend on several factors, e.g., how important the promise was to her or how much she had already altered her conduct in expectation that you would keep your word.

Alternative B₂ : Apologize, explain, and offer a justification.
In accepting this alternative, as with alternative A, you accept
the obligation imposed by your promise. In this alternative,
however, you justify breaking your word by pointing to the
impossibility of keeping it given something else that is a
higher or prior obligation, so that it would now be wrong for
you to keep your promise. For example, you and your wife
agreed years ago that you would support her parents after
they retired if their social security and pension income
proved inadequate. When you promised your daughter to pay
her college expenses, you made no proviso on this point
because it seemed there would be no problem. Unforeseen
events have arisen (a very high rate of inflation, pension fund
bankruptcy, exorbitant medical expenses), so you explain to
your daughter that your obligation to her grandparents takes
precedence over your promise to her. The chief ethical
requirement of this alternative is to be sure that the
justification for breaking your promise is sufficiently
weighty, and to avoid this alternative if the only available
justification is too weak.

Alternative B₃ : Apologize, explain, and offer an excuse. If
you take this route, then as in alternatives A and B₂ , you
recognize the obligation created by your promise. This
alternative, however, is open to you only when some
genuinely new or honestly overlooked fact arises that cannot
be avoided but is decisively relevant to keeping the promise
as made, some contingency that could not be reasonably
anticipated. For instance, you unexpectedly lose your job,
try but fail to get another, and the remaining family income
is simply insufficient to put your daughter through even one
year at her expensive private college. The task for ethical
deliberation in situation 4, if this alternative is contemplated,
is to weigh whether one's new circumstances really constitute
an adequate excuse.

No matter whether you choose alternative B_2 or B_3, you will find
yourself promptly in situation 5.

☐   **Situation 5: Whether or not to make amends.** In the case of a promise
of slight weight (e.g., you promise to go to the movies with your
roommate tomorrow night), breaking it probably will not give rise to
thoughts of remedy or compensation. At the other extreme, where you
bind yourself to another person by a mutual promise in the form of a
written   contract,   there   will   be   legally   enforceable   penalties

acknowledged in advance, tacitly or explicitly, for nonfeasance by either party. In the example we have been using, once you have broken your promise to your daughter to pay her college expenses, you will certainly want to try to make it up to her in some way or other. Since you are likely to give up entirely on the idea of her going to college only as a last resort, the obvious first alternative to consider is whether your altered situation allows her to qualify for scholarship support at college. Failing that, some form of direct borrowing from a bank or other lending institution may still enable her to go to college, though perhaps not the expensive good one that you both hoped she would attend. The chief ethical considerations you face in situation 5 are whether remedy or compensation is called for at all; and, if it is, then what counts as adequate or appropriate compensation in the circumstances.

Despite the relative detail with which we have examined the example of whether or not you should make a promise, and the ethical issues that arise after you decide to do so, there is more to be said at almost every decision point. Still, the foregoing analysis suffices to illustrate how one can sort out the issues in sequence and bring into play familiar moral considerations, one by one, at each step of the way.

7   ETHICAL DELIBERATION: A Dilemma

The structure of concepts just explored sheds some light on the resources at our disposal when we face a decision and want to do the right thing. Yet the predicaments in which we often find ourselves require much more imaginative thinking than has been illustrated so far. We need to examine a situation in which our authority and powers are more limited, the risks to ourselves much greater, the consequences less foreseeable, and the constraints of duty more pronounced, in order to get a better feel for ethical decision making in real life. For this purpose, let us explore in some detail the following situation.*

A young lawyer, flushed with success after having been invited to join a large and prestigious law firm, is asked by one of the firm's senior partners to prepare a memorandum on an obscure point of law. The older lawyer explains to his new colleague that he needs the legal advice in order to provide legitimate grounds for his client to delay the development of the client's case in the courts. The young attorney does the research thoroughly

---

*Inspired by Jethro K. Lieberman, Crisis at the Bar, W.W. Norton, 1978, pp. 37-39.

and promptly, and quickly concludes that her firm cannot do what the senior partner wants done for the client; there is simply no point in law on which the client can legitimately delay the progress of the case. She reports her conclusion to the senior partner. His response thoroughly unsettles her. She is told in no uncertain terms to go back to the law books and find — invent if necessary, out of whole cloth — an argument that will do the trick. The young woman replies flatly that further research is, in her considered opinion, simply a waste of time and money both for the firm and for the client (who, of course, is being billed for the legal advice). The older lawyer retorts, "Let me worry about the costs to the client. Go back to your office and pick up where you left off on this problem. After all, we don't need to win for the client, or even stalemate the issue. All we're after is a delay to help the client; that's all he wants and let's get it for him." This shocks the young lawyer because she knows that delay of a case in the courts for delay's sake is strictly prohibited by the Canons of Legal Ethics,* and she knows that the senior partner knows this, too. Yet it seems he is asking her to conspire in a serious breach of legal ethics and to cover it up with a legal argument whose futility is bound to be revealed as soon as it gets aired in open court before the opposition attorney and the judge. What should she do?

Consider the lawyer's alternatives. Having concluded that she is being asked to engage in a conspiracy to violate the code of ethics for the profession:

1. She can go to another senior partner of the firm, explain her predicament, and ask him to intercede with the first partner to change his mind.
2. She can submit her resignation straightaway, on the ground that she refuses to do what she has been asked to do and does not want to be a member of any law firm that expects her to violate professional ethics.
3. She can report what happened to the grievance committee of the bar association, in the belief that the senior partner deserves disciplinary action because he has counseled a client in unethical practice and is also in effect forcing her to choose between resigning and collaborating in unethical conduct.

Or she can conclude that if she does either (1), or (2), or (3), her law career in town is virtually over before it started, as the word will quickly get around that she has an overdeveloped sense of rectitude; and since she cannot afford any such consequence:

---

*"In his representation of a client, a lawyer shall not ... delay a trial ..." (Disciplinary Rule 7-102(A)(1), ABA Code of Professional Responsibility, 1970)

4. She can do what the senior partner has asked her to do, and console herself by recalling the advice Speaker Sam Rayburn gave young Congressmen: "To get along, go along."

These four alternatives do not exhaust the things our young lawyer could do, but they are her major options. To take them in reverse order, we can call them the alternatives of, respectively, (4) complaisance, (3) punitive judgment, (2) dissociation, and (1) intercession.

The argument for (4) is clearly one of self-interest, and self-interest seems to argue strongly against the other three alternatives. It is in the young lawyer's self-interest to remain in the good graces of older members of the firm, and not to make a nuisance of herself by getting morally indignant at what amounts to a trifling business decision; it is also in her interest to show that she can execute promptly and intelligently *any* legal chore put into her hands, even at some cost to her principles. Probably no one will ever know that both the senior and junior attorneys trumped up flimsy legal arguments to help out a client. Besides, isn't it also a lawyer's duty "to represent his client zealously within the bounds of the law?"* Is any *law* being violated by a little delay in court?

The objection to this line of reasoning is fairly obvious. First, it is not a lawyer's *duty* to violate the ethics of the bar in order to champion a client's interests. The canons of professional ethics are every bit as much a moral barrier to what the senior partner proposes as any law. Second, we know in general that when a private interest (what the client wants, what the senior partner wants, or what the junior partner wants) conflicts with a professional duty or responsiblity, duty is always supposed to trump interest. The exceptions are difficult to state, but this case hardly seems one of them. Third, upon closer examination it is not so obvious that the path of self-interest really does lie with alternative (4), as we shall see. So, even if most young lawyers would be sorely tempted to choose (4), it is difficult to see what *ethical* grounds they could have for doing so.**

The argument for alternative (3), the course of judgment and punishment, is not very plausible. True, under the rules of the bar, the young lawyer has every *right* to file a complaint if she wants to, and to do so independently of or in conjunction with alternatives (1), (2), or (4). But here as elsewhere, acting within one's rights is not necessarily the *right* thing to do

---

*ABA Code of Professional Responsibility (1970), rules EC7-1, and EC7-19.

**It is useful to compare alternative (4) with a variant, in which the younger lawyer goes along with the senior partner's direction to invent grounds for delay, and (5) she secretly makes a full memorandum of the whole affair, with the intention at a later date of threatening to expose the unethical conduct of the senior partner unless he . . . i.e., she turns the situation into an opportunity for blackmail. Cowardly and servile as alternative (4) may be, from the moral point of view, it is at least understandable in a way that (5) could never be. Succumbing to the temptation of self-interest may be bad enough; but scheming to injure others in situations created by their folly is surely far worse.

or the *best* thing to do. Is the grievance committee really likely to believe the young lawyer's word against that of a respected senior partner (he is, after all, hardly likely to make an abject confession of wrongdoing)? Even if the committee believes her, can it really get a firm grip on any ethical violation in this instance? So far, given the facts, no delay of the courts has taken place or even been attempted; all that has occurred is talk within the offices of a law firm about moving in that direction. At the very least, it seems premature to take alternative (3) without trying alternative (1) first. If the senior partner counseling delay can be talked out of this tactic and into so advising the client, surely that is better all around. The client is averted from the unethical course of action he seeks; the senior partner is steered away from violating the ethics of the bar and from suborning a younger member of the firm; and the young lawyer has shown both integrity and resourcefulness rather than a frightened or vindictive response, and has thereby proved her value to the firm from an unexpected quarter. The more one considers it, the more one must conclude that alternative (3) is too hasty and bespeaks a somewhat rigid and uncollegial outlook on human and institutional relationships.

Alternative (2) seems recommended initially by two important considerations. First, the young lawyer knows that delay for delay's sake violates professional ethics; therefore, if she undertakes to do what the senior partner asks, she *knows* she is doing the wrong thing by the relevant standards of the profession. Moreover, she *knows* that she has no adequate moral excuse or justification for what she does if she takes this course. Second, she can plainly see how her own principles (which are those of her profession, in this instance) are violated under the circumstances. Thus, her view of herself as a professionally responsible person, not easily bought (and so forth), is instantly tarnished, with consequences for her further corruption that she cannot foretell. Even so, alternative (2) *is* abrupt; it is far more reasonable after trying alternative (1) and failing. Two further considerations need to be weighed here as well. First, if the young woman opts for alternative (2), she must realize that while it is possible this may shock the senior partner to drop his search for delaying tactics and even to urge that the senior members tear up the letter of resignation, it is more likely that the senior partner will merely turn quietly to another junior member of the firm. So her resignation really does not prevent the ethical misconduct of the firm and its client; all it does is keep *her* skirts clean. Is that enough? This leads to the second consideration. If she simply stops with resignation, and fails to take the further steps provided in alterantive (3), it can be argued that she has gone only half way down the heroic course she seems to have set for herself. Even though by virtue of her resignation she does no wrong if she fails to pursue alternative (3), she seems willing to permit others to do wrong when she might be able to prevent it, or at least secure disciplinary action if it is too late to prevent it. In other words, from an ethical point of view, alternative (2) makes somewhat more sense if taken as the preface to alternative (3); taken in isolation, alternative (2) seems both too final and too incomplete to be adequate.

Alternative (1) thus emerges as the preferred alternative. First, it alone leaves all the other options open and thereby allows for other possibilities to develop, some of which might moot the whole predicament (e.g., the client's firm is sold out from underneath the current management, thereby completely altering its legal situation). Second, given any outcome of her consultation with the second senior partner, her situation and that of all other parties involved is improved. Either the second partner agrees with her and successfully persuades the first partner from his path, or he does not. If he does, then her problem is solved thanks to his intervention. If he does not agree with her, then no matter what she does next, she can point to her good-faith effort to solve the problem quietly and loyally within the firm. If the senior partners prefer to close ranks against her, then her grounds for alternatives (2) or (3) are far more substantial. Only alternative (1) allows her the opportunity: to review the legal and ethical situation as she sees it; to do this with someone who presumably can be expected to take into account her own best interests, those of the client, and of the first senior partner; and to do all this with someone who also has greater experience with problems of legal ethics. Is she right that there is *no* legitimate basis in the law for the delay the client seeks? Is she right that what she has been asked to do is a *violation* of the canons of professional ethics? Alternative (1) gives her the opportunity to test on neutral ground her belief that the answer to both these questions is affirmative. If a negative answer can be given to either, then her problem evaporates.

We can restate the foregoing reasoning in the following way. If we rank order the four altenatives from the moral point of view, surely alternative (4) comes out worst. Both alternatives (2) and (3), however, are vulnerable to moral criticism, too, even if something can be said in their defense, as we have seen. (Whether (2) should be ranked ahead of (3), or the reverse, we leave for the reader to ponder.) Only alternative (1) is free from moral objections; moreover, by pursuing it either the problem is solved or the moral basis for each of the remaining courses of action is strengthened.

8 UTILITARIANISM

During the past two centuries moral evaluation of private conduct and public policy has been enormously influenced by Utilitarianism. According to the Utilitarian view, all ethical decisions are to be governed ultimately by the Principle of Utility, which (in one of its many formulations) states that a course of conduct is the right one for an agent if and only if it is the best alternative under the circumstances; and the best alternative is the one that has the best overall consequences, i.e., the alternative that maximizes the total balance of good over evil for all concerned.* As John Stuart Mill put it, following Jeremy Bentham, Utilitarianism is the doctrine that right action is the action that "conduces to the greatest good of the greatest number." Recent welfare economics and current cost/benefit analysis are heirs to the legacy of Utilitarianism. Because Utilitarian thinking plays such a prominent role in decision making in economics and politics (see Chapters 7, 8, and 9), it is important to examine it from the moral point of view. Several of its most distinctive features are also sources of objection to it.

First, for a Utilitarian, right and wrong in conduct are always to be calculated by reference to results, outcomes, consequences of action – *all* the results, however remote. Such calculations are difficult to make (some critics would insist they are impossible), especially in time to base a decision on them, because there are so many uncertain consequences and so many alternative courses of action to be weighed. It is little wonder they many moralists prefer to rely on ethical principles that are immune from the difficulties posed by the calculation of consequences.

Second, some notion of ultimate or intrinsic value – satisfaction of preferences, happiness, pleasure, the absence of pain, gratification of desire, or some combination of these – is needed to serve as the common denominator of the consequences, since it is the tendency of actions to cause results of this sort that must be computed. Thus, the Utilitarian embraces the principle, understood in this context, that the end justifies the means.

Third, all other moral rules or principles – from "Thou shalt not kill" to "first come, first served" – are either to be treated as corollaries, theorems, or special cases of the Principle of Utility; or else they are to be jettisoned as outmoded and superstitious baggage, relics of primitive moral thinking without rational value in ethical decision making. Fairness and integrity, for example, are usually regarded as supreme virtues, but they cannot be for the Utilitarian. At best, these ideals are subordinate to the ideal of promoting the general welfare.

Fourth, proponents and opponents of Utilitariansim alike agree that at the root of the Principle of Utility are the familiar virtues of benevolence (wishing or willing good for persons, especially other persons) and beneficience (acting so as to do good for persons). If benevolence and beneficience were not good and acknowledged to be virtues, then no one could possibly find it reasonable to embrace Utilitarianism, since what it amounts to is benevolence and beneficience generalized. Accordingly, the idea that the Principle of Utility is the foundation of all morality, *the* fundamental moral principle, goes well beyond the modest claim that

---

*In the case of ties, where alternative A has the same balance of good over evil as does alternative B, the choice of which action to take is morally indifferent to the Utilitarian. In the case where we do not *know* all the consequences of A and of B, then we cannot know what is the right thing to do.

benevolence and beneficience are virtues.

From the standpoint of ethical decision making, a Utilitarian looks at things very differently from the ordinary person. For example, the ordinary person may rest content with a certain disorder in his moral thinking, because, no matter how hard he tries, he cannot find a way to bring all his moral principles and moral judgments into harmony with each other. The Utilitarian, however, finds grounds for complaint at this intellectual disarray; for him it is irrational and unnecessary. He prizes the virtues of consistency and rationality, which he believes are conferred on his moral thinking because all his moral judgments ultimately rest on one clear and self-consistent principle, the Principle of Utility.*

Ethical decision making as seen by the Utilitarian can be illustrated by examples from several different contexts.

1. *Slavery.* Most persons today probably think not only that chattel slavery is wrong, but that it is the perfection of injustice. So did the British Utilitarians, such as Bentham and Mill, who were among the most vigorous critics of the slave trade and of chattel slavery. Yet the moral theory of Utilitarianism permits — in fact, it requires — opposition to the practice of slavery on moral grounds if and only if it can be shown that the relative total costs of a social system with slavery outweigh its relative total benefits. This means that a Utilitarian might find, to his surprise, that he has to accept, even defend, slavery as a morally proper institution for a given society under certain conditions. Perhaps such conditions have never actually existed, or at least no longer obtained after the early 1800s. But perhaps they did; or perhaps in a century from now they will, so that on balance the best thing to do would be to enslave some whole class or race or sex, or to breed a subspecies for slavery (as Aldous Huxley portrayed with the test tube babies known as the Epsilon Minuses in his novel, *Brave New World*).

What is true of the Utilitarian approach to slavery is true of the Utilitarian approach to every other social practice. What is and what is not morally desirable depends entirely on the facts. Categorical and unqualified opposition on moral grounds to slavery, the death penalty, torture, censorship, sexploitation, child abuse, or any other indignity and brutality is impossible for a Utilitarian. He must always bear an open mind toward any course of action or social policy, however ugly and repellant he may find it, on the chance that impartial analysis of the circumstances and consequences show that this action or policy is, after all, the best thing to do according to his criterion of right conduct.

2. *Cannibalism.* Most people have a horror at the very thought of eating the flesh of others, and of being eaten by other people after death. Still,

---

*Utilitarians are not the only moral thinkers who repudiate pluralism of ultimate principles. Kant, for example, with his Categorical Imperative, was equally monistic.

history is full of cases where survivors have fed on the blood and meat of dead companions, when no other food was available. Piers Paul Read's story about the Andean crash victims, *Alive*, is only the most recent case. The Utilitarian can easily justify cannibalism of this sort by pointing to the beneficial results on balance. The benefits outweigh the costs to the survivors, to the deceased, and to anyone else affected by the cannibalism, when compared to the relative benefits and costs of the alternatives. If someone objects that eating human flesh is forbidden, anathema, the Utilitarian is likely to reply either that this shows the objector is superstitious, or that he accepts some non-Utilitarian moral theory, or that he has miscalculated the consequences and wrongly opposes what in fact is the best thing to do in the circumstances.

3. *Triage.* During the First World War, when advance hospitals immediately behind the front lines were wholly inadequate to cope with the flood of casualties, French medical supervisors devised the following scheme. As the wounded arrived, they were immediately sorted into three groups. One group consisted of the fatally wounded; since nothing could be done to help them, they were to be left to their fate. No medicines or nursing services were diverted to alleviate their agonies. The second group consisted of the wounded whose condition was so severe that even if they lived they would be of no further use to the war effort. After being patched up at the advance hospital they were transferred to a rear base hospital for proper treatment. Those in the third group were the focus of immediate surgical and other medical services at the advance casualty station. They consisted of all the wounded who, if promptly and effectively treated, could probably return to duty at a later date. Ruthless though it may seem, triage maximized the saving of lives and maintenance of an effective fighting force under conditions of extreme scarcity. It also proved relatively simple to administer, always an advantageous features of any selection process in emergencies. It seems easy to justify on Utilitarian grounds.

Another example of what amounts to triage is the proper method of apportioning one's energies as a teacher. The method is attributed to Kant, who is supposed to have said that he found the students in his classes could be sorted into three kinds. First, there were those (few?) who were so stupid and lazy that it was a complete waste of his valuable time and energy to offer them any serious instruction; this group he virtually ignored. Second, there were those (even fewer?) who were so brilliant and eager to learn that all he could do was to get out of their way lest he impede their rapid progress; so he did. The third group (no doubt the largest) was the one to which he devoted almost all his energies. It consisted of all those students bright and self-disciplined enough to profit from his pedagogical efforts, but not so brilliant and ambitious as to make significant progress on their own. Since they could show marked improvement if and only if he worked hard with them, that is exactly what he did. Kant was a conspicuous anti-Utilitarian, so there is in this example the implication, if the story is not apocryphal, that triage in the classroom can be justified on non-Utilitarian grounds.

To argue for or against accepting the Principle of Utility as the supreme principle of morality, and therefore to organize ethical decision making in its terms, goes well beyond the scope of the present discussion. Utilitarianism, even though it is not widely accepted among moral philosophers, continues to be much discussed. Its close examination has shed considerable light on the problems of constructing and validating any theory suitable both for individual and collective decision making from the moral point of view.

9   THE OBJECTIVITY OF ETHICS

Many find it difficult to take ethics seriously because they believe that in matters of conduct, all that counts in the end is sincerity, "doing your own thing," what Existentialist philosophers have called "authenticity." Beyond this, they believe, there is only arbitrary preference or self-interest. Objectivity in ethics — the idea that some ethical judgments are true (and all other judgments incompatible with them, false), that some principles of conduct are the best principles for everyone to live by — is thought to be impossible, or at least highly implausible and unprovable. The assumption throughout this chapter, however, has been just the reverse. Within certain boundaries and given certain assumptions, ethical decision making should be viewed as the task of finding the right answer to questions of conduct. The notion that ethical judgment is a matter of disguised personal preference, opinion, or taste, is rejected. What is affirmed is that ethical decision making can be a rational and objective discipline, such that two people, given all the same facts and other information relevant to the problem of choice, and the time and patience to deliberate thoroughly, would arrive at the same result and for the same reasons. If they do not, then either the question is not one of right and wrong in conduct after all, or one or more of the contingencies just mentioned bars the way to agreement, or one (or both) of them is in error.

This view cannot be proved here; that is why it is frankly advanced as an assumption. It is possible to show, however, that it is not so naive or preposterous as it may seem. Consider again the situation of Robinson Crusoe, or anyone bent on pursuing his own interests. Surely, it is reasonable to assume that there are better and worse ways for such a person to achieve the maximum satisfaction of all his interests, that is, there is some state in which the person obtains the maximal satisfaction of all his interests, he should find out what that state is, and can then endeavor to achieve it. Furthermore, given the world as it is and given his nature, it is not unreasonable to believe that there is only one or a small number of ultimate goals he could achieve (some might prefer to say instead 'kind of person he could become'). For him to believe otherwise is simply a vain illusion, based on ignorance or wishful thinking, or both. If that is true, why is it any less plausible that the problems of ethical decision making in general should have better and worse answers? It is certainly conceivable that for one solitary person, there is some one course of action among the alternatives open to him that maximizes his self-interest and that the person might come to know and pursue it. Why, then, is it any less conceivable that in a given society there should be one course of action among the alternatives that is the best way for everyone to satisfy their interests? Selfishness, of course, as well as other factors, may make some persons uninterested in or incapable of trying to find this course of action, or in pursuing it once it is identified. But these are not reasons to think that there *is* no answer, and thus are not reasons for rejecting the assumption of objectivity in ethics.

For our task, this assumption is extremely important. If it is not granted, then ethical decision making becomes either impossible, or arbitrary and unreasonable, or else it collapses into something else (such as the decision making practiced by a set of persons each of whom is interested in nothing but his own good). Whatever interest there is in ethics as a disciplined mode of thought about human conduct derives from the tacit assumption that not all moral principles and ethical judgments are equally sound, that not all conduct evaluated from the moral point of view is equally good. All we have done is to make this assumption explicit.

10   CHOOSING A WAY OF LIFE

Human conduct as seen from the moral point of view characteristically involves considerations of rights and duties, just as moral training typically involves inculcation of the virtues. We see ourselves and others as ethical creatures when we weigh the making of an obligation (promising something to someone), the discharge of a duty (staying at the telephone, as the job requires, even though it does not ring), the exercise of a right (giving permission to a friend to use our camper for a vacation trip), and so on. A morally virtuous person, roughly, is one who accepts and performs his obligations, discharges his duties, does not trespass on the rights of others in exercising his own, and respects others as he respects himself.

Moral perplexity often takes the form that it does because rights and duties arise from different and independent sources, and sometimes converge in unexpected ways. A person faces a moral dilemma when he finds he is under conflicting or incompatible obligations, e.g., he has promosed to pay back a long-standing debt only to discover that his child is in need of expensive medical attention and the insurance is insufficient to cover the cost. Or a person finds she is in a conflict between her clear duty and an opportunity to serve the general welfare, e.g., she has made a promise to execute the unwritten testament of a dying relative only to learn that he wants to spend his large estate on a crackbrained scheme; once he is dead no one else will know his wishes, and she could easily divert the estate into some socially useful enterprise, with praise all around for the deceased's philanthropy. A fair proportion of what can properly be called ethical decision making falls into the category of resolving moral perplexity of the sort illustrated above.

How much of a general nature can be said about the right thing to do in such cases? "Keep your promises," "tell the truth," "help those in need," "avoid waste of useful resources," "forebear violence and revenge" — are all maxims of right conduct, ethical rules of thumb in most ethical theories since Plato and the Bible. What passes for common sense in moral matters, as well as what is strictly entailed by most ethical theories, however, does not treat these maxims as inviolable. Nor is there any reason to believe that in their totality such maxims form a complete or consistent set. Most ethically sensitive people believe that each has its exceptions, and it is not difficult to think up cases in which the right thing to do is to tell a lie, break a promise, take violent measures, or ignore someone in peril. It is sometimes possible to advance good moral reasons against doing what one has a perfect right to do, or in favor of ignoring or violating another's rights, or in favor of withholding from someone what he thoroughly deserves. Laying down a strict and general higher-order rule that defines exactly when it is right (or not wrong, or the lesser evil) to break a promise or tell a lie is virtually impossible. To expect such rigor in moral decision making is probably to pursue a will-o'-the-wisp. Where it seems possible to achieve this rigor, it is usually because one has fallen back on sheer intuition or is relying on some ethical doctrine mechanically applied. In neither case is the rigor well grounded. The intuition is likely to be arbitrary, and the ethical doctrine indefensible. About the most one can say without fear of contradiction is that where the ethical problem or dilemma is one of complying with versus overriding a maxim such as "keep your promises," some reasons will be better than others, no reasons are likely to be conclusive in every possible situation, and one must be especially cautious before accepting any solution that clearly favors oneself at the expense of others.

In some (perhaps rare) situations, there may be no determinate answer to the questions: what is the right thing to do? or what would be best for all concerned? Rather, one must view any proposed answer to such questions as a symptom or an expression of a whole way of life, much as Christians view Jesus on the cross as the symbol of a self-sacrificial life, a single act that sums up the way to live and die. But not everybody sees the crucified Jesus as a metaphor for his or her life, and there may be no way to convince a person who fails to do so that he or she is wrong. Most attempts to get around this problem of ultimately undecidable moral questions do so by denying that such cases exist or by insisting that there is some all-embracing solution for every occasion of apparent conflict, or that the question is no longer a *moral* question. Perhaps. Yet there is a danger here of impoverishing the actual complexity of our moral world. The cost of this enriched structure is the possibility of ultimate disagreement in ethical decision making, of questions that cannot be answered rationally. If Aristotle had been right, and there was but one Good for all men, no matter in what epoch they lived and regardless of their sex, birthright, natural gifts, and so forth, then there could not be tragic choices, true moral dilemmas, in which good and right are arrayed on both horns of the dilemma. But Aristotle seems to have been wrong. There *is* a role for ideals and goals in the choice of how to live that cannot be ignored, and there are wide limits within which these ideals and goals may range.

11 CONCLUSION

The scope of human conduct subject to ethical appraisal is virtually unlimited. This book is organized as though this were not so, because in each chapter we look separately at ethical, medical, economic, and political decision making. We should not confuse a useful division of labor, however, with a doctrine that decision making occurs in separate categories or settings that are labeled medical, political, and so forth. There are recognizably distinct methods and assumptions, goals and purposes, in decision making, and they allow us to contrast and compare economic decision making with legal decision making, and so on. Yet *any* act or decision by *anyone* is subject to evaluation and criticism from the moral point of view. This is easy to overlook because the verdict to be rendered for many of our acts and decisions from the ethical point of view is a simple and uncontroversial "go ahead, there's nothing morally wrong with that; do what you want to."

Whether one should go on to say that all points of view except the moral are incomplete or inconclusive, and thus logically subordinate to the ethical, is a matter of philosophical controversy and cannot be argued here. We know that what may be a sound economic decision may be a moral disaster. What we do not seem to know is which point of view to adopt. Suffice it to say that the ethically sensitive person is wary of artificial or arbitrary limitations on the range of issues to be brought under scrutiny from the moral point of view. Ethical decision making may not be the be-all and end-all of human decision making. Yet if it is not, what is?

12 SELECTED BIBLIOGRAPHY

Classics

Aristotle. *The Nichomachean Ethics.* ed. and tr. W.D. Ross (1925).
Hobbes, Thomas. *Leviathan.* (1640; many editions).
Kant, Immanuel. *Groundwork of the Metaphysics of Morals.* (1786), ed. and tr. H.J. Paton (1956).
Mill, John Stuart. *Utilitarianism.* (1861; many editions).

Modern Sources

Baier, Kurt. *The Moral Point of View.* New York: Random House, 1965 (revised edition).
Bedau, Hugo A., ed. *Justice and Equality.* Englewood Cliffs, N.J.: Prentice-Hall, 1971.
Gauthier, David P., ed. *Morality and Rational Self-Interest.* Englewood Cliffs, N.J.: Prentice-Hall, 1970.
Geach, Peter T. *The Virtues.* Cambridge University Press, 1977.
Gert, Bernard. *The Moral Rules.* New York: Harper & Row, 1973.
Lemmon, E.J. "Moral Dilemmas," *Philosophical Review,* 1962.
Mackie, J.L. *Ethics: Inventing Right and Wrong.* New York, Penguin Books, 1977.
Rawls, John. "Outline of a Decision Procedure for Ethics," *Philosophical Review,* 1957.
Rawls, John. *A Theory of Justice.* Cambridge, Mass.: Harvard University Press, 1971.
Smart, J.J.C., and Williams, Bernard. *Utilitarianism For and Against.* Cambridge University Press, 1973.
Warnock, G.J. *The Object of Morality.* London: Methuen & Co., 1971.

Other Works Cited

American Bar Assocation. *Code of Professional Responsibility.*
Huxley, Aldous. *Brave New World.*
Lieberman, Jethro K. *Crisis at the Bar.*
Rand, Ayn. *The Virtue of Selfishness.*
Read, Piers Paul. *Alive: The Story of the Andes Survivors.*
Riesman, David, *et al. The Lonely Crowd.*
Schlesinger, Arthur M., Jr. *Robert Kennedy and His Times.*
Schulberg, Budd. *What Makes Sammy Run?*

Chapter 5
Individual and Social
Decision-Making Processes

1   INTRODUCTION

One of the major objectives of this book is to provide the reader with a set of tools and concepts that may help you to make more effective decisions. In truth, social psychology has little by way of tools to offer the study of decision making. Nor, for that matter, does the discipline have a set of particularly key concepts or theoretical models to propose. What social psychology can contribute is an approach to the study of the decision-making process that specifies in a particular way the social conditions under which decisions are made. The role of social psychology is thus not so much to offer a theory of decision making or an analysis of decision-making techniques, but rather to provide some insight into the factors, needs, and concerns that affect the particular decisions people make. Through the research conducted by social psychologists, both in the laboratory and in the field, it may be possible to specify more clearly than before the host of reasons people have for the particular decisions that they make.

1.1   An Illustration: Intervention in Emergencies

Try to imagine yourself in the following situation. It is 3 o'clock in the morning, and you are awakened from your sleep by the sounds of someone

Percy H. Hill et al., Making Decisions: A Multidisciplinary Introduction

screaming in the street below your bedroom window. You reluctantly climb out of bed and look out the window, and see a young woman with her hands raised defensively in front of her face, apparently fighting off a man's attack. The man seems to be wielding something shiny in his right hand, possibly a knife. The woman is crying for help. Just as you wonder what you should do, the man runs away. A few minutes later, however, the same events are repeated. Again there are the screams and cries, again the man appears, and again he disappears when the woman calls out for help. Finally, after several more minutes have elapsed, the man returns again; the woman cries for help once more, but the attacker finally succeeds in his mission; the woman lies bleeding in the street and, as you later discover, is quite dead.

As a student of decision making, what would you have done in this situation? Quite possibly many of you believe that you would have intervened on behalf of the victim, perhaps by rushing to her assistance, by shouting out your bedroom window, or by simply phoning the police. Be cautious, however, before you declare your unswerving commitment to such altruistic behavior in this situation. In point of fact, an incident rather similar to the one described actually occurred some years ago in a residential section of New York City, resulting in the murder of a young woman named Kitty Genovese. When the police arrived on the scene and began their investigation, it turned out that this crime had been witnessed by thirty-eight people looking out of their apartment house windows; *none* of these perfectly respectable witnesses intervened in any way! Possibly they were motivated by different concerns from you, who perhaps would have intervened with little hesitation. On the other hand, perhaps the social situation surrounding the attack on Kitty Genovese was really so powerful that virtually anyone would have been led to behave in the same passive manner. Perhaps the most altruistic of concerns would have been overwhelmed by the presence of even more powerful social forces.

In the immediate aftermath of the Kitty Genovese murder, social psychologists began to look more closely at the circumstances surrounding this event. The question that they posed for themselves, and subsequently attempted to answer through experimental research, was *why* people tended to behave as they did in this situation. How could the nonintervention of these thirty-eight bystanders be explained, particularly in terms of the social and psychological forces at work? Note that these social psychologists did not ask what the people should have done or what tools would enable people to make more effective decisions in situations such as this. Rather, it was the explanation, analysis, and prediction of social behavior that interested the social psychologists.

Although at the time of the Kitty Genovese murder it was widely believed that urban apathy explained people's refusal to help those in distress, two social psychologists (Latané and Darley, 1968) were not satisfied with this hypothesis. Instead of assuming that someone should have intervened because there were so many people looking on, they argued that it was precisely *because* each observer suspected that there were lots of people looking on that no one intervened. Latané and Darley conducted a series of laboratory experiments in which they found that the greater the number of bystanders to an emergency, the less likely or the more slowly any one bystander would intervene and provide aid.* In explanation of this finding, the investigators suggested that the larger the number of bystanders, the more likely it is for any one person to reason that he is no more responsible for what is going on than anybody else (Latané and Darley refer to this as *diffusion of responsibility*), and also no more guilty than his neighbor if anything bad should happen (*diffusion of guilt*).

In summary, the research on bystander intervention can be viewed as an illustration of the typically social psychological approach to the study of decision making. The question of *why* people behave (decide) as they do is the focus of inquiry. And in the case of bystander intervention, in particular, the answer appears to be that behavior is shaped by the real or imagined presence of other people who share in the individual's sense of responsibility or guilt. What looks at first like a series of isolated, passive, disconnected individuals is in fact a group of sorts, in which individual decisions are inextricably related to the social context in which they are made.**

1.2 Two Assumptions

Before proceeding further, two related assumptions must be clearly stated. First, it is assumed that one can meaningfully distinguish decision making at an individual (intrapersonal) level from the process as it occurs at increasingly complex levels (interpersonal, intergroup, organizational, and international). Second, it is assumed that those factors that affect decision making at an intrapersonal level are likely also to affect interpersonal processes, which in turn will have an effect on the way that decisions are made in groups, in organizations, and in nations. The assumption here is that decision making occurs at progressively more complex levels, much like concentric circles whose inner rings are included within those located more peripherally. Intrapersonal considerations influence the shape of decision making at an interpersonal level, and these processes may in turn shape

---

*In one study, Latané and Darley (1968) asked male undergraduates to wait in a room for several minutes before beginning "a study of urban life." The participants waited either alone or in groups of three. After a minute or so, some harmless but frightening white smoke began to issue into the "waiting room" through a wall vent, and continued to do so for several minutes. The researchers found that participants who were asked to wait alone reported the smoke to the experimenter much sooner and more often than those who waited with two others like themselves.

** Other examples of individual decision making with collective overtones and consequences include the decision to turn on one's auto headlights at dusk, the decision to have a certain number of children, and the decision to give one's child a particular first name.

decision making in increasingly complex social arrangements. Social psychologists have been primarily interested in the study of intrapersonal and (especially) interpersonal phenomena. Hence, discussion in this chapter will be lmited to decision making at these two levels. (See Chapter 6 for material dealing with groups, organizations, and nations.)

2 THE INTRAPERSONAL DECISION-MAKING PROCESS

Social psychological contributions to the analysis of intrapersonal decision-making issues may be conveniently organized around three major foci:

1. The nature of intrapersonal *conflict*, and the effects of such conflict on decision making.
2. The presence and impact of two fundamental *decision maker needs.*
3. The effects on decision-making effectiveness of various *personality traits*.

Our analysis of intrapersonal decision making will conclude with a brief look at one particularly important consequence of decision-making conflict: the process of entrapment.

2.1 Intrapersonal Conflict and Decision Making

Imagine a decision maker standing before two closed doors, only one of which can be opened. Imagine further that the decision maker is completely and utterly indifferent regarding his choice of door; he experiences *no* conflict about which of the two alternatives to choose because he simply does not care. Under these circumstances, the decision maker may be expected to choose rather easily, and to experience neither satisfaction nor regret as a result of having opened one door rather than the other.

Life, unfortunately, is not typically structured so simply. More often than not, we are *not* indifferent to the choices that we make. Rather, we tend to have strong feelings about the alternatives we elect to pursue, as well as the ones we leave behind. Like Robert Frost's traveler in the yellow wood, our choices remind us of the "road not taken." Decisions have consequences, some positive and some negative, and as a result these decisions almost invariably contain the elements of conflict.

2.1.1 Approach-Approach Conflict

Imagine that you have to register for one of two courses, both of which sound marvelously interesting but unfortunately are scheduled to meet at the identical time period. Or, imagine that you are trying to choose between two equally attractive jobs, restaurants, or dates. In each of these situations, you are asked to choose between two goals that are positively valued, and that you therefore wish to approach. Such conflict has been identified by Lewin (1935) as *approach-approach* conflict. Characteristic of such conflict is the fact that the closer the decision maker comes to choosing one alternative, the more likely he is to be torn by (reminded of) the positive features of the nonchosen alternative — the road not taken. In an approach-approach conflict, the decision maker may be expected to vacillate between the positive goal objects, and to be plagued by indecision until he can find some way to choose.

2.1.2 Avoidance-Avoidance Conflict

If only the world were made up of nothing but approach-approach conflicts; how exquisite the pain of being forced to choose between heaven and paradise! Instead, it is too often the case that the decisions we are asked to make consist of a choice between alternatives that, rather than being equally appealing, are equally repulsive or painful. Such conflict, in which a decision maker is confronted with two negative goal objects, each of which he hopes to avoid, is described by Lewin as *avoidance-avoidance* conflict. Here the decision maker must choose between the lesser of two evils, the devil and the deep blue sea. Would you rather suffer by staying up all night to study for an exam, or would you rather not study and thereby be sure of failing the exam? Would the child rather eat his spinach, or would he rather go straight to bed? In conflicts such as these, as in approach-approach conflicts, the decision maker is likely to vacillate, uncertain about which way to turn. The closer he gets to one of the negative goal objects, the more unattractive this choice is apt to appear in relation to the other goal object, and the more likely the decision maker is to approach this alternative choice — only to find, of course, that it appears increasingly unattractive the closer he gets.

2.1.3 Approach-Avoidance Conflict

It is often the case that a single goal object has associated with it both positive and negative features, resulting in what Lewin has described as *approach-avoidance* conflict. Consider these conflicts: candy is delicious, but fattening; it would be nice to go swimming, but the water is cold; it would be fun to ask her out on a date, but what if she says no. In each of these situations, the individual must decide whether or not to approach a goal object about which he is truly ambivalent. The more the decision maker approaches the goal object in question, the more aware he becomes of its negative features (the swimmer dips his big toe in the water and finds the water is as cold as ice). On the other hand, the more the decision maker moves away from (avoids) the goal object, the more salient its positive features become (sitting in the confines of his room, the swimmer thinks that a dip in the lake would be mighty refreshing). Thus, it is characteristic of approach-avoidance conflict that the decision maker is simultaneously pushed and pulled by the forces at work within him, until an *equilibrium point* is reached. At this point, the two forces are equal in intensity but opposite in direction, and it is here that the decision maker will experience the greatest conflict between opposing tendencies.

2.1.4 Double Approach-Avoidance Conflict

Complicating and enriching matters a bit further is the fact that most of the multiple alternatives available to a decision maker have both positive and negative consequences. Thus, a choice between two goal objects often becomes a choice between courses of action about *each* of which the decision maker is truly ambivalent.

Imagine a situation in which a person has decided to buy a car. After reading through numerous magazine articles and consulting with friends, he succeeds in reducing the vast array of possible purchases to two dramatically different alternatives: a Porsche or a Ford Pinto. Being the good student of decision making that he is, the consumer sits down one day and develops a list of the potential advantages and disadvantages of owning each car. A partial version of this list might look something like the listing in Table 5-1.

Armed with his list, the decision maker now attempts to choose between the Porsche and the Pinto, perhaps by applying the decision matrix techniques (discussed in Chapter 8). This decision may prove to be more difficult to make than he first expected. Each of the goal objects has both positive and negative features, leaving him in a state of genuine ambivalence about not one but *both* of the possible choices. The decision maker is damned if he does and damned if he doesn't, no matter which of the cars he decides to buy.

These, then, are the four basic types of intrapersonal conflict with which a decision maker is likely to be confronted. These conflicts differ in the number of goal objects (choice alternatives) available, and they differ in

Table 5-1.   Illustration of Double Approach-Avoidance Conflict:
Choosing between a Porsche and a Ford Pinto

		PORSCHE		FORD PINTO
ADVANTAGES (+)	(1)	Prestigious	(1)	Readily available in your choice of colors and styles, too.
	(2)	Fun to drive (lots of buttons to push, gauges to watch, etc.)	(2)	Easy to maintain and repair
	(3)	Well made (likely to last a long time)	(3)	A "patriotic" choice (funneling money back into the American economy)
	(4)	Safe to drive (low center of gravity, excellent suspension, cornering ability, etc.)	(4)	Inexpensive to purchase
DISADVANTAGES (−)	(1)	*Very* expensive (although you can probably get a loan)	(1)	Bland appearance
	(2)	Hard to repair	(2)	Poor engineering (car likely to last only a few years)
	(3)	Expensive to maintain and insure	(3)	Low resale value
	(4)	Increased possibility of theft	(4)	Potential fire hazard (possibility of gas tank explosion in the event of a rear end collision)

the symmetry of positive or negative features associated with each goal object. Common to the four types of conflict is the fact that they are likely to produce in the decision maker the ambivalence, uncertainty, and vacillation that lead to perpetuation of the conflict. Eventually, we may assume, it becomes intolerable for the decision maker to continue in a state of uncertainty and conflict, and he makes a *choice*. He chooses A or decides against doing so; he chooses alternative X or instead selects alternative Y. In any event, the decision maker finds some way to reduce the conflict he experiences by making a choice, and then engaging in the cognitive work necessary to protect and justify this choice. Let us turn now to a consideration of the sorts of needs that may govern the habitual ways in which people resolve intrapersonal conflict.

2.2   Fundamental Needs of the Decision Maker

People have a wide variety of needs, some of which are shared while others are not. Although other needs may indeed have a bearing on decision making, and although decision makers will clearly be affected in different ways, it appears that two needs in particular — *simplicity* and *consistency* — are likely to prove especially important.

2.2.1 The Need for Simplicity

The world is a complicated, intriguing, and at times an overwhelming place. In the course of our daily lives, we are continually bombarded by countless social and nonsocial stimuli. In order to organize this welter of information, and render it more manageable, we need to simplify our cognitive world. We do this by developing *models* — lenses that permit certain information to enter the cognitive system to the exclusion of other information. Models help us to organize our perceptual environment and, in so doing, they transform a world that is in reality a continuum of grays into a more manageable array of blacks and whites.

A decision maker in conflict about which of several alternatives to choose is likely to vacillate only for so long. After some period of time, this state of continued uncertainty is likely to prove intolerable, and the decision maker's need for simplicity is likely to dictate commitment to some course of action. In choosing between two equally attractive or unattractive alternatvies, the decision maker is likely to go out of his way to discriminate among them. This discrimination, no matter how finely tuned it may be, allows the decision maker to distinguish a wise choice from a foolish one, and thereby to choose one goal object to the exclusion of the other.

The need for simplicity is both a blessing and a curse. Its great virtue is that it enables the decision maker to impose a framework that organizes a set of choices and events in such a way that action can be taken. By developing simplifying typologies that lend structure to his cognitive world, the decision maker can better sort out those values, courses of action, and outcomes that he believes are important in relation to those that he views as less important. On the other hand, the need for simplicity can also be a liability, to the extent that it blinds the decision maker to the true sublety of the choices available to him. Transforming a world of true continuity into one of perceived polarity may rob the decision maker of the sensitivity to nuance that is essential for truly effective decision making.*

2.2.2 The Need for Consistency

Decisions are not usually made in isolation. Rather, they emerge in a personal context that includes the decision maker's own prior history, the set of others with whom he interacts, as well as the larger enviornment

---

*For example, consider the stereotype that little girls are "made of sugar, spice, and everything nice," while little boys are "made of snakes, snails, and puppy dog tails." Armed with such a conception, the perceiver is able to reduce a world of true continuity and complexity to a simple bipolar category system in which *all* boys and girls can be pigeonholed. "Real boys" and "real girls" are those who conform to the perceiver's *Weltanschauung;* everyone else is a deviant. The terrible liability of such an outlook is that it mutes the perceiver's sensitivity to the textured individuality and uniqueness of others, even as it forces the persons so viewed to regard themselves in the same stereotypic light.

through which he moves. In choosing among alternative options, the decision maker typically needs to behave in ways that maintain or restore consistency among the several attitudes, beliefs, and values that are part of his personal context.

Social psychologists have long understood the importance of maintaining attitudinal consistency. Some years ago, Heider (1958) advanced an explanatory model known as *balance theory*, which stipulates some of the ways in which consistency is maintained. Heider said that the individual has a need to develop an attitudinal system in which the component attitudes are in balance (are consistent) with one another. Attitudinal imbalance is stressful, and motivates the person to restore consistency as quickly and easily as possible, along pathways that are specified by Heider's theory.

Other theorists, such as Newcomb (1953) and Osgood and Tannenbaum (1955) have similarly pointed to the importance of attitudinal consistency, and have outlined the steps by which such consistency can be maintained or restored. On the basis of the experimental and theoretical work of these social psychologists, as well as others, it is abundantly clear that a sound analysis of the circumstances surrounding a particular decision must take into account the decision maker's need to maintain attitudinal consistency.

Apart from this need to maintain consistency among his several attitudes, a decision maker also needs to maintain consistency between his attitudes and his actual behavior. This attitude-behavior consistency can develop in either of two rather different ways. On the one hand, a decision maker (e.g., a voter) may hold a particular attitude (e.g., the South African policy of apartheid must be abolished), which in turn leads to behavior that is consistent with this attitude (e.g., voting for a candidate who promises to impose immediate and intense desegregation pressure on the South African government). In this sequence, it is the attitude that leads to the behavior. On the other hand, a decision maker may occasionally find himself first behaving in a particular way (e.g., kicking the door), and only subsequently discovering what his underlying motive or attitude must have been (e.g., since he kicked the door, he must be feeling angry). Here it is the behavior that shapes the attitude.

Once a decision maker has committed himself to the selection of a particular alternative, powerful pressures are likely to arise that lead him to justify the appropriateness of his choice not only to other people but to himself as well. The process by which this justification unfolds, and the circumstances under which it is likely to be more or less powerful in its effects, have been described in detail by Festinger (1957) in his *theory of cognitive dissonance*.

Recall the earlier illustration of a consumer trying to decide between buying a Porsche or a Ford Pinto. [See Table 5-1] Each of the two alternatives had associated with it both positive and negative features, placing the decision maker in a double approach-avoidance conflict. The buyer would be expected to vacillate between his two choice possibilities; the closer he gets to purchasing one car, the more striking are both the several possible virtues of the other vehicle as well as the drawbacks of the car under consideration.

Imagine that after much hesitation and suffering, after consulting his friends as well as his almanac and horoscope, a choice is made — the decision maker commits himself to buying the Porsche. Having done so, we may expect the decision maker to begin immediately the sort of cognitive work that will permit him to justify his commitment to this particular course of action. Even though the two cars were really quite equal in their overall appeal, the decision maker is likely to rationalize his choice of the Porsche in four related ways:

1. By playing up the virtues of the chosen alternative ("a Porsche sure is a neat and incredibly safe car, made to be enjoyed for a lifetime!").

2. By playing down the virtues of the nonchosen alternative ("a Pinto is yech! Everybody's got one of these things, and it's not really as cheap as I thought; besides, do I *really* think the national economy will be affected by the kind of car I buy?").

3. By playing down the drawbacks of the chosen alternative (a Porsche is not really *that* expensive, when you consider how long it will last; and why worry about maintaining and repairing it — the car will probably never break down or need work; as far as the possibility of theft goes, that's why I've got insurance!").

4. By playing up the disadvantages of the nonchosen alternative ("a Pinto is a garbage can on wheels; it'll probably fall apart the moment you drive it out of the showroom; it can be resold only for junk; it's so poorly made you're likely to get yourself killed; in fact, you've got to be crazy to drive one of those heaps!").

And so it goes. Out of the uncertainty, ambiguity, and conflict concerning which of two alternatives to choose, the decision maker somehow manages to select one option over the other. Having done so, despite the fact that each alternative has both advantages and disadvantages, he then often proceeds to bring his attitudes into line with his behavior: if he chose X over Y, he reasons, it must be because X is somehow more attractive (or less unattractive) than Y.

The upshot of the preceding analysis is that in order to understand why decisions are made as they are, one needs to appreciate the human proclivity to behave in ways that are both simplifying and consistent. To impose order upon the multitude of choices with which they are confronted, decision makers tend to simplify — and occasionally oversimplify — for example, by forming dichotomous, categorical judgments out of what may really be continuously distributed information. Moreover, in their appraisal of the various courses of action available to them, decision makers typically attempt to develop choice alternatives that are consistent with their attitudes and with the personal context in which their decisions are made. Finally, having committed themselves to a particular choice, decision makers tend to develop attitudes that are consistent with the alternative chosen; the choice that was made tends to be rationalized as the correct or most desirable one, while the roads not taken tend to be seen as having been avoided for good reason.

The fact that decision makers tend to behave in ways that are simplifying and consistent should not be construed as implying that the process cannot be influenced or that it is necessarily an irrational process. The needs for simplicity and consistency should be viewed as constraints that impact the decision-making process, constraints that cannot be easily changed, perhaps, but that can be better understood. Such understanding, in turn, can be used to help make decision makers more aware of the forces that typically act upon them, thereby encouraging greater vigilance than before.

2.3 Personality Traits and Decision Making

Lewin (1936) has theorized that an individual's behavior may be understood as a function of two parameters: E (environment) and P (person). E consists of all aspects of, and elements in, the individual's physical and social environment. P, on the other hand, consists of the individual's underlying needs, beliefs, and values, the set of enduring predispositions (personality traits) that he carries with him from situation to situation. Without clear analysis of E, P, and the interaction of E and P in any particular situation, one cannot hope to truly understand the meaning of an individual's behavior.

We have seen that decision makers are motivated by several common needs that affect the manner in which alternatives are developed, evaluated, chosen, and justified. These shared needs form an important part of the P component of any decision. The remainder of P consists of the set of traits that may be different (rather than be common) from one decision maker to the next, and that are likely to influence decision-making effectiveness. Let us now briefly consider several of these personality traits.

2.3.1 Tolerance for Ambiguity

People differ in their underlying willingness or ability to tolerate ambiguous information. All people find ambiguity and uncertainty intolerable after a while. Some, however, are far less tolerant of ambiguity than others; they prefer information that is concrete rather than more abstract; they prefer problems wth simple solutions to those that are more complex; and so forth.

As Janis and Mann (1977) have observed in their important recent book, effective decision making requires a willingness to think carefully before acting — to canvass thoroughly all alternative courses of action, to weigh the rewards and costs associated with choosing each alternative, and to search for and be willing to assimilate new information relevant to the further evaluation of available alternatives. A person who has a high tolerance for ambiguity will probably be both willing and able to engage in each of these phases of the decision-making process. A decision maker who is intolerant of ambiguity, on the other hand, will tend to be far less patient. Instead of living with uncertainty for a time, while alternatives are canvassed, evaluated, and reevaluated, he will tend to take action prematurely, thereby reducing his chances of making a truly effective decision.

2.3.2 Self-Concept

Self-concept refers to the set of feelings that people have about how they look in their own eyes and in the eyes of others. People with a positive self-concept tend to have greater self-esteem and self-acceptance, and tend to be less anxious about what others think of them, than those with a more negative view of themselves.

Self-concept may be expected to influence decision-making effectiveness in two related ways. First, individuals with a relatively negative self-concept will experience greater general anxiety than those who think more positively of themselves, and this anxiety may well lead to a state of stress that makes a thorough search for and evaluation of alternatives extremely unlikely. Second, because of their greater concern about how they look in the eyes of others, decision makers with a relatively negative self-concept may be unduly sensitive to social pressure; instead of doing what *they* believe is right, they may find themselves doing what they believe *others* believe is right. For both these reasons, individuals with an unfavorable self-concept are less likely to make an effective decision than those who have a more positive view of themselves.

2.3.3 Locus of Control

Rotter (1966) has argued for the existence of a personality variable called *locus of control,* defined as the subjective probability that outcomes are determined by self-effort (internal control) or by outside agency (external control). In effect, the world can be thought of as consisting of two extreme personality types, *internals* and *externals.* Internals are people who believe that their outcomes are dependent upon their own behavior; by choosing one course of action rather than another, they determine their own rewards and costs, and thereby shape their own destiny. Externals, on the other hand, believe that the outcomes they experience are independent of their behavior; rewarding or costly outcomes are determined by fate, luck, chance, or other people, but not by anything that the externals themselves may do.

The variable of locus of control is likely to affect a decision maker's ability and willingness to search out and thoroughly evaluate information. To the extent that a decision maker believes that the locus of control over outcomes is external to him (that events are largely beyond his control), he is likely to invest very little care and effort in the study of alternatives. Why bother, after all, if one's ability to influence outcomes is minimal anyway? Conversely, a person who perceives the locus of control over outcomes to be more internal is likely to take the search process far more seriously and will probably do a better job.

2.3.4 Risk-Taking

Independent of the particular social situation in which they are placed, people differ in their underlying willingness to take risks. Some people go out of their way to avoid situations in which it may prove necessary or desirable to take a chance. Others seem to thrive on risk and actively seek out situations in which it may pay to gamble.

It may be that the most effective decisions are made by people who are neither extremely high nor extremely low in the willingness to take risks. A decision maker who is high in risk-taking propensity may fail to do a careful enough job of screening alternatives, and may end up choosing alternatives that are unnecessarily risky. Conversely, a decision maker who is unduly concerned about risk-avoidance is apt to be so constrained in his search for and evaluation of alternatives that he has great difficulty committing himself to a decision; moreover, the decision itself may prove to be unnecessarily conservative. It is the individual with an optimal willingness to take risks who knows when to continue the screening of alternatives and when to stop, when to pursue a relatively risky course of action and when to avoid it, that is likely to prove most effective.

Four personality traits have been briefly described, each of which influences the quality of decision making in a different way. Other personality traits obviously exist, and many of these no doubt play an important role in decision making as well. The four traits presented should therefore be viewed as illustrative rather than exhaustive. Contextual considerations play an extremely important part in the decision-making process, and it is this context to which most of the attention in this book is directed in one way or another. But, Lewin's P is also important, and we should not lose sight of the fact that the individual brings to the decision-making situation a set of enduring predispositions, his personality, that exerts a powerful influence on the way in which the decision process unfolds.

2.4 Entrapment

The term *escalation* refers to an increase in the perceived or actual size of a conflict. Given this definition, *entrapment* may be formally defined, in turn, as a special form of escalation in which the parties involved expend more of their time, energy, money, or other resources in a conflict than seems appropriate or justifiable according to some external standard(s).

2.4.1 The Dollar Auction

Imagine that you have been invited to a party with a number of other people. To keep the gathering lively, the host suggests that the group play a little game. He proceeds to take a dollar bill out of his pocket and announces that he will auction off this dollar to the highest bidder. That is, people will be invited to call out bids (5, 10, 15 cents, etc.) until no further bidding occurs, at which point the highest bidder will pay the amount he bid and will win the dollar in return. The only feature that distinguishes this auction from traditional auctions, your host points out, is the rule that the *second highest* bidder will also be asked to pay the amount bid although he obviously will not win the dollar. For example, if Jane has bid 30 cents and Joe has bid 25 cents, and the bidding stops at this point, the auctioneer-host will pay Jane 70 cents ($1 minus the amount she bid) and Joe (the second highest bidder) will have to pay 25 cents. Bids are to be made in multiples of 5 cents, and the auction will end when one minute has elapsed without any additional bidding.

At this point, the game begins. One person bids a nickel, another bids a dime, someone else jumps the bidding to a quarter, and the bidding proceeds at a fast and furious pace until about 50 or 60 cents is reached. At around this point, the number of people calling out bids begins to decrease, and soon there are only three or four people still taking part. (You, of course, have decided at the outset to observe what happens from the sidelines rather than make a hasty decision to get involved.) The bidding continues, at a somewhat slower pace, until the two highest bids are $1 and 95 cents. There seems to be a break in the action at this point, as the two remaining bidders seem to consider what has happened. Suddenly the person who bid 95 cents calls out $1.05, and the bidding begins once again. Soon the two remaining bidders have escalated matters so far that both bids are over $4. Then one of the guests suddenly escalates the bidding by offering $5, the other (who has already bid $4.25) refuses to go any higher, and the game ends. The host proceeds to collect $4.25 from the loser and $4 from the "winner." Some winner. Some party game. Some host.

A bizarre tale? Not at all. This devilish game is known as the Dollar Auction and was developed by Shubik (1971), who claims that he used the Yale University cocktail party circuit as his proving ground. Several researchers have had people play this very game under controlled laboratory conditions and have found that the participants typically end up bidding far in excess of the $1 prize at stake, sometimes paying as much as $5 or $6 for a dollar bill.

The interesting question, of course, is why decision makers in the Dollar Auction behave in what appears to be a rather irrational manner. What motivates them to bid initially and to persist in this course of action, eventually bidding far more for a prize than the prize is objectively worth? Thanks primarily to Teger's (1979) careful and extensive Dollar Auction research, this question has been largely answered. Teger has found that when participants in the Dollar Auction are asked afterwards to give reasons for their behavior, their responses tend to fall into one of two major motivational categories: economic and interpersonal. Economic motives include the desire to win the dollar, the desire to regain losses, and the desire to avoid losing more money. Interpersonal motives include the desire to save face, a desire to prove that one is the best player, and a desire to punish the other person.

In the early stages of the Dollar Auction, economic motives appear to predominate. People begin the bidding with the hope of winning the dollar bill easily and inexpensively. Their bids increase a little bit at a time, in the expectation that their latest bid will prove to be the winning one. If the other person reasons the same way, however (as is often the case), the bidding continues to escalate. At some subsequent point in the Dollar Auction, the decision makers may begin to realize that they have been sucked into a rather treacherous conflict. They turn around, in effect, comprehending that they have already (perhaps unwittingly) invested a portion of their own resources in the auction, and now begin to pay particular attention to the amount they stand to lose. Thus, in the course of the auction, the players seem to shift from a goal of maximizing winnings to one of minimizing losses. Eventually, and especially after one player has bid $1 for the dollar bill (more generally, when investments exceed the objective worth of the prize), interpersonal motives begin to come to the fore. Even though the players know they are sure to lose, each may go out of his way to punish the other, making sure that the other loses even more, and each may become increasingly concerned about not being made to look foolish by giving in to the continued aggression of his adversary. Thus, as the conflict escalates, and as entrapment occurs, there is a marked shift from an orientation of gain maximization to one of loss minimization, and then to an orientation that involves attempts to save face in a variety of ways.

2.4.2 Some Everyday Examples of Entrapment

Lest you think that entrapment occurs only in the confines of social psychology laboratories or at Ivy League cocktail parties, consider the following set of situations:

1. A person phones another to obtain some important information and is put on "hold." The person must decide whether to continue waiting for the other party to return (as he expects) or to hang up and try again later.
2. A person is confronted with the choice of walking to his destination for an appointment, or continuing to wait for a bus that he expects will get him to his destination faster and in greater comfort.
3. A couple in a deteriorating marriage must decide whether to continue their relationship (in the hope that their differences will soon be reconciled) or to dissolve it.
4. Having already invested many millions of dollars in the development of the Concorde supersonic transport plane, the French and British governments must decide whether to go ahead with plans to put the Concorde into production (in the face of worldwide opposition to such a plan) or to scrap the project.
5. The United States government is confronted with the choice of continuing a "holding pattern" of remaining in Vietnam (in the hope and expectation of victory) or withdrawing its troops.

2.4.3 Characteristics of Entrapment

Each of the above illustrations (some social, others nonsocial) constitutes a situation in which entrapment has occurred or may occur.

Common to these examples, and countless others not described here, are a number of features.

First, notice that the same parameter (time, money, and human lives) may be viewed *both* as an investment and as an expense. The passage of time (in examples 1 through 3) and the outlay of other resources (in examples 4 and 5) represent *investments* to the extent that they are viewed as increasing the chances of goal attainment (the return of the other party, arrival of the bus, marital bliss, the development of a competitive form of air transportation, or victory in Vietnam). On the other hand, the passage of time and the outlay of other resources are also *expenses* to the extent that they can be viewed in relation to the costs incurred by remaining in the situation (wasting time on the phone without getting the information, being late for the appointment, continuing in a deteriorating marital relationship, sinking money in a transportation project that may never "get off the ground," or the continued loss of American lives in Vietnam).

Second, notice that as time passes or as additional resources are invested, the cost associated with continuing in the situation increases, but so does the presumed proximity to the desired goal. Hence, the longer an individual, group, or nation remains in such situations, and the larger the expenditure of resources, the greater the conflict. The greater the conflict, the greater the pressures to act decisively, either by withdrawing or by committing oneself to remain in the situation.

Notice finally that of these two possible extreme decisions (total commitment or total withdrawal), the former is probably more likely to be made. The pressure restraining the individual, group, or nation against continued involvement (represented by the total accumulated cost associated with the passage of time or the expenditure of other resources) is more than offset by the presence of three pressures that drive the parties to remain in the situation:

a.   The reward associated with obtaining the goal.
b.   The presumed increased proximity to the goal ("light at the end of the tunnel").
c.   The cost associated with giving up on one's investment (having spent fifteen minutes on hold or at the street corner for nothing, wasting twenty years in a painful, difficult marriage, having misspent millions of dollars in the development of an SST, or having lost thousands of American lives in vain).

In summary, entrapment is a ubiquitous phenomenon, likely to rear its ugly head in virtually any situation in which a decision maker must allocate resources in order to reach a goal object that is believed to be within reach but is not yet in hand. Entrapment occurs because certain situations have the characteristic features described above. Additionally, it is important to bear in mind that entrapment also flows out of — although it does not necessarily follow from — the human needs for simplicity and consistency. If only decision makers could avoid oversimplifying their task (by misconstruing probable and possible events as certain ones), and if they could avoid the temptation to maintain consistency by justifying the course of action they have chosen (even if it is excessively costly or wrong), entrapment would occur far less often in our daily lives.

3 THE INTERPERSONAL DECISION-MAKING PROCESS

We now move from consideration of the decision maker as an asocial creature — dealing with cars, courses, and the opening of doors — to an examination of the decision-making process in the presence of, and in relation to, other people. The material on interpersonal processes will be organized as follows:

1. Development of a fundamental assumption, concerning the essential difference between decision making in a social and a nonsocial context.
2. A brief analysis of the major patterns of social interdependence, and the relationship of these patterns to the decision-making process.
3. A look at a particularly important example of interpersonal process: competitive business decisions.

3.1 Social versus Nonsocial Decision Making

In our earlier discussion of approach-avoidance conflict, one example concerned the decision of whether to eat a piece of candy that is delicious but also fattening. As tough as the decision may be for a person confronted with this conflict, one thing is clear: the decision maker does not have to take the thoughts and feelings of the candy into account in making his decision. Although our environment is generally not reactive, other people are. If you decide to push a stone, it cannot react to you — decide to chase or follow you. But if you push another person, that person is likely to react, and to do so in a deliberate way that has consequences for you. As complex as nonsocial decision making may be, there is at least no other person directly involved in or affected by the process. To be effective, decisions made by two or more people must take the preferences, expectations, and intentions of each person into account. When one considers the possibility that a particular decision reflects not only the decision maker's own preferences as well as his expectations concerning the other's decision, but also his perception of his own and the other's previous decisions, their interconnection, and the implication of any present decision for the future, it can be seen that social decision making is a remarkably complex and intriguing process.

As a simple illustration of the complexity inherent in social decision making, consider this example. You and another person, whom you have never met, never will meet, and with whom you cannot communicate in any way, are seated in separate rooms. Each of you has a piece of paper on which you are to write one of two words, heads or tails. You are told that if you both simultaneously write the same thing (both heads or both tails) the experimenter will give each of you $100. But should you write different things (one heads, the other tails) neither of you will win anything. Make your choice.

When people in our Western culture are asked to pick heads or tails in the flip of a coin, most tend to choose heads. It should come as no surprise, therefore, that most people given the above description of the heads-tails problem indicate that they would write heads; since heads is the more prominent of the two choice alternatives, it is the one on which people believe they can converge. More interesting is the type of reasoning that leads to a choice of heads. At a relatively simple level, the decision maker may reason as follows: "To decide between heads and tails, I need to figure out what the other person is likely to do. But I don't know anything at all about him, and he doesn't know anything about me. So I'll figure out what *I* would do in this situation, and assume that he is like me and will do the same thing. Let's see — I usually pick heads in the flip of a coin, so I'll write heads and assume he'll do the same thing." At a second level, the decision maker may reason like this: "The way to solve this problem is to figure out what the other person will write, and to then make my choice match his. Let's see. Given that I don't know anything about the other person, why don't I make the assumption that he's an average sort of person. Since most people would probably choose heads over tails, I'll assume that the other person will do exactly that, and I'll write heads myself so that my choice will match his." Finally, consider an even more complex chain of reasoning. "To decide between heads and tails, I need to figure out what the other person will write. But, what the other person writes will probably be determined by what he thinks I'll write. Let's see. Since he doesn't know anything about me (and therefore cannot begin to appreciate how clever I really am), he will probably assume that I'm an average Joe Blow and will therefore most likely expect me to choose heads. If he expects me to choose heads, then he'll write heads himself in order to have his choice match my own. Which means that I should write heads to make my choice agree with his choice, which in turn is based on his educated guess about what my own choice will be."

It can be seen that although these three chains of reasoning converge on the identical decision (a choice of heads), they differ widely in their complexity — in the degree and manner in which the other's preferences, expectations, and intentions are taken into account. This increased complexity, and the twists and turns to which it leads, is the emblematic feature of social decision making. Each party to a social decision must try to "get inside the head of the other," even as he acknowledges the likely possibility that the other is doing exactly the same thing to him.

3.2 Patterns of Interdependence

Interdependence is the glue of relationships, the set of bonds that link people to one another in particular ways. Two fundamentally different types of relational bonds may be distinguished, each of which will have a profound effect on the social decision-making process: cooperation and competition.

3.2.1 Cooperation

The hallmark of a cooperative relationship is the fact that the parties tend to "sink or swim together." Interests are convergent, which means that outcomes that are regarded as favorable or as unfavorable by one person will be regarded in like fashion by the other. As can be seen in Figure 1(a), it is characteristic of a cooperative relationship that the movement of one person (X) toward his own goal tends to facilitate the movement of the other person (Y) toward his objective.

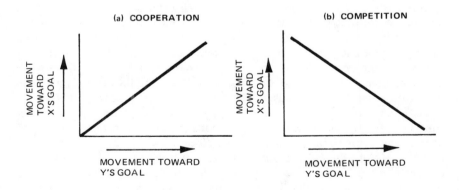

Figure 5-1. Interdependence Patterns in (a) Cooperative and (b) Competitive Relationships

Recall the example of the heads-tails problem. The participants have convergent interests in that each wants to match the other's choice and thereby win $100. If they succeed in matching, they both "swim;" but if they fail to match, they both "sink." The goals of the two participants are one and the same, which means that one person's movement toward his goal will of necessity advance the other toward his goal.

Since cooperation is characterized by converging, overlapping interests, it is also a pattern in which trust and trustworthiness are likely to emerge. If you know that our interests coincide, you will tend to trust what I say and do; in turn, you will behave in trustworthy ways that encourage me to believe in you. Social decision making in a cooperative relationship will thus tend to be characterized by trust and by a sense of positive regard among the participants. The decision makers will be able to pool their intellectual and other resources, to collaborate in the search for and evaluation of alternatives, and to make joint decisions in the belief that "two heads are better than one."

3.2.2 Competition

Characteristic of competitive relationships is the fact that if one person "sinks," the other "swims." People can do well in competitive relationships only at each other's expense, and the parties' interests are thus clearly divergent. As shown in Figure 5-1(b), the greater one person's movement toward his goal, the smaller the other's movement toward his own goal. Given the direct antagonism of interests and goals in competitive relationships, it is not surprising that such relationships are characterized by mutual dislike and suspicion. Bluffs, threats, promises, deceit, lying, and cheating become a part of the combatants' arsenal of potential weapons. Certain situations are more susceptible to lying and deceit than are others. Clearly our intent here is not to teach the reader when or how to lie, but rather to make you aware of situations in which worldly temptations to lie do exist. Being aware of the possibility of deceit should certainly increase the seriousness of decision-making efforts; no one enjoys playing the fool.

As an example of decision making in a competitive relationship, consider a simple variation of the heads-tails problem. The task, number of people, and setting remain the same as before. Now, however, one person is told that if both he and the other write the *same* (both heads or both tails) he will win $100, while the other will win nothing. Meanwhile, the second person is told that he will win $100 (and the other nothing) if he and the other write the opposite (one writes heads, the other tails). In this situation, interests are purely opposed. Each is told what the other is told; as a result one person can reach his goal only if the other fails to reach his. If a possible communication channel were to be introduced into this situation, we might expect each person to use this channel in order to mislead the other, to "sucker" the other person into behaving in ways contrary to his self-interest.

3.3 Competitive Business Decisions

Many business decisions are made under competitive conditions where the actions of one's rival must be considered prior to determining one's own best strategy. The need to "get inside the head of one's adversary" becomes particularly acute when the number of rival firms is so small that each firm unmistakably recognizes its mutual interdependence, and where the existence of antitrust laws prohibit collusion. Each is aware that a contemplated policy change could so affect one's rival that retaliation in an identical or related form would be a certainty. A thorough analysis of the benefits and costs of a proposed policy change by one party must therefore include the costs associated with the adversary's probable form of retaliation.

3.3.1 Game Theory as an Aid to Business Decisions

Businessmen frequently find themselves in the position of trying to outguess their rivals. As much as each would like to know precisely how his adversary will react, only an inept rival can be expected to permit his countermoves to be predicted with any degree of accuracy. One solution to the problem of competitive choice behavior is provided by *game theory*, a method of economic analysis first developed by Von Neumann and Morgenstern (1947). In game theory, each party tries to determine his rival's most profitable counterstrategy to his own best moves, and then devises his own strategy accordingly.

As an illustration, let us consider a hypothetical version of the competitive struggle between MacDonald's and Burger King for relative shares of the fast food market, where it is assumed that as one company's share grows the other's share decreases. Suppose that each has three possible courses of action: lower prices, raise prices, or increase advertising outlays. The outcome of any pair of strategic choices may be summarized in a payoff matrix, such as the one presented in Table 5-2. The numbers themselves can be thought of as the best estimates of the resulting share of the market by the marketing departments of each firm. Let us assume that both marketing departments are equally adept at forecasting; let us further assume that both rivals are considering the same set of possible payoffs. There is thus no need to record each company's share of the market, since one company's share is simply equal to 100% minus the other company's market share. The entries in Table 5-2 are therefore recorded as percentage shares of the market for Burger King.

Table 5-2.   Matrix display of outcomes in a two-person game.
(Numbers represent percentage shares of the overall market for Burger King, as a result of each combination of strategies by the two "players.")

		McDonald's Strategies		Increase Advertising Outlays
		Lower Price	Raise Price	Outlays
	Lower Price	56	62	51
Burger	Raise Price	41	54	44
King's Strategies	Increase advertising outlays	55	65	53

Given that both sides have the information contained in this table, each must decide upon a strategy without knowledge of the other's countermove. A cautious approach to this problem entails assuming the worst and acting accordingly. Thus, Burger King can assume that if it chooses to lower price, McDonald's will choose to increase its advertising outlay, leaving Burger King with a 51% market share. If Burger King raises price, it can assume that McDonald's will opt to lower its price, leaving a 41% market share. Finally, if Burger King chooses to increase advertising outlays, it can assume that McDonald's will do likewise. Given this rather dreary outlook, the best that Burger King can do is seek the best of these minimum payoffs, by choosing to increase advertising outlays. This decision rule (picking the best of the worst) is called a *maximin strategy*.

McDonald's, also employing a cautious approach, would find that if it chose to lower price, Burger King would also choose to lower price, resulting in a 56% market share. (Remember that large payoffs, while good for Burger King, are bad for McDonald's.) The worst possible payoffs for McDonald's, resulting from each of its other two strategies, are 65% and 53%. The best that McDonald's can do is to pick the strategy that results in the lowest of these payoffs, i.e., increase advertising. This decision rule (picking the worst of the best) is called a *minimax strategy*.

In this particular example the payoff matrix is said to have an *equilibrium*, a point on which the maximin and minimax strategies converge.* These decision rules also have some rather interesting properties.

---

*Although not all game matrices have an equilibrium point, our treatment will consider only those that do.

First, they offer "down-side protection," in the sense that no further damage can be inflicted upon either party if it opts for its respective maximin or minimax strategy. Thus, if Burger King chooses its maximin, its market share can fall no lower than 53%. This rule holds whether both act simultaneously or one leads and the other follows. Second, if one participant chooses its maximin (minimax), then the best that the other can do is to choose its minimax (maximin) strategy. Finally, if one participant is poorly informed, likes taking risks, or for some other reason does not employ a maximin strategy, then it may be to the other's advantage to change strategies and thereby gain at the former's expense.*

Although our example is purely hypothetical, it is meant to illustrate the social and psychological structure of many real competitive situations. Outcomes are not easily predictable, of course, let alone the possible choices among strategies and counterstrategies. All this notwithstanding, it is extremely important to know when one is in a game-like setting. Managers who engage in consistent, patently obvious patterns of decision making may soon find themselves out of a job. Avoiding predictability is a key to success. How easy it would be if one only knew what the competition was about to do next. Small wonder that industrial spying has become a part of the competitive struggle among business concerns.

3.3.2 Bargaining and Business Decisions

Constant-sum games, such as the Burger King-McDonald's struggle, can provide useful insights into business decision making. However, at least as many problems in the real world are of the non-constant-sum variety, such that both parties can win, both can lose, or one can win at the other's partial expense. It is in precisely such a context, where parties can both help and hurt each other, that bargaining occurs: cartels can increase the profits of all participants, peace negotiations can be more productive than war, collective bargaining can benefit both management and labor given the alternative of a strike.

In the literature, nonconstant-sum two-person games tend to be divided into two classes: cooperative and noncooperative. In the cooperative case, it

---

*Note that the preceding analysis has been presented in the context of social decision making. Elsewhere in this volume the reader is exposed to many of the same terms, but with one fundamental difference. Here the opponent is a person or firm that acts and reacts, and is out to do everything possible to limit the success of the other player. In the treatment presented in Chapter 9, the second "player" is not an opponent, but rather is nature. As the reader will see, the optimum strategy in games against nature may be anything but minimax (maximin).

has been argued that participants will be sufficiently rational to discover ways of utilizing the opportunities available. For example, suppose a payoff exists that would benefit both parties, but requires that each adopt a different strategy than the one currently being employed. Suppose also that a change by either alone would greatly benefit the nonchanger at the expense of the one that did change. In this example, a simple promise to change would be insufficient since each would have an incentive to cheat. But, if the parties were able to enforce their promises, possibly by placing side bets with a third party, who guarantees to underwrite any loss that results from a broken promise, the mutually preferred payoff could be attained.

Noncooperative cases illustrate several interesting features of conflict and bargaining situations. To the person who walks into a bank and claims to be carrying a bomb in his valise (whether he actually is or not), disclosure of intent is necessary if one is ever going to win one's point (i.e., get the cash). Unlike conflict situations that call for secrecy, it is important here that the commitment (threat) be irrevocable and that it be communicated unambiguously. A bluff that is perceived as a bluff can hardly be expected to work, nor can a true threat that is similarly perceived. A winning strategy in the game of "chicken" (a constant war of nerves that pits two drivers approaching each other with their left wheels on the center line in the road) may consist of having the driver remove his steering wheel and toss it out the window — provided that he does so in full view of the other driver. In many instances, it is the person making the first move who wins. If both commit themselves simultaneously (the tactic being equally available to both), it could result in a standoff (or, in the game of chicken, in a disaster!).

It is not always advantageous to make strong, irrevocable commitments. One runs the risk, in doing so, of (being seen as) establishing an unreasonable, untenable position. For example, strong advance commitment by union leaders to a specific wage proposal may force a nasty choice between a crippling strike and the public embarrassment (and possible loss of elected office) that would result from having backed down. Indeed, in many bargaining situations weakness may be strength; it may be wiser to accentuate one's (apparent) weakness while simultaneously playing down one's (true) strength. The ongoing battle for public opinion in labor-management negotiations is a case in point. There was a time when labor automatically received most of the public's sympathy. Today, one can observe management urging the general public to understand that higher wages must be passed along to the consumer as higher prices, and that it is "in the public's best interests" that they (management) resist "unreasonable" union demands.

In summary, it has been argued that cooperation and competition are polar opposites, implying widely divergent consequences for the decision-making process. Remember, however, that real-world decision situations do not neatly sort into these two patterns. It is more often true that relationships are not rigid and contain a varied mixture of cooperative and competitive motives. In any given relationship, some interests may be shared while others are in direct opposition; one person may want to strike a bargain that is as personally or competitively advantageous to him as possible, but may require the consent of the other party if any agreement at all is to be reached. To fully understand why decision making occurs as it does in a particular relationship, then, it is essential that the balance of existing cooperative and competitive motives be taken into account.

4 SELECTED BIBLIOGRAPHY

Baumol, W.J. *Economic Theory and Operations Analysis*. 4th ed. Englewood Cliffs, N.J.: Prentice-Hall, 1977.

Chernoff, H., and Moses, L.E. *Elementary Decision Theory*. New York: John Wiley and Sons, Inc., 1959.

Darley, J.M., and Latane, B. "Bystander intervention in emergencies: Diffusion of responsibility." *Journal of Personality and Social Psychology*. 1968, *10*, 215-221.

Festinger, L. *A Theory of Cognitive Dissonance*. Stanford, Calif.: Stanford University Press, 1957.

Heider, F. *The Psychology of Interpersonal Relations*. New York: John Wiley and Sons, 1958.

Janis, I., and Mann, L. *Decision Making: A Psychological Analysis of Conflict, Choice, and Commitment*. New York: Free Press, 1977.

Latane, B., and Darley, J.M. "Group inhibition of bystander intervention in emergencies." *Journal of Personality and Social Psychology*. 1968, *10*, 215-221.

Lewin, K. *A Dynamic Theory of Personality*. New York: McGraw-Hill, 1935.

Lewin, K. *Principles of Topological Psychology*. New York: McGraw-Hill, 1936.

Luce, R.D., and Raiffa, H. *Games and Decisions, Introduction and Critical Survey*. New York: John Wiley and Sons, Inc., 1957.

Newcomb, T.M. "An approach to the study of communicative acts." *Psychological Review*, 1953, *60*, 393-404.

Osgood, C.E., Tannebaum, P.H. "The principle of congruity in the prediction of attitude change." *Psychological Review*, 1955, *62*, 42-55.

Raiffa, H. *Decision Analysis*. Reading, Mass.: Addison-Wesley, 1968.

Raven, B.H., and Rubin, J.Z. *Social Psychology: People in Groups*. New York: John Wiley and Sons, Inc., 1976.

Rotter, J. "Generalized expectancies for internal versus external control of reinforcement." *Psychological Monographs*. 1966, *80* (1, Whole No. 609).

Rubin, J.Z., and Brockner, J. "Factors affecting entrapment in waiting situations: The Rosencrantz and Guildenstern effect." *Journal of Personality and Social Psychology*. 1975, *31*, 1054-1063.

Rubin, J.Z., and Brown, B.R. *The Social Psychology of Bargaining and Negotiation*. New York: Academic Press, 1975.

Schelling, T.C. *The Strategy of Conflict*. Cambridge, Mass.: Harvard University Press, 1960.

Shubik, M. "The dollar auction game: A paradox in noncooperative behavior and escalation." *Journal of Conflict Resolution*. 1971, *15*, 109-111.

Teger, A.I. *Too Much Invested to Quit: The Psychology of the Escalation of Conflict*. New York: Pergamon Press, 1979.

Von Neumann, J., and Morgenstern, O. *Theory of Games and Economic Behavior*, 2nd ed., Princeton, N.J.: Princeton University Press, 1947.

Chapter 6
Decision Making in Politics

1   INTRODUCTION

If only we could study decision making in politics according to some
obvious plan. If only an underlying logic could be found for those decisions
that are the very stuff of our political life. If only we could integrate an area
that is, by its very nature, sprawling and multi-layered. Alas, we can do none
of these things and so you, the student of decision making, will have to hold
in check your passion for order. Just as there is little order in politics, so
there is little order in political decision making. That makes a certain sense,
of course, since politics and decisions are one and the same.

Politics is deciding who gets what. It is the decision-making process of
any group that makes rules for its members. Politics is also the process of
deciding who decides. It is not self-evident who has the right to decide for
anyone else, or even if anyone has that right. Consequently, we are faced with
a political universe in which who decides, what is to be decided upon, and
according to what rules, become the core questions. To complicate matters,
these concerns cannot be addressed once and for all. Since it is typically
assumed that decision making on one issue should dictate the decision
process on other issues, political concerns are likely to emerge repeatedly.

Percy H. Hill et al., Making Decisions: A Multidisciplinary Introduction

Just because you are willing to accept the decision of the nine Justices of the Supreme Court that schools must be integrated does not mean that you are willing to have the Supreme Court decide whether you may or may not have an abortion.

To get some idea of just how complex a single political decision can be, let us look briefly at one case that superficially appears to be rather simple: President Carter's 1978 move to establish full diplomatic relations with the People's Republic of China. How should this decision be broken down into its component parts? As students of decision making, how should we analyze this decision, explain it, understand it, compare it, and use it? Consider the following possibilities, each of which constitutes a perfectly reasonable way of slicing the same piece of decision-making pie.

1.1 The Decision to Recognize China Seen as a Public Policy Decision

Carter's gesture in 1978 was simply the last in a series of small steps that go back at least as far as Nixon's trip to Peking in 1972. It was a logical outgrowth of a broad policy with several aims: to achieve peace by maintaining a delicate balance among several powers, including Western Europe, Japan, China, the Soviet Union, and the United States; to do business with just about anyone who can pay; and to move away from the simplistic ideological warfare that characterized the worst days of the Cold War.

1.2 The Decision to Recognize China Seen as an Institutional Decision

Carter's overtures to Vice-Premier Deng Xiaoping constituted yet another example of the "Imperial Presidency." It is clear that the president moved without much consultation with Congress on such questions as the fate of Taiwan, or the effect this rapprochement would have on delicate arms negotiations with the Soviet Union. All things being equal, the power to chart this country's course still resides in the Oval Office.

1.3 The Decision to Recognize China Seen as a Bureaucratic Decision

Before Carter moved on China he consulted with several government bureaucracies, including the departments of State, Defense, and Commerce (each had an input into the way the decision was finally made). Indeed, Carter's ability to make decisions was so sharply constrained by these bureaucracies that he was reduced to managing the decision within the limits that these governmental organizations imposed.

1.4   The Decision to Recognize China Seen as a Small Group Decision

Like most recent presidents, Carter had a small coterie of trusted advisors with whom he discussed everything. The decision to recognize the People's Republic of China was an outgrowth of a series of meetings of this group, whose members included such disparate figures as Hamilton Jordan, Stuart Eizenstat, James Schlesinger, Cyrus Vance, and Zbigniew Brezinski. Although there is no evidence of a single small policy-making group in this case, all of Carter's advisors supported the Chinese overture. As a result, he heard not a single dissenting voice from those who were closest to him.

1.5   The Decision to Recognize China Seen as an Interest Group Decision

Above all, the private sector in this country stood to gain if American goods could be sold to 800 million more customers. It is well known that the American business community has been champing at the bit in recent years, straining to gain access to the vast untapped market of Chinese who might be, say, thirsty for a Coke. Therefore, our government was merely responding to the interests of big business, a national constituency that knows Washington, above all, must protect our capitalist way of life.

1.6   The Decision to Recognize China Seen as an Individual Decision

The decision to recognize China was made by one man, and one man only. Whatever the information that came pouring into the White House, whatever the cacophonous clamor of needs and preferences that reached the president's ears, in the last analysis it was he who decided. "The buck stops here," Harry S. Truman intoned, and in 1978 it stopped at the desk of Jimmy Carter.

To some degree, the decision to recognize China was all of the above. It was a public policy decision as well as an individual decision; even though it was a small group decision, the small group was influenced by big business. In short, none of the above perspectives by definition necessarily excludes any of the others. Even so, when our concern is to describe what happens in the real world, trying to understand how a particular decision really came to be made, it is not very helpful to assert that "everything matters." Even though everything *does* matter, it is also true that some factors have a greater weight than others on any given decision. So, the essential task of those who would come to understand a political decision is to analyze the factors that caused this particular decision to come out the way it did.

Our interest here is not in how a decision *should* have been made, but rather how it *was* made. Of course, some in political science would occupy themselves with value more than fact, with "ought" more than "is," with a *prescriptive* rather than *descriptive* mode of analysis.* Because we must confine our concern in this chapter, we will limit our focus to the matter of how decisions are actually made in everyday political life.

Most of you will become neither practicing politicians nor practicing political scientists, but you are and will continue to be citizens. We believe that you will be more astute observers of, and the wiser participants in, the role of citizen to the extent that you understand the way in which the hundreds of political decisions at every level of government finally are made.

We will approach the task by steadily narrowing the focus of inquiry. We will begin with an overview of the system as a whole; next, we will examine the special decision-making properties of organizations; third, we will look at large and small groups; and finally we will consider the individual as a decision maker. Before we begin, however, one caveat: do not expect this kind of an investigation, directly, to teach a skill. There is no device, technique, or model that will specifically instruct you how to make good political decisions. The name of this discipline notwithstanding, politics is still more art than science; the tools at our disposal are far from exact. The aim therefore is modest: merely to provide some insight into the whole political decision-making process by looking at several of its component parts.

2 PUBLIC POLICY (SYSTEMIC) DECISIONS

To understand how government works, take a look at how public policy is made. Policy is a course of action deliberately embarked upon by government; it reflects public goals and consists of public programs. At every step along the way, there are decisions to be made. Which goals should have first priority? Which programs will best serve our diverse goals? How should we go about implementing proposals already decided on? Unfortunately, policy makers are almost always reduced to choosing

---

*One of the central concerns of such prescriptive theorists is the problem of social choice. How should the tastes, preferences, or values of individual persons be amalgamated and summarized into a collective choice, a single decision?

among what appear to be equally strong alternatives, equally defensible values, and equally deserving advocates. When Congess enacts a law that increases the mandatory retirement age from 65 to 70, such a change may be fine for the energetic and able-bodied senior citizens who want to stay on the job five years longer. But it may not be so good for the young job seekers who find themselves unable to break into their professions because there are fewer jobs available, or for the middle-level manager who is stuck for five more years in the same slot because the hierarchy above him is closed. It is precisely because of the conflicts inherent in any system that makes even the faintest claim to being a participatory democracy, that governments end up compromising. Public policy is usually a give and take of some sort, an attempt to find a middle road that reconciles different demands. Usually no one ends up completely satisfied, but no one group is entirely shut out, either.

How, precisely, does our government finally settle on a particular compromise? Ideally, government should go through the rational decision-making process also described elsewhere in Chapter 3.

1. It should make a preliminary appraisal of the problem (e.g., reduction in air pollution).
2. It should identify the goals and rank order them (e.g., cleaner air would probably vie with economic development).
3. It should canvass the possible alternatives (e.g., cutting off federal aid to states that do not have an acceptable antipollution plan, shifting budget outlays from highways to mass transit).
4. It should consider the consequences of each of the alternatives (e.g., cutting off federal aid would cause economic hardship).
5. It should select the alternative that most closely matches the preferred goals (e.g., perhaps the government would settle for somewhat cleaner air at less cost, rather than perfectly clean air).
6. It should establish a plan for implementation.

At first glance this process seems reasonable enough; it is not such a demanding sequence that it would be impossible to follow. It does raise additional questions, however. Will different parts of the government, and different persons in the same part, perceive the problem in the same way, even in a preliminary appraisal? Can their different perceptions be easily eliminated in favor of one outlook? Can we usefully rank order our goals when goals differ, and when they change even in the short run? Do we have the resources, especially the necessary full information, to examine all the alternatives in each policy-making situation? Are the variables always so certain that we can predict with accuracy the consequences of choosing one rather than any of the other alternatives? And can we foresee enough of what will actually happen during implementation to plan such implementation precisely?

In response to questions such as these which point to the imperfections both of the real world and of the rational model of policy making, political decision theorists have introduced the term *disjointed incrementalism* to describe how they believe policy is actually made.

> It is decision making through small or incremental moves on particular problems rather than through a comprehensive reform program. It is also endless; it takes the form of an indefinite sequence of policy moves. Moreover, it is exploratory in that the goals of policy making continue to change as new experience with policy throws new light on what is possible and desirable. In this sense, it is also better described as moving *away* from known social ills rather than as moving *toward* a known and relatively stable goal. (Braybrooke and Lindblom, 1970, p. 71.)

Two main types of incremental decision making are hypothesized. The first involves a change that largely repeats frequent previous change (e.g., an increase in the minimum wage); the second involves a nonrepetitive change viewed at the time as merely a minor alteration in policy (e.g., the Rehabilitation Act of 1973 prohibiting discrimination against the handicapped). Both of these are implemented and also characterized by strategies or dodges "developed for dealing with very complex problems — strategies that are especially well adapted to public policy analysis." (Lindblom, 1966, p. 24.) These include:

1. *Satisficing decisions* — decisions that fall short of maximizing the desired value but are not too high in cost and so are good enough.
2. *Remedial decisions* — decisions that are designed simply to rectify a condition from which it is desirable to escape.
3. *Serial decisions* — decisions that are specifically understood to be only the first in a long series of related decisions.

The framework of disjointed incrementalism seems to be a great improvement upon more rational models of policy analysis. It does a better job of explaining political reality. It addresses the problems of real-life policy making by admitting only the politically relevant alternatives; by keeping all costs in range; and by reducing the number of alternatives to be explored, the information to be gathered, and the complexity of the analysis. It at least allows us to agree on what it is that we are against. Consider as an example the way in which the federal budget is put together. Each year's budget is based on the outlays of the preceding year. Shifts in allocations tend to be small. In any given fiscal year, defense spending may be up, but (barring a war) it will not go up by a quantum leap. In another year, the funding for general training and employment programs may be down, but it tends not to drop drastically. No attempt is made to assemble a budget that will respond to *all* our needs. A budget that is good enough will do, especially if it responds to the loudest demands. Finally, nothing so characterizes policy as the product of compromise as does the budget. Guns and butter are locked in a contest from which both will emerge as the winners and as the losers: there will never be enough guns for the most ardent proponents of high military spending, nor enough butter for the most fervent devotees of social programs. On the other hand, there will always be some guns and some butter, with most advocates getting just enough most of the time to prevent them from getting really dissatisfied with how the system works. The implication is that disjointed incrementalism contributes significantly to the stability of the system; it helps maintain the status quo.

2.1 The Anatomy of a Single Policy Decision

So far, we have considered the general character of public policy in America, and seen how real-world politics dictates policy output so as to give it a conservative cast. Disjointed incrementalism helps us to understand how this policy formation at this general level is developed. Our task now is to analyze and understand how any single policy decision is actually reached. To accomplish this task, we must examine the mechanics involved, the participants, the settings, the groups, the system of information processing, the power relationships — in short, all the components that determine the outcome. One investigator who has done some key research in this area is Graham Allison; his book, *Essence of Decision* (1971), takes a careful look at the 1962 Cuban missile crisis. Allison identifies three basic frames of reference for use when thinking about foreign affairs. (Actually, they apply as well to domestic political decisions.) Each frame of reference is, in effect, a conceptual lens through which one might view a given set of events differently.

- Model I, the *Rational Actor Model* as Allison labeled it, is the frame of reference used by most laymen and analysts to understand decisions in foreign affairs. Decisions are to be seen as "the more or less purposive acts of unified national governments" (p. 4). The actor is the national government and the "action is chosen as a calculated solution to a strategic problem" (p. 13). Since the underlying premise of this model is that action is the result of rational choice, it is hardly surprising that Allison gives it rather low marks for explanatory power.

- Model II, the *Organizational Process Model*, holds that the happenings of international politics are the results of organizational processes. Actual occurrences are organizational outputs; organizational routines constitute the range of effective choice open to government leaders confronted with any problem; and organizational priorities structure the situation within which the leaders must decide.

- Model III, the *Government Politics Model*, contends that the decisions and actions of governments are political resultants: *"Resultants* in the sense that what happens is not chosen as a solution to a problem but rather results from compromise, conflict, and confusion of officials with diverse interests and unequal influence; *political* in the sense that the activity from which decisions and actions emerge is . . . bargaining among individual members of the government." (p. 162)

Allison's perspectives are not all-inclusive. Three additional models have been devised to point to some of the variables he neglects; they are intended to supplement, not replace, the three models Allison proposes. Analysts of public policy decisions thus have no less than six conceptual lenses through which a governmental action can be viewed.

- Model IV, the *Small Group Process Model*, sees public policy decisions as the resultant of small group processes. The model is derived from two facts: the first, long understood by social psychologists, is that small groups have their own special dynamic; the second is that much public policy is formulated in small group situations. The quality of the decision depends on the interaction among members of the small group making the choice. The range of alternatives in this model is no greater than the sum total of choices offered by the group's members, and this range structures the situation so that the group (or leader) has to decide within the limits of its constraints. Some of this model's organizing concepts include the personalities of the participating actors, the actors' constituencies, their parochial priorities and perceptions, and small group dynamics (e.g., leadership style, group norms, group cohesiveness). Particular attention is directed to the many factors that intervene between an issue and a decision, especially the matter of what actually happened while the small decision-making group was in session.

- Model V, the *Dominant Leader Model*, defines a policy decision as the resultant of the personality and behavior of the dominant leader. This model's explanatory power is derived from the belief that "the buck stops here." The range of alternatives is limited to those considered by the leader; the final choice is simply whatever the leader selects; and it is a consequence of the leader's traits and circumstances. It is assumed that the dominant leader is able to control all pertinent bureaucracies, small groups, and individuals; that the leader largely determines the flow of information as well as access to this information; and that the leader's personal needs and political constituencies therefore have primary impact on the final choice he makes. In the instance of the Cuban missile crisis, this model suggests that the main explanation for the decision to blockade rests in the person of President John F. Kennedy. It is assumed that an examination of *his* actions during those thirteen days of crisis, and *his* personality and political perspective, provide the best possible understanding of what happened, when, and why.

- Model VI, the *Cognitive Process Model*, contends that decisions are the resultant of the abilities of political actors to decompose complex policy problems. An ability to pursue a rational course of action is constrained by our limited capacity to process information and disseminate data. This cognitive process defines the decision making that occurs. General and invariant characteristics of the human mind are of primary importance: the tendencies to conceptualize decision problems in terms of a single value, to associate but a single outcome with an available alternative, to restrict consideration to a relatively small number of variables, to resolve uncertainty by generalizing, to use analogies as shortcuts to reaching a decision, to ignore discrepant information or assimilate it to pre-existing beliefs, and to undertake premature cognitive closure. According to this model, some of the consequences that adversely affect the quality of decisions are: first that past events are too often used as analogies to contemporary ones; second, that policy tends to be stagnant, because those who are most involved in its implementation have been in similar jobs for a long time and therefore tend to be guided by old images and to resist innovation; and third, that the system as a whole resolves its dilemmas by disjointed incrementalism, with small steps being taken that lead to solutions that are only "satisficing."

Theoretically, any of the six models can lead to alternative explanations of the same decision. (Allison's book is a case in point.) They are *not*, however, mutually exclusive. The chances are good that in analyzing any given decision, two or even more of these models will prove to be helpful in coming to understand what really took place. Finally, no claim is being made that these six models are all-inclusive. It is certainly possible that as the field of political decision analysis grows, other models will be developed to add to this list.

3   ORGANIZATIONAL DECISIONS

The United States government is an organization, and so is the New York State government. The Department of Defense is an organization, and so is the New York State Highway Department. The Consumer Safety Products Commission, the Food and Drug Administration, the Forest Service, the Social Security Administration, the Veterans Administration, the Office of Management and Budget, and the United States Postal Service – all are organizations. The place where you work will almost certainly be an organization, as is the college or university in which you are now a student. In our society, preschool children and nonworking housewives are the only large classes of persons whose lives are not affected by being part of an organizational setting. Certainly it is true that to talk of politics in America is to talk of bureaucracy in America – which, in turn, is to talk of the organization as a social system.

Organizations have special decision-making characteristics, and a formal structure with certain invariant traits. The result is that routines and patterns of decision making tend to develop that are more or less standard from one organization to the next. Thus, to understand thoroughly the workings of one organization is to know something about the workings of any other. You will know something about how decisions are made in the State Department if you understand how decisions are made in your own college or university. Both, for example, have someone sitting at the top, the chief executive, who is responsible for making policy decisions. The executive is charged with making decisions that further the purpose of the organization, and then communicating these decisions to those persons further down in the administrative hierarchy who are actually responsible for implementing them. The President of the United States may decide that our government should establish formal relations with the People's Republic of China, but he depends on those lower in the pyramid to execute this decision. Similarly, the president of your university mandates a cut in the size of the departments of English, history, and anthropology, but he depends on others to effect that cut.

Max Weber, in the course of his studies on what he labeled *bureaucracy,* was the first modern theorist to try to identify the characteristics of organizations. Typically, organizations are planned and created to accomplish specific objectives; their *raison d'être* is simply to get the job done. According to Weber (1947), organizations have the following characteristics:

1. Labor is divided by skills and authority, and responsibility is defined by law and administrative regulation.
2. Each job, each office, is independent of its occupant. The job is permanent, the individual temporary.

3.   Authority is increasingly centralized. At every stage of the organization there are superiors and subordinates, arranged in a pyramidal hierarchy of powers.
4.   The organization operates according to general rules. Individual employees act in accordance with the formal definitions and requirements of their jobs.
5.   For the sake of organizational continuity, written records are kept.

It follows from this litany of traits that organizations, as decision-making systems, tend to behave in rather special ways. Indeed, there is a gradually developing literature on organizational decision making, pioneered by, among others, Herbert Simon, 1978 Nobel laureate in Economics for his work in problem solving and decision making. As long ago as 1945 he published a book, *Administrative Behavior*, whose very subtitle, *A Study of Decision-Making Processes in Administration Organization*, suggests the merits of isolating organizational decision from all others. More recently, Simon has also pioneered the introduction of such modern decision-making techniques as mathematical analysis, models, and computer simulation. (See the discussions of forecasting and trend analysis in Chapter 12.) Implicit in all of the organizational literature, and explicit in some of this work (e.g., Simon's *The New Science of Management Decision*), is the assumption that to learn about organizations and decisions is to improve the quality of executive (i.e., organizational) output.

Perhaps the quickest way to grasp some of this material is to begin with Simon's proposition that the basic features of organizational decision making are not very different from those of other kinds of decision making. Certain constraints limit us at every level. We have already alluded to the way in which we would ideally like to make decisions. For example, we would like to identify every possible alternative, and every possible consequence of each alternative. We have also already spoken of how actual policy makers circumvent such impossible demands by a series of small decisions that usually do no more than cope. Organizations (and, as we soon shall see, individuals) do much the same.

Consider for a moment the problem of perfect, or complete, information. Organizations, like people, like systems, are physically unable to possess full information. Even if they could, the cost of obtaining such information in each case where a decision has to be made would be prohibitive. So what do organizations do? They converge on those decisions that do a good enough job, minimally sufficient to solve the most pressing problems. Consider the implications for organizational decisions of this one assertion:

1.   Organizations settle for satisficing decisions; they do not even seek to make the optimal choice.

2. Organizations, especially when faced with routine, repetitive decisions, undertake a stable, sequential search process that terminates as soon as the first satisficing alternative has been located.
3. Organizations do not seek out problems for decision making; instead they make only the decisions they are forced to consider by the problems that confront them. Also, there is a desire to avoid uncertainty; as a result, solutions that provide quick feedback are most likely to be chosen.

All organizations are happiest when following set routines. Any student who has ever tried to put together a program of study outside of a regular major, or tried to cope with a lost passport, or tried to register to vote without proof of age in hand, knows full well that the people who staff organizations are distinctly uneasy when confronted by anything out of the ordinary. They are superb at making and executing "programmed" decisions, those that are usual for them. Each organization develops programs and standard operating procedures that can be tapped at any moment to deal with familiar situations. The problem arises when organizations are forced into making nonprogrammed decisions, possibly provoked by a crisis of some sort. Here an organization is quite helpless, straining to send quick messages to its flailing subunits, rather like a giant struggling to gain control over its unwieldy limbs.

This brings us to another point: most of the evidence notwithstanding, it appears that organizations are not altogether resistant to change. A new challenge, demanding a fresh response if the organization is to survive, may force it to adopt new procedures. A sudden increase or decrease in financial resources, for example, may induce dramatic change. A business firm that has spent the last few years operating in the red will have to alter its programs and standard operating procedures if it is to survive.

This leads to a final point. Any organization, like any individual, is interested above all in its own health and survival. Since an organization tends to have a single task, or primary responsibility for one set of problems, it is limited in its interests and concerns. Those who staff it tend to develop limited perceptions and special priorities. Decisions are made, then, from a narrow perspective and, in fact, even when the goal of two separate organizations is the same, they may decide on different ways to reach it. The conflict between the Navy and the departments of Defense and State in the Cuban missile crisis is a perfect case in point. Their goals were identical — the prevention of both a nuclear holocaust and Russian domination — but the preferred modes of attaining them were in conflict. The point is that organizations decide on the basis of what they perceive to be in their own interests. What benefits them is what they will agitate for. They want more personnel, more money, a broader area of jurisdiction, and more independence from the effects of decisions made by other organizations. An organization, in short, sees the world through organizational glasses — anything that benefits it is good, period, and anything good for the organization is good for all those who staff it.

Oddly, social scientists have only recently brought organizations under their close scrutiny. As recently as 1954, *The Handbook of Social Psychology* had chapters on small groups, mass media, industrial social psychology, leadership, and voting behavior; but none on organizations. Yet as we have seen, organizations play an enormously important role in our lives. If one would understand political decisions as they are reported every morning on the front page of the *New York Times*, just knowing that the formal structure of an organization gives it a particular decision-making dynamic, and that so much of government is organization (i.e., bureaucracy), should provide some special insight.

4   GROUP DECISIONS

4.1   Large Latent Groups

By definition, a large latent group is one with so many members that the action of any given member does not matter much one way or the other to the behavior of the group. People organize into such groups because they expect it will help them advance their interests. Any given group cannot meet all of its members' individual needs; it can promote one or more particular interests that the members have in common. Any nation, including the United States, is an example of a large latent group, whose common interest (e.g., protection from attack by another country) can be served only by various compulsory payments (e.g., taxes, military service). "Despite the force of patriotism, the appeal of the national ideology, the bond of a common culture, and the indispensibility of the system of law and order; no major state has been able to support itself through voluntary dues or contributions." (Olson, 1965, p. 13.)

There are some important distinctions between formal organizations and large latent groups, and between both of these and small groups. Consider the importance of group size in relation to the production of public goods, goods shared equally by all members of the group. In a small group, it is likely that some of the members will find that their personal gains are exceeded by the costs incurred; the system seems inequitable to them, but there is little they can do about it. For example, husbands and wives will work to feed their families, even if they are the only ones in the family laboring hard every day. But in a large latent group, where there are so many members, the contribution of any one person will be imperceptible; thus, the motivation to be a "free loader" and not contribute at all is high. After all, the tax dodger benefits from the deterrence provided by the nation's expensive arsenal of antiballistic missiles every bit as much as does the loyal taxpayer.

Another key difference between small groups and large latent groups that must concern the student of decision making is that the small group is more effective; it is far more likely to take action. In the Senate and House of Representatives, legislation on particular items is considered by committees; the future of General Motors is decided in the board room; for direction and coordination, your dormitory will turn to its dorm government; and to get any kind of national program, we turn to our elected representatives. Voting, indeed, is one method of aggregating the values of large latent groups, of making a social choice. We decide who should decide.* In a very large group that is usually the maximum extent of a member's decision-making power.

Of decision making in large latent groups, two things may be said. First, because of a low motivation to contribute to a public good, some element of coercion will be involved, some decisions imposed, and some dues extracted. Second, because a large group is inefficient in furthering its interests, small groups will emerge within it to do its business. These small groups may or may not truly represent the popular will. But in a democracy, at least, their powers and authority are subject to decisions by the majority.

4.2 Intermediate Groups

The intermediate-sized group plays such an important part in our political life that although there is no formal theory on how such groups decide, it cannot be altogether ignored. Consider the legislatures that function at the state and federal levels. The United States Senate has 100 members, and the House of Representatives has 435. Neither of these bodies is a formal organization (recall section 3 above). There is no hierarchy, for example, nor is labor divided by skills and authority (except in a few cases), nor are legislators responsible to anyone above them. (They are accountable to their constituencies.) Nor are our legislatures large latent groups. Their numbers are not *that* large, nor is it the case that the contribution (or lack thereof) of any one member goes unnoticed. Nor are they small groups. They are too large for that and, although most members of the Senate and House do come to know each other, their actual face to face contact is limited (especially in the House where members have only two-year terms). Social incentives,

---

*We set aside here the question of who really has power in America.

therefore, play only a modest role. It appears, then, that the Senate and the House (as well as similarly structured legislatures) are something apart, neither fish nor fowl. If we look closely, however, it turns out that they are part fish and part fowl. They incorporate aspects of the organization, aspects of the large latent group, and aspects of the small group.

How are they like organizations? Each office is independent of its occupant; if senators die, or are voted out of office, they are promptly replaced. Each legislature operates according to a specified set of rules; jobs are clearly defined; and any given law is passed according to prescribed measures. Written records are kept; *The Congressional Record* alone is testimony to the power in legislatures of the printed word. How is a legislature like a large latent group? A common interest is shared in legislating effectively. But each individual's interest also lies elsewhere. In fact, since legislators are primarily accountable to constituencies that are outside the group — constituencies that determine whether legislators may keep their jobs — there is a built-in limit to the extent of institutional (or group) loyalty, as well as to the motivation to contribute to a public good. And how, finally, are the Senate and House like small groups? They are like them to the degree that small groups in the form of committees and subcommittees dominate their work life. We have already said that if you want action, turn to a small group. That axiom has clearly been uncovered by our lawmakers, who conduct most of their business in groups of twenty or fewer.* To a considerable degree, then, our legislatures are subject to the dynamics and incentives that characterize small group life. But, because the men and women who serve as our representatives are responsible more to us than to the small group, and identified more as members of the whole (e.g., the House) than as members of the part (e.g., the House Subcommittee on Labor Standards), the structural factors that have the greatest impact on legislative decision making remain difficult to pin down.

One way to begin to understand decisions in intermediate groups is to look at how the individual members decide. In the House and Senate, there are certain traditions and patterns that provide some insight into this process. Here is a partial list:

1. The desire to get re-elected suggests that if a legislator's constituency sends clear signals on a given issue, they will be heeded rather than ignored.
2. The variety of issues and sheer mass of relevant information are so great that legislators become specialists. They have an impact on the decisions of their colleagues to the extent that their expertise is acknowledged and their lead followed.

*For example, the House Committee on Appropriations has about fifty members. But it divides its labor among a dozen or so subcommittees ranging in size between five and eleven members. In 1951, Senate subcommittees had an average of 5.4 members and House subcommittees an average of 7.8.

3. Group affiliations, especially political party affiliations, will affect their decisions.
4. Institutional courtesy and reciprocity will contribute to the outcome on any given vote: "I'll vote yes on your pet bill if you'll vote yes on mine."
5. Interest groups determine legislators' votes, especially if they have a lot of money to contribute to campaign chests, or clout to get out votes.
6. Strong personal leadership can influence choice. Names like William Fulbright and Wilbur Mills became so well known because these men had an impact on how their Senate and House colleagues acted.

4.3 Small Groups

Many of the most important executive, legislative, and judicial decisions are reached in small group situations. Decisions reached by the cabinet or the National Security Council, by the Senate Committee on Foreign Relations or the House Trade Subcommittee, or by the Supreme Court, are all small group decisions. Indeed, because of the relative efficiency of the small group, it is often called upon when the going gets roughest. The ex-com group (seventeen members) that did all the deciding during the Cuban missile crisis is a perfect case in point. There is an extensive body of literature in the social psychology of small groups that is relevant here. Let us confine ourselves to the work of Irving Janis, who makes explicit the links between small group behavior and political decision making. Struck by what appeared to be the incredibly faulty planning during the Kennedy administration of the Bay of Pigs invasion of Cuba, Janis set out to explore whether some kind of psychodynamic factor prevailed in the decision-making group that might have interfered with mental alertness of its members. Based on the analysis of four cases of "major fiascos" and two cases of "well worked out decisions made by similar groups," Janis concludes that there is a high risk of imperfection in all small group decision making, especially if the group has a high sense of cohesiveness. He labeled this fatal flaw *groupthink*, a "mode of thinking that people engage in when they are deeply involved in a cohesive in-group, when the members' strivings for unanimity override their motivation to realistically appraise alternative courses of action." (Janis, 1972, p. 9)

Janis diagnoses the sources of groupthink errors as follows:

1. Limited discussion in which the full range of alternatives is never examined.
2. Selection of a course of action that was initially preferred by the majority and never subjected to critical examination.

3. Failure to reconsider choices that were initially rejected.
4. Inadequate search for expert advice.
5. Selective bias in response to factual information.
6. Failure to consider fully the drawbacks of the preferred choice and to develop a contingency plan.

The more a group is characterized by a high level of esprit de corps, argues Janis, the more likely it is to substitute groupthink for independent critical thinking. This conclusion is especially useful since it allows for the formulation of remedies, or at least of strategies to minimize the likelihood that groupthink will occur. These include, first and foremost, the awareness that groupthink exists (and, therefore, the conscious attempt to avoid it); and also a recognition of dangers inherent in even the preferred choice, the search for full information, the need for meetings of subgroups, leaderless sessions, encouragement of freewheeling discussion, and role definitions that remove the label of expert and turn every member into a generalist. Thus, Janis' research is specially relevant where Model IV (from section 2.1) is employed.

5   INDIVIDUAL DECISIONS

Offhand, one might assume that the study of individual decision making is simpler than the study of group decision making. Deciding to go and see Woody Allen's latest movie is easy, easier anyway than deciding which movie to see if you insist on Woody Allen but your date demands the latest remake of "Invasion of the Body Snatchers." As the discussion of the social psychological aspects of decision making points out (see Chapter 6), even solo choice is not without its complications. Many factors enter into an individual's decision, factors that must to some extent be sorted out anew each time a new decision is to be made.

In our discussion of the individual decision in politics, we will look first at the presidential decision and then at the voting decision. In both cases a quick way to begin to understand the decision is to consider personality and position. Personality encompasses such factors as traits, values, needs, drives, and habits; it is assumed that all these form some kind of structure that remains relatively stable over time. By *position* we mean the place of the individual in the whole society (e.g., is he a president or a janitor?), and also the place occupied at the moment of decision (e.g., does the president have a working majority in Congress for the bill he wants to push through this month?).

5.1 The President as Individual Decision Maker

We all know that presidents have different styles of decision making. Compare the following:*

How Roosevelt collected information in order to reach a decision:

> So eager was the President for intelligence, no matter how great the ensuing clutter and confusion, that *he deliberately organized his office to cast as wide a net as possible*. Not content with the varied advice in the Cabinet, he established in July 1933 an Executive Council. . . . Still not content, he established later in the year, the National Emergency Council. . . . Week after week they [Cabinet and Councils] gave Roosevelt a vivid picture of the vast array of problems. . . . And more, they exposed the heads of . . . agencies firsthand to Roosevelt's contagious drive and enthusiasm. Sitting confidently in the midst of his admiring lieutenants, telling stories, making jokes, knocking heads together, urging action, demanding quick reports and recommendations, Roosevelt almost singlehandedly gave pace and direction to New Deal battalions. (Burns, 1956, pp. 173-174)

How Eisenhower delegated authority, as he had learned to do in the Army:

> The essence of Eisenhower's system of administration, Anderson writes, "was *his belief in the delegation of authority*". . . . Eisenhower's carefully charted system did save him from immersion in trivia; decisions were so thoroughly staffed that by the time they got to him a great deal of extraneous matter had been sliced away and he could say yes or no. . . . But the system has its costs. To his natural disinclination to be "bothered" was added . . . his staff's disinclination to "bother" him. "But the less he was bothered," as Richard Neustadt noted, "the less he knew, and the less he knew, the less confidence he felt in his own judgement." (Barber, 1972, p. 163)

How Carter tries, sometimes at a cost, to forge "clean decisions":

> Last June [1977] Carter was approaching a decision on the B-1 bomber, [and] he was caught in a political cross fire. He met with both sides and called for memos from the Pentagon, the State Department, the National Security Council staff and other agencies. Then he retired to his study to pore over the memos. . . . As if he were back at Annapolis doing a staff study, *he wrote out the pros and cons on a yellow legal pad – 47 arguments in all*. Neatly, in the margin, he assigned numerical weights to each. . . . The arithmetic went against the B-1. So did President Carter. . . . Above all, Jimmy Carter is a problem solving President and that essential cast of mind explains many of his strengths and weaknesses as a leader. . . . But his rush into decision making and problem solving has taken such precedence over vital political functions that Mr. Carter has paid a price – never more obviously than on the energy program. (*New York Times Magazine*, January 8, 1978, p. 30)

---

*Italics in the following quotations are added.

Style is not trivial. It affects the content of the decision. How the president gathers information, how he relates to and uses his staff, how sensitive he is to the political environment in which the decision must be accepted and implemented, how interested he is in maximizing his power — all these will inevitably determine not only the process but the outcome of that process. No argument is being made that style is more important than, say, ideology. But both can be said to emerge from, or reflect, personality as it has been forged by background and experience. Take the case of Jimmy Carter. Not a single president-watcher would dare ignore his roots: the South, the Church, the soil, etc. Nor would one dismiss his particular life history: the Carter family, Annapolis, engineer-businessman-farmer-governor, etc. The stuff of biography, in sum, is what we need in order to really understand individual choice.

At the same time, nothing illustrates the need to consider position along with personality as well as presidential decision making. To understand what goes on in the Oval Office, we must consider not only the man, but also the office, itself. The White House as a setting for decisions has been the subject of a book by a Kennedy aide, Theodore Sorensen (1963), who concluded that the enduring nature of the White House environment makes it inevitable that presidential decisions will constantly be molded by the "same basic forces and factors." (p. 7) He argues that the chief executive will always have to contend with a uniquely large volume and array of decisions. Decisions, Sorensen points out, are forced upon the president by the calendar; each year, for instance, he must make major choices when drawing up the annual budget. But for most decisions there is no pattern, no established criteria. Some presidents reach out and find decisions to make. Others decide only when absolutely required to do so. Finally, there are the limits imposed by the White House setting. Contrary to popular belief, presidents are hemmed in at almost every turn. To the extent that the *imperial presidency* ever existed, it did so only under a special set of circumstances. It fell apart as soon as conditions were less than optimal. Certainly in the area of domestic politics all presidents must learn to cope not with too much decision-making power, but with what is, from their vantage point, too little. No doubt Sorensen, after his almost three years in the White House, was particularly sensitive to the constraints. It was he who pointed out that presidents are limited by what is legally permissible, by available resources, information, and prior commitments. He also noted that each individual decision is shaped by presidential politics, presidential advisors, and the special presidential perspective. What we have, then, is a decision-making situation in which the man and the office (personality and position) are indivisible. If President Jimmy Carter decides that his administration will suffer the evils of unemployment to combat what he sees as the greater dangers of inflation, that decision must be seen as an outgrowth of this particular man as he occupies the Oval Office at this particular moment in time.

Personality and position, in short, are the keys to any analysis of presidential decision making. Can it be that these same two variables will unlock the mysteries of the voting decision, the humble choice that is as close to political action as most of us ever come?*

5.2 The Voter as an Individual Decision Maker

The voting decision has been the object of considerable academic attention, for at least two reasons. First, we like to think of it as the foundation of our political system. Although some people question whether, for example, there was a significant difference in 1976 between the Democrat Carter and the Republican Ford, it is certainly one of the more enduring political themes in this country that we (almost) always have a real choice between (at least) two different candidates, parties, and platforms. It is through this choice that we are supposed to exercise some control over our destiny at local, state, and national levels. Second, the voting decision is usually our only political participation of any kind and it becomes, therefore, the most readily available measure of the political intelligence of every man. Some studies have concluded that our electoral choice merely reflect our political socialization, not an informed analysis (e.g., Campbell, et al., 1960). Others have found that "voters are not fools," that they do, in fact, choose in their own interest (Key, 1966). In any case the voting decision has a central place in political science and its two aspects — *whether* we vote and *how* we vote — have been analyzed and at the same time seen as large-scale indicators of the vigor of our *participatory democracy*. Our concern here is with why people vote the way they do when they vote. By examining the voter's personality and position in the system, we can gain some understanding of how a decision is made.

In large part, we are politically what we were socialized to be as children and adolescents. The main agents of political socialization are family, peers, schools, the media, and whatever other groups are socially relevant to the individual. With regard to the voting decision, the family plays the dominant role. It gives us our first awareness of an attachment to the system and it supplies us with our most basic identifications and

---

*Many of us do not even come this close. In the 1976 presidential election only 53.3% of the electorate bothered to vote.

attitudes. Because the family has the best access and strongest emotional ties to the child (and early adolescent as well), it is in a unique position to shape *political man*.

Party identification, the sense of attachment some of us feel towards a given political party, is the single most important cue to the voting decision.* And the family bestows it. When the party preference of both parents is the same, up to 80% of adults and children also report that preference. Party identificaion is usually learned by around the age of seven or eight and, to the extent that it is strong and endures, it serves as a cognitive filter through which we see and interpret the political universe. If, for example, we are dyed-in-the-wool Democrats, our need for new information at voting time is relatively low. We will support candidates and approve of party platforms simply because they are stamped Democratic.

Other identities, too, have been acquired from our families, or at least from our early life, which tend to have a further impact on party preference. If your father was a steelworker, the chances are that you will lean toward the more liberal party; if he was a banker, toward the more conservative one. (Too few mothers are steelworkers or bankers at present in our society to have a comparable influence with fathers!) The region in which you were raised, the community in which you spent your early years, your religious affiliation, each can also affect your voting habits. For example, Alabama has a Democratic tradition and Kansas a Republican one; Democrats tend to dominate politics in big cities, and Republicans in small and medium-sized towns and big city suburbs; since the early 1930s Roman Catholics and Jews have tended to support the Democrats, and Protestants the Republicans.

Of course, an individual's development does not end with adolescence. Things happen to us in adulthood that change the opinions and attitudes that served us perfectly well when we were younger. There are people, for example, who came from a poor home but who, by the sweat of their brow or the jackpot in Las Vegas, improved their station in life and, as a result, altered their political perceptions and priorities. For reasons not yet completely understood, we have shown an increasing tendency to move away from the politics of our parents. The number of independents is growing and although it is not clear how many are truly independent, that is, completely free of all party preference, they are certainly an important new force in our political life. What factors influence how independents decide to vote? Clearly, family background and early life experience play a lesser role, and current place in the socioeconomic system a greater one. To explain the

---

*Party identification is also a strong indicator of whether we vote. What is important here is not the particular party we identify with, but how strong our attachment is. Strong party identification is particularly effective as a mobilizer of lower socioeconomic groups to the polls.

independent vote, attention has been focused on issue-voting, and the charismatic appeal of the individual candidates.

The most recent research suggests that issues have greater salience for the voting decision than had previously been estimated. When voters were asked which issues were important *to them*, rather than researchers telling them which issues *should* be important, unexpected results were obtained. An elderly couple, for example, might have little to say on whether or not the United States should recognize China, and thus seem quite ill-informed to the interviewer who asks them about it. But this same couple might be very knowledgeable about, and voice strong opinions on, the subject of Medicare. They might well cast their vote on the basis of which candidate reflects their preference on that single issue. There is also good evidence that we are more vulnerable than ever to the candidates' personal qualities. Of course, in local elections, where we have little exposure to the contenders, we will tend to fall back on that old reliable indicator, party identification. But in a long campaign for an office with high visibility, where the candidates repeatedly come into our living room thanks to television, it is more likely than ever that we will decide according to how we feel about them personally. It is the more mature, the more intelligent, the more capable, the more trustworthy, the more independent — or the wittier, handsomer, sexier — candidate who gets our vote.

Although the voting decision has received what some might deem an excessive attention from academics, it is not all that resistant to common sense. We have seen how personality and position feed into it. Look at your own most recent experience as a voter. How did you come to make your choice? How do you think you will choose the next time around? The chances are that if you think about it for a few moments, you will conclude you make this decision in much the same way that you make other decisions. You canvass the alternatives, that is, the candidates and the parties. You make some effort to gain information about the alternatives, but the chances are that you will not be willing to incur great costs in time or money to become more informed. You tally the advantages and disadvantages of each of the alternatives. You vote for the candidate who you feel has the greatest number of favorable attributes. If no candidate appears to have an advantage over the other(s), you vote for your party affiliation. If neither candidate nor party appeals, and if no issue arouses you, you may decide not to decide, that is, not to vote at all.

An argument can be made for the proposition that *all* political decision making boils down to individual decision making. Who, after all, comprises the system, the organization, the large latent group, and the small group, if not a population of individual decision makers? We have seen that individuals in groups do not decide as do individuals acting alone. Yet it is probably also true that to understand the decision-making process in a group of any size, the attempt must be made first to understand the process in ourselves.

6   CONCLUSION

What does the study of decision making in politics have to recommend it? At the risk of banality, we can say that it educates us about what happens in our political life, and why; about what happens in our own personal and professional lives, and why; and that it instructs so that we might, as practicing decision makers, learn from what happened and do better the next time. There seems to be little doubt that the study of decision making in general can help us to use our full intelligence to make wiser political choices. We would do well, therefore, to conclude this discussion by making a list of the steps that should be followed in undertaking a rigorous decision analysis. Even though decision making in politics has been presented so far as primarily a descriptive rather than as a prescriptive discipline, there is no reason why we should not end on a different note by offering these words of advice:

1. Pay attention to who has made, or is making, the decision, and in what setting.
2. Evaluate the central actors (if there are any) especially in terms of their personality and position.
3. Consider the interpersonal dynamics of the decision-making group.
4. Take into account the influence of the social and political environment within which the decision making has taken, or is taking, place.
5. Chart a history of the political decision, especially in relation to prior similar decisions.
6. Outline the rational model of decision making as it applies to the particular situation, and compare this with what really happened.
7. Review the six models of decision making and try to take advantage of the explanatory power of one or two of these models.

Undertaking some of these steps some of the time will help to increase your awareness of how decisions are reached. But in this best of all possible worlds, awareness is not merely enlightening. It may also yield practical benefits. Students can count on better understanding, and politicians can count on better choices. Each of us should also find that knowing something about how decisions are made is knowing something about how to live a better life.

7   SELECTED BIBLIOGRAPHY*

Allison, Graham. *Essence of Decision.* Boston: Little, Brown, 1971.
Barber, James D. *The Presidential Character.* Englewood Cliffs, N.J.: Prentice-Hall, 1972.
Becker, Theodora, and Feeley, Malcolm. *The Impact of Supreme Court Decisions.* New York: Oxford University Press, 1973.
Braybrooke, David, and Lindblom, Charles. *A Strategy of Decision.* New York: Free Press, 1970.
Burns, James MacGregor. *Roosevelt: The Lion and the Fox.* New York: Harcourt, Brace & World, 1956.
Campbell, Angus, Converse, Philip, Miller, Warren, and Stokes, Donald. *The American Voter.* New York: John Wiley and Sons, 1960.
Dahl, Robert. *Who Governs?* New Haven: Yale University Press, 1961.
Dawson, Richard, Prewitt, Kenneth, and Dawson, Karen. *Political Socialization.* Boston: Little, Brown, 1977.
DeRivera, Joseph. *The Psychological Dimension of Foreign Policy.* Columbus, Ohio: Charles Merrill, 1968.
Downs, Anthony. *An Economic Theory of Democracy.* New York: Harper & Row, 1968.
Fenno, Richard. *Congressmen in Committees.* Boston: Little, Brown, 1973.
Garson, David. *Power and Politics in America.* Lexington, Mass.: D.C. Heath, 1977.
Hargrove, Erwin. *Presidential Leadership.* New York: Macmillan, 1966.
Janis, Irving. *Victims of Groupthink.* Boston: Houghton Mifflin, 1972.
Janis, Irving, and Mann, Leon. *Decision Making.* New York: The Free Press, 1977.
Jervis, Robert. *Perception and Misperception in International Politics.* Princeton, N.J.: Princeton University Press, 1976.
Jones, Charles. *An Introduction to the Study of Public Policy.* North Scituate, Mass.: Duxbury Press, 1977.
Key, V.O. *The Responsible Electorate.* Cambridge, Mass.: Harvard University Press, 1966.
Langton, Kenneth P. *Political Socialization.* New York: Oxford University Press, 1969.
Lindblom, Charles. *The Policy Making Process.* Englewood Cliffs, N.J.: Prentice-Hall, 1966.
Lowi, Theodore. *The End of Liberalism.* New York: Norton, 1969.
March, James, and Simon, Herbert. *Organizations.* New York: Wiley, 1958.
Mills, C. Wright. *The Power Elite.* New York: Oxford University Press, 1959.
Neustadt, Richard. *Presidential Power.* New York: John Wiley and Sons, 1960.
Nie, Norman, Verba, Sidney, and Pervocik, John. *The Changing American Voter.* Cambridge, Mass.: Harvard University Press, 1976.
Olson, Mancur. *The Logic of Collective Action.* Cambridge, Mass.: Harvard University Press, 1965.
Pressman, Jeffrey, and Wildavsky, Aaron. *Implementation: How Great Expectations in Washington are Dashed in Oakland, or Why It's Amazing That Federal Programs Work at All.* Berkeley: University of California Press, 1973.
Ranney, Austin. *Governing.* Hinsdale, Ill.: The Dryden Press, 1975.
Ripley, Randall, and Franklin, Grace. *Congress, The Bureaucracy and Public Policy.* Homewood, Ill.: The Dorsey Press, 1976.
Rourke, Francis. *Bureaucracy, Politics and Public Policy.* Boston: Little, Brown, 1976.
Schlesinger, Arthur M. Jr. *The Imperial Presidency.* New York: Popular Library, 1973.
Simon, Herbert. *Administrative Behavior.* New York: Free Press, 1948.
Simon, Herbert. *The New Science of Management Decision.* New York: Harper, 1960.
Sorensen, Theodore. *Decision Making in The White House.* New York: Columbia University Press, 1963.

---

*There is a considerable political science literature on decisions concerning Pearl Harbor, Korea, Cuban missile crisis, Vietnam, and Watergate.

Steinbruner, John. *The Cybernetic Theory of Decision.* Princeton: Princeton University Press, 1974.

Verba, Sidney. *Small Groups and Political Behavior.* Princeton: Princeton University Press, 1961.

Verba, Sidney, and Nie, Norman. *Participation in America.* New York: Harper & Row, 1976.

Weber, Max. *The Theory of Social and Economic Organization.* New York: Oxford University Press, 1947.

Chapter 7
Utility and Decision Making: Individual and Group Choice

1 INTRODUCTION

"Whatever made you buy that silly-looking hat?"
"Say what you will — I like it!!"

All of us have our own personal yardsticks of value, which on occasion we triumphantly apply in bold defiance of the values of others. Clearly, we have two people here with differing opinions as to the value of the hat. The introduction of a third person could easily produce another view of its worth; a fourth, still a different view; and so on. Yet the admitted differences of value among individuals should not dissuade us from confronting the importance of utility in decision making.

2 INDIVIDUAL WELFARE

The term *total utility* refers to the total well-being (welfare, satisfaction) that an individual derives from his or her total situation at a point in time.

Percy H. Hill et al., Making Decisions: A Multidisciplinary Introduction

Included are all things, real or imagined, that affect the individual's welfare whether they be positive or negative in their influence. The usual array of consumer goods and services is invariably included, as well as some less obvious items, such as the welfare of other people, the local crime rate, the noise from a neighbor's motorcycle, the effect of government regulations on home and work environments, future consumption, free band concerts, expected benefits of a college education, the value of time, and even the climate.

Futhermore, total utility is purely subjective; each individual determines her own or his own total utility. While the items that constitute total well-being may not differ among individuals, the variations in ultimate decisions reached by these individuals derive from the difference in the weights or values assigned by each individual to the various items. Increasing the number of items of positive value or decreasing those of negative value would obviously improve an individual's total welfare. As used in utility theory, the term *value* should not be confused with market price. While the latter is an easily identifiable objective quantity stated in monetary terms (e.g., dollars and cents), the former is a subjective concept uniquely determined by each individual.

Unfortunately, most of us cannot have as much (or as little) of everything as we would like. Instead, our choices tend to be limited by our income, education, skills, opportunities, the environment, and, if nothing else, time. Invariably, the decision to do one thing is at the same time a decision *not* to do something else. For each choice that we make, we must forego or sacrifice some other opportunity. The most highly valued alternative that is sacrificed when one makes a choice is known as the *opportunity cost* of that choice. Your choice to read this book now means that you have decided not to sleep, play tennis, enjoy the company of a friend over a cup of coffee, and so forth. Clearly, the resources (including time) that are used to do one thing cannot be used to do something else. In this sense it is indeed true that "there is no such thing as a free lunch." Every undertaking has its costs, however hidden, remote, or subjective they may be. Furthermore, since they include expected benefits that were sacrificed in the form of the *unchosen* alternatives, there is no way that costs can be directly measured by someone else. Only the decision maker can estimate the value of what has been foregone on the roads not taken.

As a practical matter, individual decison makers find it convenient and reasonably justifiable to examine only a portion of the items which affect their total utility by assuming that all other items are unaffected and invariant to changes in the particular items under consideration. Thus, we could ask whether an individual's welfare was enhanced by consuming more or less of a particular bundle of goods (A) as opposed to a different bundle

(B) when the only change in the initial situation is in the market prices of (A) and (B). This assumption of *ceteris paribus* (other things being equal) is a very handy methodological simplification and is used extensively by decision makers. If preferences pertaining to a subset of items that is a part of one's total utility are independent of those in other subsets, then optimizing decisions by subsets are valid. What we may be willing to accept as "other things being equal," however, may not always be very straightforward or clear. If nothing else, should some of those "other things" not remain "equal," it would force the decision maker to confront the importance of those particular items and to weigh them against the costs and benefits of the subset under consideration.

Note that it is the individual who is the judge of his own welfare. In a relatively free society, such as the United States, we proceed on the assumption that the individual, with limited exceptions, knows what is best for himself. Thus, Bill tells us that he would rather date Julie than Martha, or if he simply reveals through his actual choice a preference for Julie, we would conclude that he was better off with Julie than with Martha (both being possible choices). Though we may disapprove of the choice, we are unlikely to be persuasive in arguing that Martha would have been a better choice for Bill. With the exception of children, persons declared mentally insane, drug addicts, and others who are unable to understand or evaluate the choices available to them, an individual's preferences are the standard by which we judge that person's welfare.

It would be useful if there existed a *cardinal* unit of measure of utility as there does for distance (e.g., feet, yards) and volume (e.g., quarts, gallons). We would then be able to determine not only how much better off an individual is in one situation as opposed to another, but we would also be able to make interpersonal comparisons and determine just how much better off one individual is than another. The latter sort of judgment would be particularly useful in group decision making. Unfortunately, no such cardinal measure exists.* In the analysis of individual decisions, however, considerable progress has been made using *ordinal* measures of utility. This merely requires that the decision maker be able to rank alternatives from most to least preferred, a judgment we assume most individuals can make. There is no need to identify a common yardstick for all individuals or to identify exactly the size of the units on each individual's own yardstick. Confining ourselves to ordinal measures, however, virtually

---

*Although the search has gone on for more than a century, the only acceptable measure has been developed by John von Neumann and Oskar Morgenstern (1947) and their followers. This measure is limited to choices involving risk (lotteries, fire insurance) and is applicable to an individual only; it does not allow for interpersonal comparison.

forecloses the possibility of interpersonal utility comparisons. Adding one person's first five choices, for example, to those of others yields no intelligible result.

3   MARGINAL UTILITY

Although a distinction has been made between subjective value and market price, you may be wondering whether there is a connection between the two. Some two centuries ago, Adam Smith had a similar concern. He was baffled, however, by the fact that ordinary water, a necessity of life and therefore presumably of high subjective value, had a low market price, whereas diamonds (not a necessity and presumably of low subjective value) had such a high market price. He eventually concluded that subjective value and market price were separate and unrelated concepts.

Today, students who have been exposed to an introductory course in economics know that a connection nevertheless does exist between the two concepts. By dividing market price determination into demand- and supply-side influences, and concentrating on marginal rather than total utility (something Adam Smith was unable to do since these concepts were not introduced until nearly a century after his death), the linkage becomes more apparent, especially on the demand side. An individual's *demand* for a good or service is defined as a schedule of the quantities of the good or service that one will willingly purchase at various prices in a given time period. *Marginal utility* is defined as the increment in an individual's total utility that comes from the last unit of the good or service acquired.

As a consumer you may be willing to buy a particular hat for $10 because the added utility you expect to derive from the hat is greater than the added utility that you can get from any alternative use of the $10. After buying this first hat, however, imagine yourself buying a second one. It too will add to your total utility, but will it add as much as the first one did? How about a third hat? The opportunity to vary hat color, style, and so forth may be appealing, but at some point you will probably find that the increment in total utility associated with the last hat is less than it was for the next to the last one acquired. This point at which the marginal utility diminishes will be the same neither for all products nor all persons.

Given that a person is free to buy or not to buy the last hat, then, if its marginal utility is less than the marginal utility of its highest valued alternative, the only way that the person would willingly buy the hat is if its market price, and thereby its opportunity costs, were lowered. This relationship, larger quantities demanded at lower prices, is the most common manifestation of the link between utility and demand. Though admittedly sketchy, it is this link that makes it possible to resolve Adam Smith's paradox. In part, the market price of water is low relative to diamonds because we derive less value from the last little bit of it used. It is the interaction of these demand-side influences with those on the supply side, particularly the relative abundance of water, that results in the lower market price of water.

4   A MODEL OF INDIVIDUAL CHOICE

Given a seemingly endless array of items of value, the possession or use of which could enhance an individual's welfare, and given a limited income constraining one's options, a consumer must choose from among the selections offered at the market prices in effect at that time. Although the model to be presented below is one drawn from the field of economics, you will soon see that it has much wider applicability.

The key behavioral assumption of the model is that the individual is a *rational economic being* ("economic man"), who attempts to maximize his utility subject to the income and price constraints given.* It is further assumed that the individual is able to order his preferences, and that these preferences are transitive. Transitivity implies that if a consumer prefers A to B and B to C, then he must also prefer A to C (i.e., it assures us that preferences at this point in time are consistent and noncontradictory.)

The notion of a rational person, however, requires some clarification. Unlike its use in common speech, the term is not prescriptive; it does not refer to how people ought to behave, or to tacit moral standards in terms of which a person's goals should be evaluated. As used by economists, *rational* merely implies that a consumer will use the most efficient means available to achieve the goal of personal utility maximization.

To illustrate with a simple example, let us assume that all goods and services have positive utility,** but that the increment in utility associated with an additional unit of a good or service decreases as we acquire more of it (i.e., the *marginal utility* of all goods and services is diminishing). Subject to one's income and price constraints, the consumer will make selections designed to maximize his or her own welfare — in short, to "get

---

*While it is possible to introduce additional constraints, such as a fixed number of ration coupons or prescribed quotas for certain goods, it is not necessary in our treatment of the subject here. Religious, social, and other so-called constraints can be handled by simply assuming that the consumer alters the utilities of the items with which these constraints are associated.

**We have already noted that utility functions can, and most likely do, contain items with negative utility; items that we would willingly pay a positive price to be rid of. To simplify the example, such items are excluded here.

one's money's worth." Technically, this occurs when the ratios of marginal utilities (MU) to price (P) for each item are equal; or, with n items, when:

$$\frac{MU_a}{P_a} = \frac{MU_b}{P_b} = \ldots\ldots\ldots = \frac{MU_n}{P_n}$$

To see why this is so, let us suppose that MU_a/P_a is greater than the other ratios. Clearly then, by spending one dollar less on some or all of the other goods and services, and using that dollar to buy more of good a, the individual's total welfare would increase since the utility added by another unit of a is greater than the utility given up by consuming less of something else. As the quantities of the various goods selected change, so too do their marginal utilities, thus tending to restore the equality in the ratios. As a practical matter it may be impossible to equate exactly all such ratios, especially when dealing with goods in large indivisible quantities. The assumption only requires that the consumer tries to get his money's worth, or maximize utility.

By now you are undoubtedly aware that utility theory, based as it is upon rather ephemeral, erratic, and nebulous notions of value, leaves considerable room for those who would wish to manipulate opinions to suit their own ends. Caveat emptor ("let the buyer beware") is particularly relevant in a world of advertising, media hype, and political propaganda. The fact that large, expensive advertising campaigns are conducted to entice consumers to purchase a particular good or service indicates that people in business believe in such models of consumer behavior. Technically, advertisers know that if they can raise the marginal utility that a consumer associates with their product, the ratio of the product's marginal utility to its price will rise, and that rational consumer behavior will take care of the rest (i.e., lead to more sales).

The usefulness of this particular model is especially important in a capitalist society that relies heavily upon a free market system. Trying to predict the behavior of a single individual can be painfully frustrating. Predicting the general behavior of a large group of consumers tends to be a much easier task. For example, policy makers in the United States today believe that an increase in the price of gasoline, ceteris paribus, will cause a decrease in gasoline consumption. But given the nature of individual preferences, one would be hard pressed to predict whether a particular individual would consume less or, if so, how much less. The development of advanced statistical techniques that make use of historical prices and market sales have greatly improved the art of forecasting general consumer behavior; unfortunately, they have not been as useful in predicting individual behavior.

The model of individual choice behavior is also relevant in a controlled economic system, in which market prices and consumer incomes are centrally determined by government decree, so long as consumers are given some freedom of choice. One way to conserve a scarce resource for a specific use, say steel for the military, would be to directly prohibit its use in consumer goods. An indirect method to the same end would be to raise the price of steel-using consumers goods and leave the allocation of the scarce steel to consumer choice. By setting prices high enough, and assuming a model of consumer behavior similar to that described here, government planners could achieve the desired results. They would not have the same degree of certainty in reaching their goal as direct controls would provide; but neither would they have the economic, social, and political costs associated with those controls.

Thus far we have concentrated on the spending of money. To provide a feel for the wider applicability of the model, let us suppose that you want to get admitted to medical school and that your immediate problem is studying for final examinations. How should you allocate your scarce time? Would you spend as much time studying for your finals in economics and music as you would for your finals in chemistry and biology? Possibly, but not very likely. Rather, you would divide your time among your courses until the marginal utilities of the last minute spent on each was equal. The same rule would apply for the allocation of any scarce resource among competing uses. According to Nobel laureate Paul A. Samuelson (1976), the "marginal equilibrium condition is not merely a law of economics; it is a law of logic itself" (p. 436).

5   THE VALUE OF INFORMATION

We are all subjected to varying degrees of incomplete, false, and misleading information. Even so, most of our decisions are not made in a vacuum. We have a pretty good idea of what to expect when we buy a pair of jeans; when we buy the services of an auto mechanic, our expectation is probably vaguer. In each case, we continually alter our expectations on the basis of our own experiences and those of others. Although rational behavior does not preclude making errors, as long as people use their experiences to avoid repeating their errors, the model of individual choice discussed above should provide a reasonably accurate description of actual behavior.

As much as individuals may wish to have the best possible information before making a choice, it should be recognized that information itself is not always free or easily accessible. The quest for information should be subjected to· the same test as that applied to the purchase, or acquisition by the expenditure of effort, of any other good or service. If and only if the utility of the additional information per unit of expenditure is thought to be greater than the utility of that which is sacrificed to acquire the information, then rational behavior would predict that the individual would seek out the information. However, like any other good or service, information also is subject to diminishing marginal utility and at some point one will find it not worthwhile to go further. The information itself, of course, can be imperfect and eventually prove to be worthless, even damaging, or, turn out to be far more beneficial than we could ever have imagined. Our choice would be a lot easier if we had perfect foresight. Unfortunately, it is the perceived value of the information *prior* to its acquisition that is important in the decision of whether or not to acquire it.

6   RISK AND UNCERTAINTY

Following the work of Frank Knight (1921) contemporary economic theory makes a distinction between risk and uncertainty. *Risk* refers to situations in which outcomes can vary, but where the probabilities of each is known or at least can be estimated. Thus, lottery tickets, insurance, sports betting, and short-run predictions of rain all involve risk in this sense. In such cases, the optimal strategy is to choose the alternative whose utility is highest when weighted by its probability of occurrence. Thus, in a choice between two equally priced lottery tickets, each having the same payoffs but different probabilities of winning, the decision maker would be expected to choose the ticket that has the highest probability of winning. The crucial assumption here is that the decision maker attaches no particular value to the probabilities themselves, i.e., derives no utility from "taking *long* shots" or "doing things the hard way." If this assumption does not hold, then the simple multiplicative rule will not yield the optimal choice.

Uncertainty is said to exist when outcomes cannot be predicted, even in probabilistic terms. For example, a young woman is trying to decide which of two equally priced automobiles to buy. One is better suited for city driving, while the other is better for highway driving. Assuming that she is not yet settled into a permanent job and locality and does not particularly want to be tied down, she is probably uncertain about where most of her driving will be done. Similar uncertainties arise when we are confonted with choices that are weather sensitive and where conventional weather forecasts are of little or no help, as when we plan an outdoor picnic on a specific day two months hence. It is also true of many situations where probabilities do exist, but where one's ability to find out those probabilities is severely limited. In such cases it is as though we are "choosing in the blind." (See Chapter 9, as well as the references cited at the end of this chapter, for further discussion of this topic.)

7   SOCIAL CHOICE — A NORMATIVE APPROACH

In matters of public choice, decisions are often made by ballot, with each voter registering one vote. Issues are decided by a majority, plurality, two-thirds, or any other fraction of the votes cast. There are many different ways in which votes are taken and counted, each presumably designed to promote the highest possible degree of fairness. The question of what is and what is not a fair method of voting has intrigued scholars for generations. How should public choice be determined? Are there any normative theories that can guide us?

If we assume that the well-being of the community as a whole (social welfare) depends upon the level of individual welfare, then unanimous consent would be an obvious voting rule. If a measure can secure unanimous approval, then it is reasonable to infer that everyone believes he is not harmed by it and that some believe they are made better off. If so, then the measure must be an improvement in social welfare. (This is known as Pareto criterion, after Vilfredo Pareto, the Italian economist who formulated it some seventy years ago.) The appeal of this criterion is that by insisting upon unanimity of opinion (or, what amounts to individual veto power), it avoids the crucial issues associated with interpersonal utility comparisons. As a guide to practical questions of social choice, however, it has severe limitations. How many legislative measures would pass if unanimous approval were required?

Spurred by the work of Kenneth J. Arrow (1951), scholars are again devoting considerable attention to the relationships between individual and group choice. Given that the individual preferences of the members of a group are unique, the problem is one of reconciling those preferences with a group decision. Arrow began by stating several plausible criteria for social decisions and then examined their implications. He proved rigorously that it was impossible for a society to choose among alternatives without violating at least one of these criteria. Our attempt here will be to indicate the essence of his argument without the rigorous mathematical proofs. His criteria are:

1. Social preferences should be transitive, thus providing a consistent ordering of all feasible alternatives.
2. Social choice should be responsive to the preferences of the members of the community and should not change if an alternative that otherwise would have been chosen becomes more highly preferred by some individuals.
3. No individual should enjoy a position of having his or her preferences take precedence over those of others in the community.
4. As between two alternatives, the choice should not be affected by preferences over any other alternatives.

Let us illustrate how difficulties can arise. If voters had to choose between only two alternatives, majority rule would suffice. But suppose we have three alternatives and three voters, each of whom has ranked the alternatives according to his or her own preferences as summarized in the table below (1 being the highest ranking).

Alternatives Voters	X	Y	Z
Able	1	2	3
Baker	2	3	1
Charlie	3	1	2

It has long been known that such rankings can violate the transitivity criterion. From the table above we notice that a majority (Able and Baker) prefers X to Y. A majority (Able and Charlie) also prefers Y to Z. Consistency would require the majority to prefer X to Z. Alas, this is not so, as a majority (Baker and Charlie) prefers Z to X.

In practice, votes on candidates or issues are often taken in pairs. Notice that in the example above if we were to begin with a choice between X and Y, a majority would prefer X. Dropping Y and then comparing X to Z would close the voting. Clearly, this is an arbitrary procedure, but it is one often used to avoid intransitivities.

The relaxation of the second and third criteria would yield discrimination and dictatorship, respectively — hardly outcomes that would be deemed compatible with a system of citizen sovereignty. In other words, social choice has to be either inconsistent or undemocratic.

At first glance Arrow's criteria appear to be ethically appealing. Actually, scholars have wanted to place yet more constraints on the social choice process (cf. Mueller, 1976). To avoid the impossibility result, however, even his criteria must be relaxed. Further examination has shown that the fourth criterion in particular is considerably more restrictive than it at first appears.

This criterion can best be illustrated by an example. Suppose a group is trying to decide on a common menu for a banquet and the choice is between roast beef and lobster, with preferences split 50 — 50. This criterion requires that the choice be limited to a consideration of just these two alternatives. Furthermore, it requires that only rankings be considered and that intensity of preferences, no matter how measured, must be disregarded. Thus, even though one half of the group felt so strongly about its choice that it favored lobster not only to roast beef but to all other possible choices, and the other half preferred roast beef to lobster but preferred virtually all other possible choices to either of the two, the criterion requires that the choice be uninfluenced by the other "irrelevant alternatives."

Their inclusion, of course, would result in a rank ordering that would clearly reveal a group preference for lobster.

Admittedly, the intensity of feeling cannot be unambiguously measured. One advantage of the criterion is that it eliminates the possibility of willful misrepresentation of preferences. Once this criterion is relaxed, we may find ourselves confronted with situations where it might pay to lie about our own preferences. Some would argue, however, that the introduction of irrelevant alternatives would provide some indication of the intensity of feeling. Logrolling (vote trading) has also been suggested as a way in which one can express intensity of preferences. For example, consider the two issues (L and M) to be decided by group choice as presented in the table below. The numbers in the matrix represent the net utility gains and losses to each of the three voters if either measure is passed. (They are intended for illustrative purposes only since in fact such numbers would be virtually impossible to obtain.)

Issues / Voters	L	M
Fields	-3	-3
Gordon	7	-3
Hall	-3	7
Totals	1	1

If left to majority rule both issues would fail (Fields and Hall vote against L, and Fields and Gordon vote against M). If Gordon and Hall could somehow get together and make known their respective preferences, it is very possible that they would agree to trade votes. Hall will vote for L as long as Gordon votes for M. If both measures pass, each will experience a net utility gain of 4. While Fields suffers a loss by the passage of each measure, passage also results in a net utility gain of 1 on each issue for the group taken as a whole. Through vote trading, Gordon and Hall are said to be expressing the intensity of their preferences just as they would when trading privately in the marketplace. However, the question remains of whether, as in the private market transaction, total welfare is enhanced. In the table above, if we change the two 7s to 5s the same trading of votes could occur but the total effect for the community is minus 1 (rather than a plus 1) on each issue. The proponents of logrolling usually point to parks, schools, and national defense as examples of issues where vote trading is a potentially useful way of revealing preferences and reaching optimal choices. Its critics cite tax loopholes and pork-barrel projects as examples where vote trading leads to inefficiency, unfair and unnecessary taxation, and a lowering of social welfare.

However we may feel about Arrow's work, by addressing some of the oldest and toughest questions a free society faces, he has drawn attention to the pitfalls and perils in the analysis of social choice.

8   CONCLUSION

Individual choices are essentially the product of our own subjective values. Each individual must eventually decide which particular alternative is best for himself or herself. Uncertainties, imperfect information, limited ability to predict the future, and external influences such as advertising can and do affect our choices. To maximize utility, subject to any constraint, the individual must look to the margin. The fundamental rule of logic is that total utility is at a maximum whenever the ratios of the marginal benefits per unit of constraint are equal for all alternatives.

Reconciling individual choice with group choice, however, has been shown to be a much more difficult task than one might have initially presumed. Indeed, from a normative point of view, Arrow has shown that it is impossible to arrive at a group choice in a democratic society without violating at least one of the criteria that one might expect to hold in any democracy. Given that group decisions are made in our society with less than unanimous approval, this result should alert each of us to the fact that social gains can mean losses, possibly terribly damaging ones, to certain individuals.

9   SELECTED BIBLIOGRAPHY

Alchian, A.A. "The Meaning of Utility Measurement," *American Economic Review.* Vol. XLIII, March 1953.

Arrow, K.J. *Social Choice and Individual Values.*Cowles Commission Monograph No. 12, New York: John Wiley and Sons, Inc., 1951.

Baumol, W.J. *Economic Theory and Operations Analysis.* 4th ed., Englewood Cliffs, N.J.: Prentice-Hall, 1977.

Buchanan, J.M. *Cost and Choice.* Chicago: Markham, 1969.

Chernoff, H., and Moses, L.E. *Elementary Decision Making.* New York: John Wiley and Sons, Inc., 1959.

Friedman, M., and Savage, L.J. "The Utility Analysis of Choice Involving Risk," *Journal of Political Economy.* Vol. 56, August 1948.

Knight, F.H. *Risk, Uncertainty and Profit.* Boston: Houghton Mifflin Co., 1921.

Luce, R.D., and Raiffa, H. *Games and Decisions, Introduction and Critical Survey.* New York: John Wiley and Sons, Inc., 1959.

Mansfield, E. *Principles of Microeconomics.* 2nd ed., New York: W.W. Norton, 1977.

Mueller, D.C. "Public Choice: A Survey," *Journal of Economic Literature.* Vol. 14, No. 2, June 1976.

Papps, I., and Henderson, W. *Models and Economic Theory.* Philadelphia: W.B. Saunders, 1977.

Pareto, V. *Manuel d'Economie Politique,* Paris: Girard, 1909.

Raiffa, H. *Decision Analysis.* Reading, Mass.: Addison-Wesley, 1968.

Samuelson, P.A. *Economics.* 10th ed., New York: McGraw-Hill, 1976.

Smith, A. *An Inquiry into the Nature and Causes of the Wealth of Nations.* (1776; 5th ed., 1789), New York: Modern Library, 1937.

Stokey, E., and Zeckhouser, R. *A Primer for Policy Analysis.* New York: W.W. Norton, 1978.

Von Neumann, J., and Morgenstern, O. *Theory of Games and Economic Behavior.* 2nd ed., Princeton, N.J.: Princeton University Press, 1947.

Chapter 8
Decision Matrix

1 INTRODUCTION

Once a number of alternatives has been identified and understood in sufficient detail, the use of a decision matrix may facilitate the choice of the the alternative that best suits the decision maker or the situation. A decision matrix is used most effectively when there are more than two alternatives; its efficiency increases as the number of alternatives increases. This technique has a wide range of applications. It can be used to select which product to put on the market, what major to select in college, what stock to purchase, which automobile to buy, who to promote to higher position, as well as which engineering design concept to select as the one that best meets certain specifications. This decision aid forces a detailed analysis of each alternative in light of imposed criteria and the weighting of criteria based on the decision maker's own utility value. The discussion of the decision matrix technique will be presented in the context of a *case study*. Put yourself in the position of the individual described and follow his analysis of alternatives to an ultimate decision.

2 CASE STUDY

A young dentist is about to establish himself in private practice and must spend $25,000 or more on the purchase of a dental chair and operating unit. He was able to purchase a slightly used chair through a friend for $6000; the chair is of the lounge type, rests on an air pedestal, and is fully automatic. The dentist must now decide which operating unit to purchase. (The selection of this unit is one of the most important economic decisions a dentist makes, for it can affect his practice of dentistry for many years.) The unit is usually composed of high-speed and low-speed drills, hot and cold water and air syringes, saliva ejector, cuspidor, water filler, and all controls. Many units also include an interoral light. A dentist will use this unit during almost every procedure for six hours each day, four to five days a week, for 40 to 48 weeks a year for twenty to thirty years. The efficiency, comfort, and to a large extent the quality of his work will depend upon the selection of a unit with which he is completely satisfied.

3   IDENTIFY ALTERNATIVES (STEP 1)

The first step in the decision process is to identify all the alternatives in dental units that seem reasonable given the type of practice, space limitations, and general preferences of the dentist. This can be accomplished by visiting manufacturers, dealers, or dental supply houses and examining available units, having each demonstrated, and reviewing sales literature and claims. The dentist should familiarize himself with the functioning of the unit, maintenance, durability, availability of service and parts, and other considerations important in its efficient and comfortable use.

Let's assume that he has reviewed carefully all of the units available to him and has identified the following five as those among which his selection must be made:

1. Company (A) offers a fixed unit. This unit is fixed to the floor on a post adjacent to the dental chair and supports various instruments on brackets or arms supported by a central column, with electrical supply, air, water, and vacuum being fed through its center. The column or post also supports the dental light and bracketed tray.
2. Company (B) offers a tray unit. The tray unit is rather small (the manufacturer describes it as "miniature") and is composed of a central dental tray bracketed onto the chair. This tray carries the essential components but contains no cuspidor. Power is fed up through the base of the chair and through the arm supporting the unit. This unit can be adapted to the chair the dentist has already purchased.
3. Company (C) offers a mobile cabinet unit. This unit is contained in a roll-up cabinet with electricity, air, water, and vacuum fed through an umbilical tube attached to a cabinet and wall or floor outlet. Such a

cabinet gives the dentist complete flexibility in where he wishes to place it, but the umbilical tube (1.5 to 2.0 inches in diameter) does present a hazard to the feet.

4. Company ⒟ offers a counter-mounted unit. Like a laboratory bench, this unit is mounted into a specially contoured counter. When seated, the patient is then moved into close proximity to the unit, procedures are performed from this work surface, with the dentist and chairside assistant seated on opposite sides of the dental chair.

5. Company ⒠ offers a chair-mounted unit. This unit is the simplest of the five in that it mounts to the rear of the dental chair and contains a hand-held cuspidor that is given to the patient to use during the procedure. One advantage of this unit (according to the manufacturer) is that all components are out of the patient's sight. A disadvantage is that hoses connected to the drills and syringe will come into contact with the dentist's legs if he practices while seated from the back of the chair.

4   ESTABLISH SELECTION CRITERIA (STEP 2)

The second step in the decision matrix process is to establish criteria that will serve as a basis for selecting one unit over another. These criteria vary enormously from person to person because they reflect what is really important to the individual decision maker, what he is comfortable with, what he demands, and what he will accept. For the case at hand, the following list of selection criteria was prepared and ordered in importance according to the imaginary preferences of our hypothetical dentist. Since the units have roughly the same initial cost, a cost factor was not included as one of the criteria.

Each item has been given a number according to its order of importance. Since there are nine criteria and since Comfortable to Use (we hypothesize) is the most important, it is given the highest score. Weighting factors are now determined by summing up the scores and dividing the total into each.

	Criteria	Order	Weighting Factors
ORDER OF IMPORTANCE ↑	Comfortable to Use	9	9/45 = .20
	Durable (Long lasting)	8	8/45 = .18
	Reliable (Low downtime)	7	7/45 = .16
	Solid-State Electronics	6	6/45 = .13
	Easily Repaired (Maintained)	5	5/45 = .11
	Simple in Operation	4	4/45 = .09
	Flexible (Adapts to many positions)	3	3/45 = .07
	Easily Cleaned and Sterilized	2	2/45 = .04
	Functional Style (Looks good with age)	1	1/45 = .02
	Total (Sum) =	45	45/45 = 1.0

There may be situations in which two or more criteria are felt to be of equal importance. For such cases, simply list these criteria in order of importance with others and give them the same scores. Here is an example of eight criteria with three of equal importance:

6	6/29 =	.21
5	5/29 =	.17
4	4/29 =	.14
4	4/29 =	.14
4	4/29 =	.14
3	3/29 =	.10
2	2/29 =	.07
1	1/29 =	.03
29	29/29 =	1.0

5   CONSTRUCT MATRIX CHART (STEP 3)

Now that alternatives have been identified and selection criteria established, the next step in the process is the construction of a decision matrix chart of the type shown in Figure 8-1.

Alternative choices are recorded at the left of the chart, and selection criteria across the top. Weighting factors (values) calculated in step 2 are recorded opposite their respective criteria and must show a sum of 1.0.

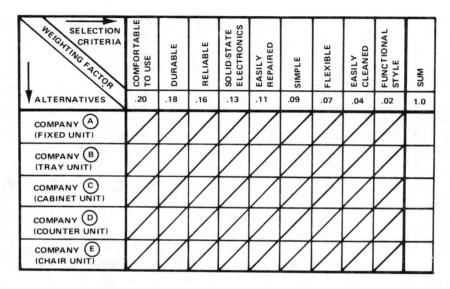

Figure 8-1. Decision Matrix Chart

6   ASSIGN RATING FACTOR VALUES (STEP 4)

The next step in the process is the assignment of rating factor values to each alternative with respect to the selection criteria. These values range from 10 to 1 (highest to lowest) and are based on the decision maker's informed opinion or best judgment. It is a good idea to assign these values for one criterion at a time, thereby comparing each alternative against that criterion. Figure 8-2 illustrates the assignment of rating factor values to the first selection criterion (Comfortable to Use). It was judged that the cabinet unit supplied by company Ⓒ was the most comfortable (hence a R.F. = 10) while the chair unit by company Ⓔ was the least comfortable (R.F. = 2).

Figure 8-3 shows rating factor values assigned to each alternative for all selection criteria. Our dentist judged that the same level of advanced technology had been applied by each company, so a rating factor value of 10 was assigned to all for the criterion designated as Solid-State Electronics. Each of the rating factors is to be assigned using the best judgment of the decision maker. It is important to be as careful as possible when assigning values and to be well informed on alternatives and criteria. The accuracy of the eventual outcome (decision) is directly dependent upon prior study and analysis of each component that enters into the chart.

WEIGHTING FACTOR SELECTION CRITERIA / ALTERNATIVES	COMFORTABLE TO USE	DURABLE	RELIABLE	SOLID-STATE ELECTRONICS	EASILY REPAIRED	SIMPLE	FLEXIBLE	EASILY CLEANED	FUNCTIONAL STYLE	SUM
	.20	.18	.16	.13	.11	.09	.07	.04	.02	1.0
COMPANY (A) (FIXED UNIT)	3									
COMPANY (B) (TRAY UNIT)	9									
COMPANY (C) (CABINET UNIT)	10									
COMPANY (D) (COUNTER UNIT)	6									
COMPANY (E) (CHAIR UNIT)	2									

Figure 8-2. Rating Factor Value Applied to First Criteria

WEIGHTING FACTOR SELECTION CRITERIA / ALTERNATIVES	COMFORTABLE TO USE	DURABLE	RELIABLE	SOLID-STATE ELECTRONICS	EASILY REPAIRED	SIMPLE	FLEXIBLE	EASILY CLEANED	FUNCTIONAL STYLE	SUM
	.20	.18	.16	.13	.11	.09	.07	.04	.02	1.0
COMPANY (A) (FIXED UNIT)	3	9	9	10	7	8	2	9	3	
COMPANY (B) (TRAY UNIT)	9	6	7	10	9	7	7	7	9	
COMPANY (C) (CABINET UNIT)	10	7	8	10	10	7	8	7	8	
COMPANY (D) (COUNTER UNIT)	6	9	9	10	6	8	2	9	3	
COMPANY (E) (CHAIR UNIT)	2	3	3	10	5	9	9	2	7	

Figure 8-3. Rating Factor Values Applied to All Criteria

7   CALCULATING THE RESULT AND MAKING THE DECISION (STEP 5)

The final step in the process is to multiply each rating factor value by its corresponding weighting factor, recording the product in the appropriate space, and summing all products. The completed decision matrix is shown in Figure 8-4. This example shows that the young dentist should make the decision to purchase the cabinet unit made by company Ⓒ . Since all weighting factors must total 1.0 and the highest rating factor value is 10, a perfect sum (highest score) would be 10. Therefore, a level of confidence in the decision made can be established from the chart by comparing how closely the score approaches 10 (or, 100%, if one prefers to use percentages). In this case the cabinet unit shows a total score of 8.75, or an 85.7% confidence level in the decision to purchase, while the chair unit manufactured by company Ⓔ shows a total of 4.93, or a confidence level of 49.3% to purchase this item.

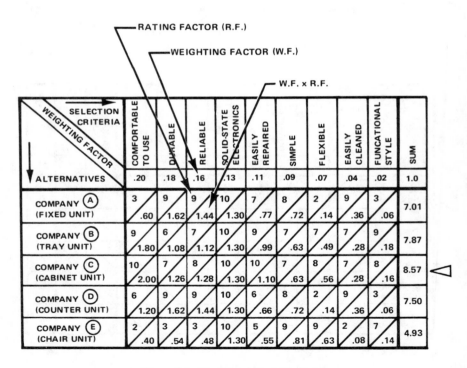

Figure 8-4. Completed Decision Matrix

8 CONCLUSION

The decision matrix also has the advantage of documenting the choice for presentation to management or other interested groups. It is an excellent communications device that clearly presents the rationale behind a given decision.

We learned in Chapter 4 the meaning of utility function, utility being the value we place on things. Each of us, regardless of discipline or general background, has a different set of utility values for a given set of things. The decision matrix technique is very sensitive to these differences in the assignment of weighting and rating factors. When two business executives come up with different choices based on the same criteria, often their disagreement can be attributed to a divergence in their respective utility functions. They will reach a better decision if they arrive at it in cooperation through the use of a single matrix.

Finally, if one is honest with oneself in the use of this technique, he will be rewarded with satisfactory results. If one begins to steer the assignment of values toward a predetermined goal, he is only fooling himself and will arrive at a decision that manipulates the technique to justify the end.

9 SELECTED BIBLIOGRAPHY

Hill, Percy H. *The Science of Engineering Design.* New York: Holt, Rinehart and Winston, Inc., 1970.

Chapter 9
Decision Making Under Conditions of Uncertainty

1 INTRODUCTION

Decision makers almost invariably choose a course of action without knowing for certain what its consequences will be. If a decision maker could know with certainty what would occur in the future, then a course of action could be selected with much greater confidence. In this chapter, we will consider statistical methods for decision making under conditions of uncertainty. These methods are prescriptions for how a person *ought* to structure and analyze a problem requiring a decision; they are not descriptions of how people actually decide. We know individuals are often neither consistent, rational, nor optimal in their analysis of a problem. In fact, it is for this very reason that it is necessary to find ways of rationally structuring a problem; otherwise, we are not likely to find its optimal solution.

Consider the following hypothetical example of decision making under conditions of uncertainty. The Atkinson Calculator Company is about to release a new machine on the market, and company executives are trying to decide whether to develop a full, partial, or minimal production schedule. The optimal schedule will depend on the projected sales for this machine.

Percy H. Hill et al., Making Decisions: A Multidisciplinary Introduction

Three levels of potential sales have been established. The sale of 750,000 or more machines would be *good*; 450,000 to 750,000 would be *fair*; a sales potential of less than 450,000 would be *poor*. Past experience with new products has shown that sales are good 30% of the time, they are fair 50% of the time, and they are poor 20% of the time. If sales are expected to be good, then the full production schedule would be the most profitable one; if sales will be only fair, the partial production schedule would be most profitable; and if sales should turn out to be poor, then the minimal production schedule would be the best choice. Table 9-1 lists the anticipated profits or losses as a function of the production schedule and sales potential. Notice, for example, that the anticipated profit of a partial production schedule on the basis of fair sales is $330,000. However, the anticipated profit of the partial schedule is still $330,000 when the sales potential is good, since there would not be any additional machines sold (perhaps because of production constraints).

Table 9-1.   Profits as Function of Sales Potential and Production Schedule

Potential Sales	Full	Partial	Minimal
Good	$600,000	$330,000	$150,000
Fair	$240,000	$330,000	$150,000
Poor	−$180,000	−$ 90,000	$ 0

Atkinson Calculator is a relatively small company in a field dominated by several larger rivals. The new machine has many novel features not present in any of the models currently marketed by the competition. If a full production schedule is chosen and sales are good, the company can expect to grow and to control much of the market before other companies can market a similar product. However, if a full production schedule is chosen but sales are poor, the company's losses will pose a serious threat to its survival. So choosing a full production schedule is risky. The minimal production schedule is safer but it lacks the potential to improve the company's relative position in the field. In fact some of the larger companies may be able to come out with a similar product in about the same time that it takes Atkinson to increase production; consequently a correct guess about future sales is crucial. Even so, company executives cannot be sure how well their new machine will sell. Throughout the rest of this chapter, the problems faced by the Atkinson Calculator executives will be used to illustrate the advantages of various formal techniques of analysis.

1.1   Maximax and Maximin Decision Rules

Consider two decision rules; the first is optimistic, the second is not. Under the *maximax decision rule*, the decision maker considers the maximum profit (the best state of affairs) for each possible course of action, and then picks the action with the greatest maximum. For example, the executives of Atkinson Calculator have three alternative actions under consideration, namely a full, partial, or minimal production schedule. The best state of affairs that could occur if a full production schedule is chosen is good sales, yielding a profit of $600,000. Given a partial production schedule, the best state of affairs is $330,000, the yield from either good or fair sales. Finally, the maximum for the minimal production schedule is $150,000. The maximax rule prescribes the course of action that "maximizes the maximums;" in this example, since $600,000 is greater than $330,000 or $150,000, it would call for a full production schedule in the hope of good sales. The maximax rule is optimistic and therefore risky; if sales turn out to be poor, the company will lose $180,000. To adopt the maximax rule is to believe you live in the best of all possible worlds.

By contrast, the *maximin decision rule* is a more conservative approach. Here, it is the worst state of affairs (or minimum) that is considered for each course of action. The three minimums for the Atkinson Calculator decision are: a $180,000 loss given full production and poor sales; a $90,000 loss given partial production and poor sales; and zero profit given minimal production and poor sales. The maximin rule states that the decision maker should choose the action that maximizes the minimums; in this example, it is the minimal production schedule, since zero profit is greater than a loss of $90,000 or of $180,000. The maximin rule is pessimistic and therefore conservative, since it focuses on the worst outcome for each alternative.

The problem with both the maximax and the maximin rules is that they do not take into account the probability of future sales. It is not risky to choose the full production schedule if poor sales are very unlikely. Likewise, if the probability of poor sales is high enough, a minimal production schedule would be prudent rather than conservative. However, before we can incorporate the factor of probability into a decision analysis, we must first examine a few elementary concepts about probability.

2   PROBABILITY

It is necessary to begin by defining a few terms, such as *sample spaces* and *probability*. After an analysis of the assignment of probability, this section concludes with a brief look at the concept of *expected value*.

2.1 Sample Space

Given a well-specified set of operations, or what we will call a *defined experiment*, the set of all possible mutually exclusive outcomes of that experiment is the sample space. For example, if our defined experiment consists of one flip of a coin, then the outcome of that experiment is either a heads or tails. The heads and tails alternatives are mutually exclusive — if one occurs, then the other cannot occur. They are also exhaustive — no third alternative is considered possible. Since the sample space is also a set, it is usually expressed by enclosing the list of alternatives within brackets. For our coin flip experiment the sample space would be expressed as S = [heads, tails]. As another example, suppose that the defined experiment consists of one roll of a pair of dice. We can define the sample space as $S = [(i,j)$, where $i = 1, \ldots, 6$ and $j = 1, \ldots, 6]$. In other words, we can consider i spots showing for one die and j spots showing for the other die.

2.2 Definition of Probability

In terms of a sample space, the definition of probability is: given S = $[O_1, \ldots, O_n]$, there are probability values, $P(O_i)$, that each $P(O_i)$ is a real, nonnegative number such that $P(O_1) + P(O_2) + \ldots + P(O_n) = 1$ and $P(O_i$ or $O_j) = P(O_i) + P(O_j)$.

By definition, the sum of all the probability values must be 1, for any sample space. Notice also that the event for which the probability is associated is enclosed within a parenthesis, e.g., the probability of outcome i or outcome j is written $P(O_i$ or $O_j)$ and is calculated as $P(O_i) + P(O_j)$.

Let us reconsider the dice experiment. There are thirty-six outcomes in the sample space as illustrated in Table 9-2. If we assign each outcome with

Table 9-2. Sample Space for A Dice Roll (Entry in each cell is the sum of the two dice).

		j SPOTS ON SECOND DIE					
		1	2	3	4	5	6
	1	2	3	4	5	6	7
	2	3	4	5	6	7	8
	3	4	5	6	7	8	9
SPOTS ON FIRST DIE	4	5	6	7	8	9	10
	5	6	7	8	9	10	11
	6	7	8	9	10	11	12

the probability, $P(i,j)$, so that $P = 1/36$, a reasonable assignment if the dice are fair. Now, to compute the probability of rolling a seven, $P(7)$, we consider all the ways in which a total of seven can be achieved. They are shown on the diagonal of Table 9-2. Consequently, $P(7) = P(1,6) + P(2,5) + P(3,4) + P(4,3) + P(5,2) + P(6,1) = 1/36 + 1/36 + 1/36 + 1/36 + 1/36 + 1/36 = 1/6$. We add the probabilities since, by definition, a seven can be achieved by $i = 1$ and $j = 6$, *or* $i = 2$ and $j = 5$, *or* . . . , *or* $i = 6$ and $j = 1$. Similarly the probability for the other totals are:

$$P(2) = P(12) = 1/36$$
$$P(3) = P(11) = 1/18$$
$$P(4) = P(10) = 1/12$$
$$P(5) = P(9)\ \ = 1/9$$
$$P(6) = P(8)\ \ = 5/36$$

2.3 Assignment of Probability

It is not always easy in practice to assign probability values. Consider the following problem. Suppose you are vacationing at a resort where gambling is legal. You see a roulette game in progress and decide to observe the action before placing your first bet. In this particular game of roulette, one can bet either on red or on black, and the wheel is divided equally into black and red sections. (Unlike the roulette games in Las Vegas, this one has no green zero and double zero where you automatically lose a bet on red or black.) After observing the roulette wheel for ten consecutive turns you find that there have been ten reds in a row. You are warmed up now and ready to bet on the eleventh turn. Should you bet red or black? What would you give as the probability of a red? When asked this question most students overwhelmingly answer the probability of red is 0.5.

Now suppose you return from vacation and go back to work. You are a research assistant in a biology laboratory, testing the effect of a new drug on rats. After injecting the first ten animals you discover that all ten have died. You are about to begin testing the eleventh animal. What would you give as the probability that this animal dies? Most people are extremely certain that it will die, and they assign a probability of death for the eleventh rat much greater than 0.5.*

These two applied probability problems pose a slight dilemma. In the roulette problem, there is a sample space, $S = $ [red, black] whereas for the biology experiment the sample space is $S = $ [live, die]. In both examples, prior experience shows us instances of one and only one of the two possible outcomes occurring. Why, then, are people so inconsistent in their assignment of probability values for the next instance in each example? We shall return to this question.

---

*These examples originated from Donald L. Meyer of the University of Pittsburgh.

Historically, three major methods have emerged for probability assignment and each will be briefly discussed: equal probability, relative frequency, and subjective assignment. The first two methods are *objective* techniques, in that the assignment of probability is independent of human information, knowledge, and belief. The third method is *subjective* in that probability does depend on human knowledge.

2.3.1 The Method of Equal Probability

The simplest technique for probability assignment is the equal probability method. Here each outcome of the sample space is made equally probable, i.e., $P(O_i) = 1/n$, where n is the number of outcomes possible. For example, in the coin flip experiment $n = 2$, so $P(\text{heads}) = P(\text{tails}) = 1/2$. For the dice example, $n = 36$, hence each of the 36 combinations of i and j shown in Table 9-2 is assigned the probability of $1/36$.

While this procedure is simple, it also has several problems that question its general applicability. There are many cases in which the assignment of equal probability is clearly absurd. For example, suppose that in a state gubernatorial election, four names appear on the ballot, one candidate each from the Democratic, Republican, American, and Socialist Workers parties. This is not the first election in the state, and political observers tell us that the American and Socialist Workers parties have an insignificantly small following. This valuable information cannot be incorporated into the equal probability method of assigning probable values, since the method ignores actual experience. According to the equal probability method, the roulette problem and the biology experiment problem are really two versions of the same thing. The ten prior observations are not to be incorporated into the probability assignment in either instance. But this is absurd. If we had 100 prior observations in the biology experiment and all 100 animals died, the equal probability method would still tell us to assign 0.5 as the probability of an animal dying. Clearly, this method is too crude to be generally used.

2.3.2 The Method of Relative Frequency

The second objective technique of probability assignment does incorporate past observations in determining probability values. Here the probability of an outcome is defined as the limit of the relative frequency of that outcome in past observations. For example, the probability of a heads in our coin flip experiment is determined by actually flipping coins. If the number of flips is N and the number of heads is $n(h)$, then the approximate probability of a heads is $n(h)/N$, or the observed proportion of heads. The qualifier *approximate* must be stressed, since P(head) is defined in terms of the limit of $n(h)/N$ as N becomes infinitely large, i.e.,

$$P(\text{head}) = \lim_{N \to \infty} \frac{n(h)}{N}$$

While the relative frequency technique of probability assignment seems quite reasonable, close examination reveals that it, too, has several problems. Often we want to assign a probability but where past frequency information is not available. This is true in all novel or unique experiments, and the relative frequency method is of little help in such cases. Also, notice that the relative frequency method would assign the same probability values in the roulette problem and in the biology experiment, even though we know that the two problems are really not the same.

Imagine that we are interested in computing the probability of a heads in our coin flip experiment. Suppose we have flipped the coin 100 times and observed 53 heads; the relative frequency probability is thus estimated as 0.53. However, suppose that before the next flip, some measurements are taken, such as that of the weight of the coin, its starting position, the forces acting upon it in motion, and its distance and angle to the floor. With this information, it is possible to compute exactly what will happen, provided we are given enough paper and the consultations of a nearby physicist. In essence the coin flip has been reduced to a complex physics problem in which it is possible to compute which side will turn up with virtual certainty. Suppose that this complex analysis yields the prediction of a tails, thereby making P(heads) virtually zero. Any objective method of probability assignment now has to face the following critical question. How can the probability of a heads change so drastically as a result of nothing more than the supply and analysis of information? If probability were really objective, entirely independent of human knowledge, such change should not be possible.

2.3.3 The Method of Subjective Assignment

Given that we understand the roulette wheel and biology experiment as different kinds of problems, we want a method that uses our prior knowledge to enable us to assign a different probability in each case. For example, we know some things about the roulette wheel. Half the wheel is red and half is black, and the wheel is carefully balanced and changed daily, so as not to become worn and hence favor either red or black. The casino is strongly motivated to ensure that the wheel's behavior is not predictable. This knowledge most likely will lead us to believe that P(red) is in a narrow range centered near 0.5; it will take a considerable amount of evidence to the contrary before we change our opinion. In the biology experiment, however, we do not have any basis to believe that the initial probability of the animals dying is in a narrow range near 0.5. Consequently, we are more likely to be open-minded concerning the numerical value of P(dying); perhaps we are prepared to accept any value between 0 to 1. Hence, after as few as ten observations we may be far more certain that P(dying) is greater than 0.5.

The subjective assignment method is more general than the previous two objective methods. It can be applied to unique situations. Moreover, it can yield identical results to the equal probability method under some circumstances. If we have no information about the sample space, then we would believe all outcomes are equally probable. Under other circumstances, the subjective assignment method is equivalent to the relative frequency technique. If, therefore, we ask whether there is such a thing as an event's *true* probability, whether each event has a *unique* probability, it looks as if the answer is negative. Any probability assignment depends upon what is known about the sample space, and what is known is never invariant.

Throughout the rest of this chapter, the subjective assignment method will be used. This technique is particularly useful in decision making, both for its general applicability and for the way it leads naturally to Bayesian methods for revising probability values. Bayes' Theorem is important in many decision analyses, and will be discussed later in relation to the Atkinson Calculator problem.

2.4 Expected Value

Another important concept in decision making is that of *expected value* or *expectation*. Expected value is like an anticipated mean or average. For example, suppose we are interested in obtaining a single representative number for the total number of spots in a single roll of dice. The total for a particular roll could be 2,3, . . . , 12, but not all of these outcomes are equally probable. The expected value weights each outcome by the probability of that outcome. For the dice problem the expected value, or $E(n)$ is:

$$
\begin{aligned}
E(n) = \ & (2)(1/36) + (3)(1/18) + (4)(1/12) + (5)(1/9) \\
& + (6)(5/36) + (7)(1/6) + (8)(5/36) + (9)(1/9) \\
& + (10)(1/12) + (11)(1/18) + (12)(1/36) \\
= \ & 7
\end{aligned}
$$

Consequently, prior to rolling the dice, if we had to guess a single number that is expected we would say 7. Also, if we actually rolled the dice repeatedly and computed the mean, then as the number of rolls becomes large, that mean should approach 7.*

3   DECISION TREES

A decision tree is a visual display of the structure of a decision problem. It looks like a tree with branches spreading out from nodes. Actually there are two types of nodes: *act* or *decision nodes* (usually represented by a small square), and *chance* or *events nodes* (usually denoted by a small circle). Branching out from an act node are all the potentially relevant decision actions that we may take. The enumeration of decision actions often depends on the judgment and creativity of the decision maker. A creative person may see some actions that others may not notice. Also, no-action is often the most reasonable action to take and it too can be included in the analysis.

Branching out from a chance node are all the possible outcomes that could occur. A chance node's branches thus constitute the sample space, with probability of each outcome shown on the branch. Finally, a value is usually placed on the end points of each chance node branch. (For the Atkinson Calculator Company, value could be expressed in terms of dollars earned.) In general, a decision tree displays the structure of the decision problem.

An example of a decision tree for the Atkinson Calculator decision is shown in Figure 9-1. The probability assignment of 0.3, 0.5, and 0.2 for the three possible sales outcomes is used since past experience with other new products yields these proportions for sales. In this example, our subjective probability is equivalent to the relative frequency method. However, if we had further information, such as market surveys or feedback from sales and promotion people, we might revise those probabilities accordingly; so it is possible that the subjective probability in this example would differ from the relative frequency.

4   DECISION RULES

Eventually we must select a criterion for making a decision, and when

---

*For example, I actually rolled my dice 60 times and obtained the following results: 5, 3, 7, 2, 7, 4, 7, 6, 2, 8, 8, 5, 3, 8, 10, 6, 7, 4, 9, 4, 8, 7, 10, 8, 3, 7, 9, 12, 5, 7, 10, 11, 5, 7, 10, 7, 4, 9, 10, 4, 12, 3, 9, 4, 4, 6, 6, 10, 3, 7, 5, 12, 9, 9, 10, 5, 8, 8, 9, 8. The average or mean of those rolls is 6.983, very close to the expected value.

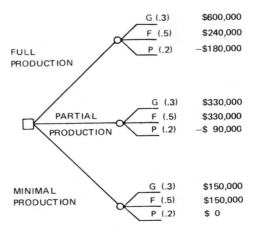

	G (.3)	$600,000
FULL PRODUCTION	F (.5)	$240,000
	P (.2)	-$180,000

	G (.3)	$330,000
PARTIAL PRODUCTION	F (.5)	$330,000
	P (.2)	-$ 90,000

	G (.3)	$150,000
MINIMAL PRODUCTION	F (.5)	$150,000
	P (.2)	$ 0

NOTE: G. F. AND P REFER, RESPECTIVELY TO
GOOD, FAIR, AND POOR SALES

Figure 9-1. Decision Tree for Atkinson Calculator Problem

we do it is likely to be one of these two rules: the *expected value rule*, or the *most-likely value rule*.

4.1 Rule of Expected Value

According to this rule, the decision criterion is chosen that maximizes the expected value for decision alternatives. For example, in the Atkinson Calculator problem each branch from the act node terminates in a chance node. According to the expected value procedure, an expectation is computed for each chance node. For example, the expected value for a full production schedule is $(0.3)(\$600,000) + (0.5)(\$240,000) - (0.2)(\$180,000)$ = $264,000. Similarly, the expected values for partial and minimal schedules are $246,000 and $120,000, respectively. Often the decision tree is redrawn to show the expected value, as in Figure 9-2. This type of tree diagram is referred to as a *folded tree* since each chance node has been folded back and evaluated. In this case the expected value rule would select the full production schedule since it maximizes *expected monetary value*.

An argument for the expected value rule is that in the long run, decisions made according to this rule will generally be best; good breaks and bad breaks tend to cancel one another. But what if a bad break results in the company going into bankruptcy? In that case the decision maker cannot

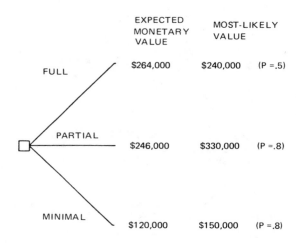

Figure 9-2. Folded Tree for Atkinson Calculator Problem

keep playing the "game" in the hope that a current loss will be canceled by long-run benefits. Hence, the expected value rule is intended for use in situations without a probable dire outcome. It would be the appropriate decision rule to use for a large corporation that makes a dozen small marketing decisions a year. For the Atkinson Calculator Company, however, a $180,000 loss is a dire circumstance. For a small company like this, the most-likely value rule would be more appropriate.

4.2 The Rule of Most-Likely Value

According to this rule, the decision maker should choose the action that maximizes the most-likely value. Figure 9-2 also shows the folded decision tree in terms of most-likely values for the Atkinson Calculator problem. For example, if full production were chosen, the most-likely event would be fair sales with a probability of 0.5; hence the most-likely *value* would be $240,000. If partial production were chosen, then either good sales or fair sales would result in the same value of $330,000; this would be the most-likely value with a combined probability of 0.8. Similarly, if minimal production were chosen, $150,000 would be the most-likely value with a probability of 0.8. Thus, the most-likely value rule leads to a choice of partial production since that production schedule has the maximum monetary value of all the most-likely values.

While the most-likely value rule is the preferred decision rule when the problem involves the possibility of dire circumstances, it can also lead to some poor decisions. First, if there are many outcomes associated with the chance node, then the most-likely outcome may not be very probable at all. For example, if there are 10 chance outcomes with probabilities 0.08, 0.07, 0.15, 0.1, 0.09, 0.11, 0.09, 0.1, 0.11, and 0.1, then the most-likely outcome will have a probability of only 0.15. Second, this decision rule does not consider the consequences if the most-likely value does not occur. For these reasons, most decision makers tend to prefer the expected value rule. For some problems, however, like the Atkinson Calculator problem, the most-likely rule works very nicely. In this problem there are not many chance outcomes and the probability of the most-likely event for the partial schedule is 0.8.

5   MEASURING SUBJECTIVE PROBABILITY

Subjective probabilities can be both assigned and measured, although their assignment may vary from one person to the next. According to one standard method of measuring subjective probability, monetary values for $X_1 \ldots X_n$ are used, and each X value corresponds to an outcome in the sample space $S = [O_1 \ldots O_n]$. For example, let us begin by setting one of the X values, say X_1, equal to one dollar ($X_1 = \$1$). To find the value of X_2, we first must imagine a gamble between O_1 and O_2. To bet O_1 you must risk X_1 dollars and to bet O_2 you must risk X_2 dollars. Now adjust X_2 so that you cannot decide which side of the wager that you prefer. (If any other outcome occurs (i.e., $O_3 \ldots O_n$), we assume you neither win nor lose the wager.) If you think O_2 is more likely, then X_2 should be greater than 1 since X_1 equals one dollar; if you think O_2 is less likely, X_2 should be less than 1. The value of X_2 should become larger or smaller to the degree that you think O_2 is more or less probable in comparison to O_1. You are setting the payoffs of a hypothetical fair bet, a wager in which you could choose either side with equal preference. Once X_2 is determined, the X_3 value should be specified similarly, except that now the wager is between O_1 and O_3. After the values of all of the X's have been determined for a particular person, that person's probability for any outcome is:

$$P(O_i) = \frac{X_i}{X_1 + \ldots + X_n}$$

For example, consider the case of a heavyweight boxing champion fighting a somewhat inexperienced challenger. The sample space for this fight would be $S = [O_1 = $ champion wins, $O_2 = $ challenger wins]. Based on what is known about these fighters over the years, the champion is clearly favored to win. If you were presented with a simple even wager (i.e., one dollar to bet either on the champion or the challenger), you would clearly prefer to bet on the champion. However, if you risk only one cent to bet on the challenger and one dollar to bet on the champion, you may prefer to bet on the challenger. The prospect of risking only one penny to win a dollar is appealing and compensates for the belief that the champion is more likely to win. If the wager were five cents to bet on the challenger and one dollar to bet on the champion, and if at that point you could not favor either side, then X_2 would be 0.05 dollars. Consequently for you:

$$P(\text{champion wins}) = \frac{1}{1 + 0.05} = 0.952$$

Following this same procedure, it would be possible for the executives of the Atkinson Calculator Company to establish their subjective probabilities for future sales.

Sometimes people are reluctant to set distinct values for $X_1 \ldots X_n$, and it may at first seem more convenient to treat all outcomes as equally probable. However, with experience, one can become quite good at establishing subjective probabilities. (For practice, you might try to determine the subjective probability for your receiving each of the possible grades, A through F, in one of your courses. Surely you do not believe that all these grades are equally probable!)

6   SENSITIVITY ANALYSIS

Suppose that the various executives of Atkinson Calculator cannot agree in their probability assignments. For example, maybe they think that $P(\text{good})$ is between 0.1 to 0.5, whereas they think that $P(\text{fair})$ is between 0.2 and 0.8, and that $P(\text{poor})$ is between 0.1 and 0.3. The midpoints of these probability ranges are the values we used earlier in the decision tree analysis. However, now we can see that there is some division of opinion. In fact, even if only a single decision maker is at work, there can still be a range for probability reflecting the uncertainty of the decision maker's knowledge. A prudent decision maker will attempt to evaluate the consequences of this uncertainty by performing a sensitivity analysis.

Sensitivity analysis essentially reworks the decision analysis for some extreme probability values. Table 9-3 lists the extreme values for the probabilities of good, fair, and poor sales. All the probabilities cannot always be at an extreme value due to the constraint that their sum must equal 1.0. Table 9-3 also shows that the optimal most-likely value decision will vary as a function of the probability assignment. If $P(\text{good}) = 0.5$, then the optimal decision is for a full schedule. However, if $P(\text{good}) = 0.1$, then a partial schedule is optimal. Consequently, the Atkinson Calculator problem is an example of a case where the decision alternative is sensitive to the probability values used.

Table 9-3. Sensitivity Analysis for Atkinson Calculator Problem

P(good)	P(fair)	P(poor)	Most-Likely Values (MLV) in $1,000 Units			Optimal Production
			Full	Partial	Minimal	
.1	.8	.1	240	330	150	Partial
.1	.6	.3	240	330	150	Partial
.5	.4	.1	600	330	150	Full
.5	.2	.3	600	330	150	Full

Sometimes all of the various assignments considered in a sensitivity analysis point to the same decision alternative. When this occurs, the decision can be said to be *robust* with respect to the variability associated with the probability assignments. If a decision is not robust, a prudent decision maker will try to obtain more information in order to narrow the range of uncertainty. In the Atkinson Calculator problem, sensitivity analysis indicates that far too much variability exists in the initial probability assignments, and more information is required. In the next section we will learn about a technique that enables us to revise initial probabilities as a function of the data collected from a marketing survey.

7   CONDITIONAL PROBABILITY, JOINT PROBABILITY, AND BAYES' THEOREM

7.1 Conditional Probability

Suppose we are to select one ball from an urn in which there are 200 balls, 100 black and 100 white. Assume also that the urn has a partition that divides it in half. On one side (side I) there are 100 balls of which 70% are white; on the other side (side II) there are 100 balls of which 70% are black. Suppose we reach in to select a ball, but without knowing from which side the ball will be taken. What is the probability that the ball selected will be black? An appropriate sample space for this problem simply consists of a listing of the 200 possible balls that can be selected:

$$S = [b_1 \ldots b_{200}]$$

where $b_1 \ldots b_{100}$ are black, and $b_{101} \ldots b_{200}$ are white. It is reasonable to view the selection of any ball as equally probable, i.e., $P(\text{ball}) = 1/200$. Since a black ball could be selected by drawing either b_1 or b_2 or . . . or b_{100} then:

$$P(\text{black}) = P(b_1) + \ldots + P(b_{100}) = \frac{100}{200} = 0.5$$

Suppose now that we know for *certain* that a ball has been selected from side II. The probability that it is a black ball is now no longer 0.5. Let us restructure our sample space conditional on the knowledge that we have selected from side II. The new sample space will be $S_1 = [c_1 \ldots c_{100}]$, where the first 70 balls are black and the last 30 are white. The probability of a black ball given that we have selected from side II is denoted as $P(\text{black}|\text{II})$ and this probability is a conditional probability. In general, $P(A|B)$ is the probability of A under the assumption that B is known. In our case, $P(\text{black}|\text{II}) = 0.7$. In essence, a conditional probability is like any other probability except that we have additional facts available that require a restructuring of the sample space and the resulting probability values.

7.2 Joint Probability

Suppose we want to calculate the probability of at least two events both occurring. For example, the probability of selecting a black ball and the probability that the ball is from side II, is a joint probability; and it is denoted as $P(\text{black and II})$. In general:

$$P(A \text{ and } B) = P(A)P(B|A)$$

Assuming that the probability of selecting side II is 0.5, where A = II and B = black, then:

$$P(\text{black and II}) = P(\text{II})P(\text{black}|\text{II}) = (0.5)(0.7) = 0.35 \qquad \text{Equation 1}$$

By interchanging the identification of A and B, we can also determine that:

$$P(\text{black and II}) = P(\text{black})P(\text{II}|\text{black}) \qquad \text{Equation 2}$$

From equations 1 and 2, we can infer that:

$$P(\text{II}|\text{black}) = P(\text{II})P(\text{black}|\text{II})/P(\text{black}) \qquad \text{Equation 3}$$

7.3 Bayes' Theorem

Equation 3 is a form of Bayes' Theorem for our urn problem. Although Bayes' Theorem has been developed rather easily in this example, it is nevertheless a profound principle. In fact, an entire body of statistical theory relies on Bayes' Theorem as the basis for all statistical inference. To understand some of the implications of Bayes' Theorem, let us return to our urn experiment.

Suppose we reach into the urn, select one ball, and it turns out to be black. What is the probability that we have selected from side II? Since the sides are unmarked, a black marble could have come from either side. Equation 3 shows us how to calculate this probability. The initial (or prior) probability that we have selected from side II is simply $P(II) = 0.5$. This is referred to as a *prior probability* because it is the probability of a hypothesis (side I or side II) prior to collecting the data of an experiment. The probability, $P(black|II)$, is a conditional probability and is called a *likelihood*. If we know that a ball from side II has been selected, then $P(black|II) = 0.7$. A likelihood is the conditional probability of the data, given the hypothesis in question. The probability of the data, e.g., $P(Black)$, is the initial probability of selecting a black ball in this experiment, i.e., $P(black) = 0.5$. Putting all this together we obtain:

$$P(II|black) = \frac{(0.5)(0.7)}{(0.5)} = 0.7$$

The term, $P(II|black)$, is the *posterior probability* for the hypothesis, given the data of the experiment. It is called posterior because it is our belief in the hypothesis after the result of one drawing from the urn. Bayes' Theorem is thus a procedure to revise our initial probability to a posterior probability, given the results of an experiment. In the next section we shall see how the uncertainty in assigning probabilities can be reduced by performing a Bayesian analysis.

8   POSTERIOR DECISION ANALYSIS

Recall that when a sensitivity analysis for the Atkinson Calculator problem was conducted, there was too much variation in the assignment of probabilities among the executives. To decrease this variation, it may help to conduct a survey in which a sample of people are questioned about their interest in the product. The information obtained in such a survey may be very helpful for decision-making purposes; however, such information is not without error. A major source of error is a result of the sampling procedure itself. Since we do not have the resources to test everyone (or what is called the *population*), we randomly test only a few. And the people we select for testing (the sample) may not reflect the values of the population; this error is referred to as *sampling error*. Generally sampling error decreases as a function of sample size, although in principle it is present whenever we sample.

This problem of sampling error can be quite complex, and occasionally requires the expertise of a statistician who can construct the likelihood values of the survey sample data given various hypotheses concerning the population. For example, suppose that our survey is conducted, and the people tested generally indicate that they like the product. Furthermore, on analyzing the survey data, the statistician gives us the following likelihood values for our sample:

P(good sample sales|good population sales) = 0.86

P(good sample sales|fair population sales) = 0.05

P(good sample sales|poor population sales) = 0.03

Notice that the sum of these conditional probabilities is not 1.0. Likelihoods do not necessarily sum to unity because each likelihood refers to a different condition or hypothesis concerning the population.(Recall that a likelihood is the conditional probability of the sample data, given a population condition.) For this survey, the sample outcome of good sales is most likely if the population sales are good, i.e., 0.86 is the greatest likelihood. However, there is a chance (i.e., 0.03) that sampling error led us to obtain the good sample sales from a population that shows poor sales. Even though we are really interested in the population sales rather than sample sales, the above likelihood values are useful in enabling us to convert a prior probability concerning population sales to a posterior probability via Bayes' Theorem.

Any Bayesian analysis involves the following: Prior probabilities; likelihood of the survey data, given some hypotheses concerning the population; the prior probability of obtaining the data; and the transformation of the prior probabilities to posterior probabilities. Table 9-4 contains these four components of the Bayesian analysis that would be conducted for the Atkinson Calculator case. The first column lists the prior probabilities, where "prior" refers to the initial belief before obtaining the survey results. The likelihoods provided by the statisticians are shown in the second column. The prior probability of the data is the sum of the values listed in the third column (i.e., 0.289). The values in the third column are the product of the prior probability and the likelihood, and these values correspond to the numerator in Bayes' Theorem. Hence, the sum of the third column is P(good sample sales) and is given by the following expression:

Table 9-4. Bayesian Analysis for The Atkinson Calculator Company

Concensus Prior Probability for	Likelihood for Sample Data Given	Prior x Likelihood	Posterior Probability
Good Sales (.3)	Good population sales (.86)	.258	.893
Fair Sales (.5)	Fair population sales (.06)	.025	.086
Poor Sales (.2)	Poor population sales (.03)	$\dfrac{.006}{.289} =$ probability of the sample data	.021

P(good population sales)P(good sample sales|good population sales) +

P(fair population sales)P(good sample sales|fair population sales) +

P(poor population sales)P(good sample sales|poor population sales)

Notice that the first term of the above expression is the joint probability of good sample sales obtained from a population that has good sales. The second and third terms are respectively the joint probabilities of good sample sales obtained from two populations, one that has fair sales and one that has poor sales. Thus, there are three mutually exclusive ways that our results of good survey sales might have been obtained. These probabilities are summed since any of these ways was possible. Finally, the resultant posterior probabilities are listed in the fouth column. These values are obtained by dividing the entry in the third column (the numerator in Bayes' Theorem) by the P(good sample sales), the denominator in Bayes' Theorem. Notice that a remarkable shift in probability values has occurred, so the survey certainly has been useful.

Table 9-5 is a posterior sensitivity analysis for the Atkinson Calculator problem. Recall that the executives did not agree in their initial probability assignments of good, fair, and poor sales (see Table 9-3). In Table 9-5, each of the possible prior probability assignments shown in Table 9-3 has been converted to posterior probabilities in a fashion analogous to the Bayesian analysis of Table 9-4.

Notice that the various executives still disagree regarding their posterior probability; however, they all now believe that good sales is the most probable outcome. They all now agree on the same optimal decision of having a full production according to the most-likely value decision rule

Table 9-5. A Posterior Sensitivity Analysis for Atkinson Calculator
Problem (see Table 9-3)

| Prior Probabilities | | | Posterior Probabilities for | | | Optimal Decision and |
P(good)	P(fair)	P(poor)	good	fair	poor	Probability
.1	.8	.1	.667	.310	.023	Full (.667)
.1	.6	.3	.688	.240	.072	Full (.688)
.5	.4	.1	.949	.044	.007	Full (.949)
.5	.2	.3	.958	.022	.020	Full (.958)

(recall section 4.2). Indeed, the sample data have been useful in the decision-making process.

9   UTILITY SCALING OF MONETARY VALUE

In analyzing the Atkinson Calculator decision so far we have dealt with value only as monetary value. However, in Chapter 4 we learned that monetary value and utility are often different. Since utility more truly represents value, it is utility that should be optimized in our decision analysis rather than monetary value. To illustrate the distinction between monetary value and utility, consider the following decision problem. Jones is trying to decide whether or not to buy accident insurance with coverage up to $100,000 in damages. The relative frequency for occurrence of such an accident is 0.0001. The insurance cost is $100. Should Jones purchase the insurance policy? Figure 9-3(a) shows the basic decision tree for this problem, and (b) shows the folded tree.

Both the maximum expected value rule and the maximum most-likely value rule tell us not to buy the insurance policy. However, are we likely to be satisfied with this outcome of the decision analysis? Probably not, since the cost of $100,000 is subjectively more than 1000 times greater than the cost of $100. Most people can absorb the cost of the policy, while the cost of a law suit stemming from a large accident would be ruinous.

One method that can be used to establish a utility scale for monetary value is called the *standard gamble* procedure. The first step in this procedure is to rank order the monetary values and label them for the Atkinson Calculator case:

Outcome	Monetary Value
A	$600,000
B_1	$330,000
B_2	$240,000
B_3	$150,000
B_4	$\quad 0
B_5	−$ 90,000
C	−$180,000

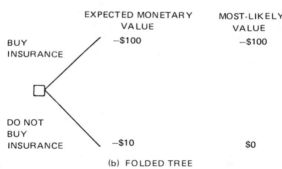

BUY
INSURANCE

BIG ACCIDENT (.0001) −$100

NO ACCIDENT (.9999) −$100

DO NOT
BUY
INSURANCE

BIG ACCIDENT (.0001) −$100,000

NO ACCIDENT (.9999) $0

(a) DECISION TREE

EXPECTED MONETARY   MOST-LIKELY
VALUE   VALUE

BUY
INSURANCE   −$100   −$100

DO NOT
BUY
INSURANCE   −$10 $0

(b) FOLDED TREE

Figure 9-3. (a) Decision Tree for Insurance Problem. (b) Folded Tree

The highest monetary value is labeled A, the lowest monetary value is labeled C, and the ones in the middle are labeled B_1 through B_5. The utility of A is always set at 100, i.e., $U(A) = 100$, while the utility of C is set at zero, i.e., $U(C) = 0$. The utility of the intermediate monetary values (i.e., B_1 ... B_5) lie between zero and 100.

Intermediate utility value is determined by means of a series of hypothetical gambles. For example, the utility of B_1 is found by establishing preference in a series of hypothetical gambles involving two choices. First, one can choose to accept a certain B_1 (i.e., a certain $330,000); or second, one can choose to take a chance on a lottery. The two results of the lottery are either: 1, with probability P of winning A (i.e., $600,000); or 2, with probability $1-P$ of winning C (i.e., owing $180,000). This gamble is illustrated as a decision tree in Figure 9-4. If P were set equal to 1, the lottery would be the obvious preferred choice. If P were set equal to 0, the certain outcome of $330,000 would be the obvious preferred choice. However, given some intermediate value of P, a person would be ambivalent between the lottery and the certain outcome. The value of P for which ambivalence results is a function either of the risk-proneness or the risk-aversiveness of the person. The problem is to specify the value of P for which there is ambivalence between choosing the certain B_1 and choosing the lottery.

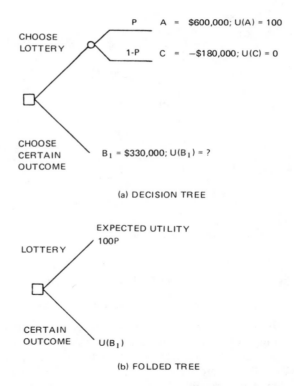

(a) DECISION TREE

(b) FOLDED TREE

Figure 9-4. (a) Decision Tree for the Standard Gamble to Determine Utility of B_1. (b) Folded Tree.

Often it is helpful to compute the value of probability, P_0, which would permit subjective probability to be scaled the same as monetary value. If $P_0 = (B_1 - C)/(A - C)$, the utility of B_1 would be directly proportional to monetary value:

$$P_0 = \frac{330,000 - (-180,000)}{600,000 - (-180,000)} = 0.654$$

However, if you were an executive of Atkinson Calculator, would you prefer a certain $330,000? Or would you prefer a lottery with probability of 0.654 of obtaining $600,000, and probability of 0.346 of losing $180,000? If you are conservative, a probability of 0.346 is too large a chance to take on a $180,000 loss; you would prefer a certain $330,000. On the other hand, if you are a risk taker, you would prefer the lottery. When most people place themselves in the situation of an executive of Atkinson Calculator, they behave conservatively. Consequently, they usually require that the probability of the $600,000 in the lottery go much higher, say to 0.83, before they find themselves ambivalent. To compute the utility of B_1, we will assume that ambivalence occurred because the *expected utility* value of the lottery choice and the certain B_1 choice were equal. Thus:

$$U(B_1) = PU(A) + (1 - P) U(C)$$
$$= P(100) + (1 - P)(0) = 100P$$

Since for our executive $P = 0.83$, $U(B_1) = 83$. The other intermediate monetary values can be determined in a similar fashion. Table 9-6 shows the executive's utility values for all monetary values.

Figure 9-5 shows a utility curve for three types of individuals. The upper branch corresponds to a conservative or risk-avoider; the lower branch corresponds to a risk-taker; and the middle branch corresponds to a person who is neither a risk-taker nor risk-avoider. Attitude toward risk is not a fixed characteristic of the person in all situations. A person might be a risk-avoider under some circumstances, but a risk-taker under others. The executive at Atkinson Calculator is basically a risk-avoider; although for low incomes (i.e., −$90,000) he is neither a risk-taker nor a risk-avoider.

10 CONCLUDING ANALYSIS OF THE ATKINSON CASE

Figure 9-6 is a final decision tree incorporating what we have discussed concerning the Atkinson Calculator problem. The probability values are the posterior probabilities after inclusion of the marketing survey data. Outcomes are evaluated in terms of their utility rather than merely their

Table 9-6. A Utility Determination For An Executive of Atkinson Calculator

Order of Preference	Objective Value in $1000	P_o	$P(B_i)$	U_i
A	600	1.00	1.00	100
B_1	330	.65	.83	83
B_2	240	.54	.70	70
B_3	150	.42	.60	60
B_4	0	.23	.50	50
B_5	−90	.12	.12	12
C	180	.00	.00	0

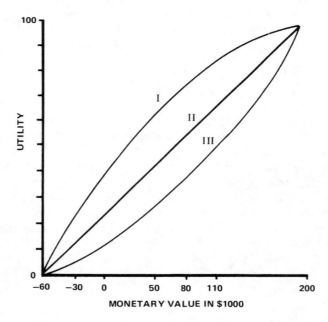

Figure 9-5. Utility curves for three types of indivuduals: I is a risk-avoider;
III is a risk-taker; and II is neither.

monetary value. From the folded tree it is clear that the Atkinson executive
will recommend a full production schedule.

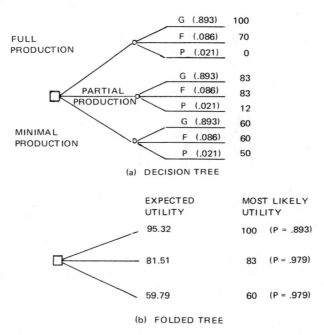

(a) DECISION TREE

EXPECTED UTILITY	MOST LIKELY UTILITY	
95.32	100	(P = .893)
81.51	83	(P = .979)
59.79	60	(P = .979)

(b) FOLDED TREE

Figure 9-6. (a) Decision Tree for the Atkinson Calculator Problem Which
Includes Utility Values. (b) Folded Tree.

11   SELECTED BIBLIOGRAPHY

Raiffa, H., and Schlaifer, R. *Applied Statistical Decision Theory.* Cambridge, Mass.:
Harvard Business School, 1961.
Trueman, R.E. *An Introduction to Quantitative Methods for Decision Making.* New
York: Holt, Rinehart and Winston, Inc., 1974.
Winkler, R.L. *Introduction to Bayesian Inference and Decision.* New York: Holt,
Rinehart and Winston, Inc., 1972.

Chapter 10
Decision Making in the Practice of Medicine

1   INTRODUCTION

A seventy-year-old man with severe vascular disease has been confined to a wheelchair for ten years. His life consists largely of watching television and reading the newspaper. He requires extensive assistance with all his activities. Over the past year his eyesight has been gradually failing; he can hardly see the television screen and has great difficulty reading. His physician determines that he has developed cataracts in both eyes. The man asks if anything can be done — he knows that surgery might be able to restore his vision. His physician explains that cataract surgery is usually quite simple and can be done at very low risk with excellent results. However, this particular man is not a good candidate for surgery. Because of his vascular disease and general debilitation, surgery would carry a very high risk. How high? Well, the physician is not sure but her best estimate is that there would be a 10% to 20% chance of the man's dying as a result of the surgery. The physician points out that she is conservative and does not want to subject her patient to undue risks. Therefore she recommends that the elderly man forego surgery and face the burden of his progressive blindness.

The above scenario is hypothetical but representative of much of medical practice. Medical decisions are made almost exclusively by the physician. Most patients are comfortable with this because they trust their

Percy H. Hill et al., Making Decisions: A Multidisciplinary Introduction

physicians to be knowledgeable and skillful. Yet few physicians have had any formal training in the process of making decisions. The content of the curriculum at most medical schools is devoted almost entirely to facts and information. Any knowledge about the process of decision making is left to the student to discover. Most medical students learn that process in their apprenticeship on the medical wards of a teaching hospital; they observe the approach of more senior physicians and try to emulate it. The tide is beginning to change, however. A few medical schools are beginning to offer instruction in the *process* of making decisions, a process not dissimilar to the approach presented in this book. Simultaneously, two outside pressures are beginning to change the process of clinical decision making. First, in an effort to contain medical costs and improve the quality of care, various government agencies and third-party payers (e.g., insurance companies) are beginning to require the physician to document and justify his management plans. Second, patients are demanding an increased role in the decision-making process. They want to be more involved in their own care and to have significant input into medical management decisions. This latter pressure has been buttressed by legal decisions that stress the need for informed consent for diagnostic or therapeutic procedures. Physicians have been held liable not only for errors of omission and commission but also for failing to inform the patient of potential complications and for failing to allow the patient meaningful participation in the decisions about his therapy.

One approach to these problems has been an increasing interest in formal approaches to clinical decision making. In this chapter, we shall provide some examples of actual medical problems in which the tools of decision analysis have been successfully applied to patient care. Certainly, the medical profession has not met this approach with open arms. Objections have been raised to this approach on the ground that it is time-consuming and too explicit. This approach underscores the fact that current medical practice is often based on inadequate knowledge and fragmentary logic. Although that knowledge is limited, we must realize that physicians must treat today's patients with information that is available now and not with the hope of better data in the future. Nevertheless, the use of formal approaches to clinical decision making promises to eliminate some of the errors that inevitably creep into all informal, implicit decision-making processes.

At the present time, there are a limited number of physicians in academic centers who utilize the tools of decision analysis in their day to day medical practice. The examples in this chapter are based on their experiences. For didactic purposes, the problems have been greatly simplified. Thus, readers are cautioned against using the data or conclusions in these examples either to question or to guide their own medical care.

2   A YOUNG WOMAN WITH CHEST PAIN

2.1   Case Description

A twenty-one-year-old college student experiences several hours of excruciating chest pain. The pain is quite sharp, localized to her right side, and markedly exacerbated by breathing or motion; she must take shallow breaths or the pain becomes unbearable. She has been coughing for the last few days but has just begun to cough up sputum containing flecks of blood. During this period she has been out of sorts, with chills and muscular aches and pains. This morning she returned from a spring vacation in Europe and, because of holiday traffic and a labor slow-down in London, was confined to a crowded plane for fourteen hours during the flight. She has been quite healthy all her life; the only medication that she takes is birth control pills. The physician who examines her thinks that she most likely was suffering from a viral syndrome, but he considers the possibility that she may have had a pulmonary embolus (a blood clot from her legs lodged in her lungs) because of her recent plane flight and because she takes birth control pills. He obtains x-rays of her chest and a special test (a lung scan) in which tiny amounts of radioactive protein are injected into her blood and used to measure its flow through her lungs. Based on these data, the physician assesses the likelihood of a pulmonary embolus to be 50%.

If a patient is known to have a pulmonary embolus, then the proper treatment involves giving medication to "thin the blood" (anticoagulants) for several months. The purpose is to decrease blood clotting and thereby lessen the chance of additional emboli. If patients with known pulmonary emboli are not given anticoagulants, the chance of re-embolization is 50%; if they are properly treated, the chance is only 15%. (In both cases, assume that the presumed precipitating cause, the birth control pills, is discontinued.) Many drugs can have untoward effects, and the major complication of anticoagulants is hemorrhage. Approximately 5% of patients given these drugs will have a bleeding episode serious enough to require hospitalization. All other things being equal, should this young woman be treated with anticoagulants?

2.2   Analysis

The first step in making this decision is to structure the problem, and for this purpose we use the decision tree notation (Figure 10-1). The square node denotes the choice — whether or not to administer anticoagulants. The upper branch of that node describes the consequences of anticoagulation; the lower branch describes the consequences of withholding that therapy. In both cases, the young woman may or may not, in fact, have pulmonary

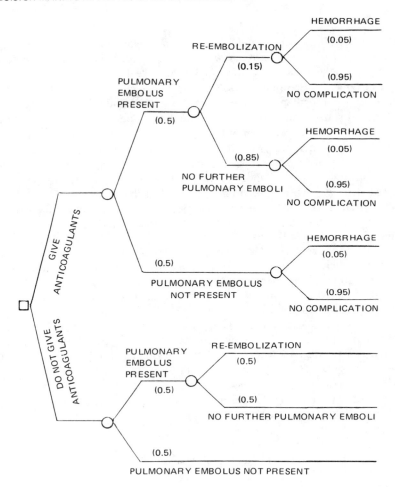

Figure 10-1. A Decision Tree for Possible Pulmonary Emboli

emboli (with probability 0.5). In the upper part of the tree, we diagram the possibility of re-embolization despite therapy (probability 0.15) and the fact that if this woman is treated, there is a chance of hemorrhage (probability 0.05). In the lower part of the tree, we note that the likelihood of re-embolization is far higher if anticoagulants are not given (probability 0.5), but there is no chance of hemorrhage.

The next step in the analysis is to assign relative values, or utilities, to each potential outcome. The establishment of a proper utility scale can be a complex task. For illustrative purposes, we shall use a simple scale. If the patient has no further problems, we assign a utility of 0; if the patient has *either* another pulmonary embolus or a hemorrhagic complication, we assign a utility of -1; if the patient has *both* another embolus and an episode of bleeding, we assign a utility of -2. On this scale, increasing degrees of negativity imply increasingly worse outcomes. For simplicity, we have tacitly assumed that hemorrhage and re-embolization are equally bad consequences.

Since this decision is truly made under the bounds of uncertainty (we do not know whether the patient has an embolus, whether she will have another, or whether she will bleed on anticoagulants), we calculate an expected utility for each course of action. The choice associated with the higher expected utility is the better management strategy. The calculation of expected utility (that is, the process of folding back the decision tree) is shown in Figure 10-2. The assigned utilities and calculated expected utilities are shown in the ovals. Calculation proceeds from right to left. The calculated expected utility of the highest chance node (re-embolization in the face of anticoagulation) is equal to 0.05×-2 plus 0.95×-1, or -1.05. Immediately below that node is the chance node, "no further emboli after anticoagulation." The expected utility of that node is 0.05×-1 plus 0.95×0, or -0.05. Moving one node to the left, we calculated the expected utility of "treated pulmonary embolus" to be 0.15×-1.05 plus 0.85×-0.05, or -0.20. The expected utility of "giving anticoagulanif pulmonary embolus is not present" is 0.05×-1 plus 0.95×0 or -0.05. Thus, the overall expected utility of giving this patient anticoagulants is 0.5×-0.20 plus 0.5×-0.05, or -0.125. In an analogous fashion, we calculate the expected utility of withholding anticoagulants to be -0.25. In conclusion, the expected utility of giving anticoagulants is higher than the expected utility of not giving the drugs; thus, this young woman should receive anticoagulant therapy.

2.3 Sensitivity Analysis

As explained in earlier chapters, one of the great advantages of the decision analytic approach is the ability to examine and modify the assumptions of the analysis to determine whether the optimal choice is affected. In this section we shall apply sensitivity analysis to two parameters: the utility of having both another embolus and an episode of bleeding, and the probability that this young woman did, in fact, have a pulmonary embolus.

Recall from previous chapters that the basic motivation of Von Neumann-Morgenstern utility theory is the axiom of substitution, i.e., reducing a complex problem with many outcomes to a logically equivalent problem with only two outcome states — one good and one bad. If there are

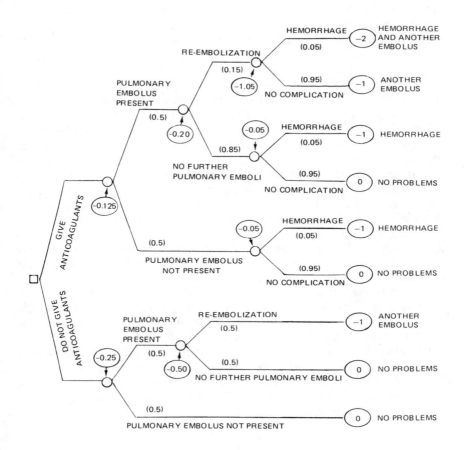

Figure 10-2. Calculating the Expected Value of Anticoagulation

only two outcomes, then the basic decision rule is elegantly simple: choose the strategy that is more likely to result in the better outcome. Our problem had three outcome states: "No problems," "another embolus *or* hemorrhage," and "*both* another embolus and hemorrhage." We chose to assign a utility of −2 to this doubly bad outcome, saying, in effect, that having two medical problems is twice as bad as having only one. It might be argued, however, that having both problems is not twice as bad as having either one alone. Clearly, if having both is less than twice as bad, then the expected utility of giving anticoagulants would be even higher, and the optimal choice would remain the same. In fact, withholding anticoagulants would not be the preferable strategy until the burden of having both problems was over 47 times as bad as having either alone. It would be difficult to imagine such a utility scale. Hence, the decision seems to be insensitive to our assumptions about the utility scale.

Although many people view medicine as an exact science and believe that the physician generally knows with assurance whether or not a given disease is present, the clinician often makes therapeutic choices without being certain of the diagnosis. In this example, we assumed that the likelihood of pulmonary embolus, based on the patient's presentation, physical findings, and laboratory test results, was 50%. Again, it might be argued that the likelihood of pulmonary embolus might be different. To analyze the sensitivity of the decision to that assumption, we use a simple graphic technique. Note that the upper chance node in each strategy branch (Figures 10-1 and 10-2) describes the likelihood of pulmonary embolus. Thus the expected utility of each of the four branches of those nodes describes the relative value of each strategy in patients either known to have or known not to have pulmonary emboli. In other words, the expected utility of treated pulmonary emboli is −0.20; of untreated emboli, −0.50, of treating patients without emboli, −0.05; and of not treating patients without emboli, zero. Furthermore, inspection of the decision tree shows that the expected utility of each strategy is a *linear* function of the likelihood of pulmonary emboli. These relations are shown in Figure 10-3, in which expected utility is shown on the vertical axis and the probability of emboli is shown on the horizontal axis. Each strategy is represented as a straight line. The two strategy lines intersect at a probability of 0.14. Thus, if the likelihood that this young woman has pulmonary emboli is anything above 14%, she should receive anticoagulant therapy.

2.4   The Concept of a Therapeutic Threshold

This decision is prototypical of an entire class of clinical choices in which therapeutic choices must be made in the absence of absolute information about the presence or absence of a particular disease. Figure 10-4 shows the characteristic decision tree for such situations. The analogy between this tree and the left-most portion of the tree in Figure 10-1 should be obvious. Here, the physician must choose to treat or not to treat a particular patient who may or may not have the disease in question. We use the symbol, p, to denote the probability that the patient does, in fact, have the disease. There are four end branches in this decision tree, and each end branch must be assigned an expected utility. The analysis can be considerably simplified, however, if one realizes that the optimal choice does

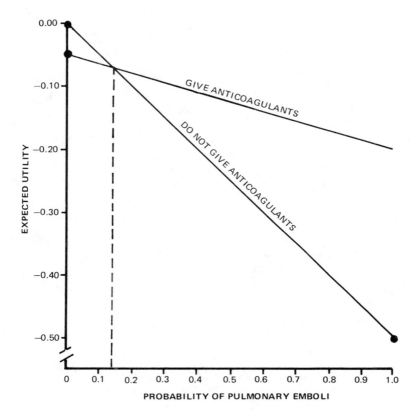

Figure 10-3. Sensitivity Analysis of Likelihood of Pulmonary Emboli

not depend on the individual utilities; rather, it depends on the differences
between pairs of utilities. The difference between treating and not treating
patients known to have the disease can be called the *benefit* of therapy. The
difference between not treating and treating patients known not to have the
disease can be called the *cost* of therapy. It can be shown that the likelihood
(p) of disease above which treatment should be given is equal to:

$$\frac{1}{\dfrac{\text{benefit}}{\text{cost}} + 1}$$

That likelihood is called the *therapeutic threshold*. If the likelihood of
disease is above the therapeutic threshold, then treatment should be given; if
the likelihood is below the threshold, then treatment should be withheld.

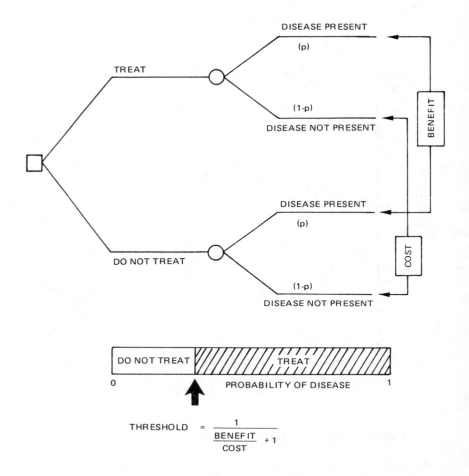

Figure 10-4. The Therapeutic Threshold

The bar graph at the bottom of Figure 10-4 shows that the therapeutic threshold divides the probability domain into two regions: a "do not treat" region and a "treat" region.

It must be realized that this threshold model assumes that the treatment decision *must* be made on the basis of currently available information. If other diagnostic tests can be performed or if delaying the decision and observing the patient will provide further information about the likelihood of disease, then one must use a decision analysis that considers these additional alternatives.

The concept of a threshold probability is not limited to medical decision making. The same formulation can be applied to any double binary choice in which one of two actions must be taken and in which the true state of the world is binary, i.e., a given situation is present or absent. For example, consider the choice of whether or not to carry an umbrella on a cloudy day. If the weatherman advises you that the likelihood of rain is 25%, if the cost of carrying an umbrella on a rainless day is 1 and the benefit of having an umbrella if it rains is 10 (on some arbitrary scale), then the threshold probability is $1/(10/1) + 1$, or 0.09. Since the likelihood of rain is 0.25 (a value well above the threshold), it would be advisable to take your umbrella.

2.5 Additional Information

The above analysis of the anticoagulation decision assumed that no further diagnostic information was available. In fact, an additional alternative exists — performing the test known as pulmonary angiogram. That procedure involves inserting a long plastic tube into a vein in the groin and passing the tube through the heart into the lungs. One then injects a radio-opaque dye and takes x-ray pictures of the lungs. This test can definitively determine whether or not pulmonary emboli are present, but the procedure causes complications in 1% of patients who undergo it. The decision concerning this procedure can be represented by the decision tree in Figure 10-5. The lower branch ("do not do pulmonary angiogram") is identical to Figure 10-2 and therefore is only presented in skeletal form. As explained above, the optimal choice is to give anticoagulants, and the expected utility of treatment without doing an angiogram is −0.125. The upper branch of Figure 10-5 depicts the consequences of performing the test. A complication of angiography was assumed to decrease the expected utility of each outcome by one. If the test were negative, then we would know that emboli are not present and would withhold anticoagulants. There would be no problems and the utility would be 0. On the other hand, if a complication occurred from the test but if the test result were still negative, then the utility would be −1. In the absence of a complication, the presence of emboli on the angiogram would necessitate anticoagulant therapy and would have an expected utility of −0.20, a value previously calculated in Figure 10-2. Thus, a positive angiogram with a test complication would have an expected utility of −1.2. Folding back the tree in Figure 10-5, we see that the expected utility of performing an angiogram is −0.11 and is greater than the expected utility of omitting the test. Thus, it would be best to subject this woman to a pulmonary angiogram and then to give her anticoagulants if the test result were positive.

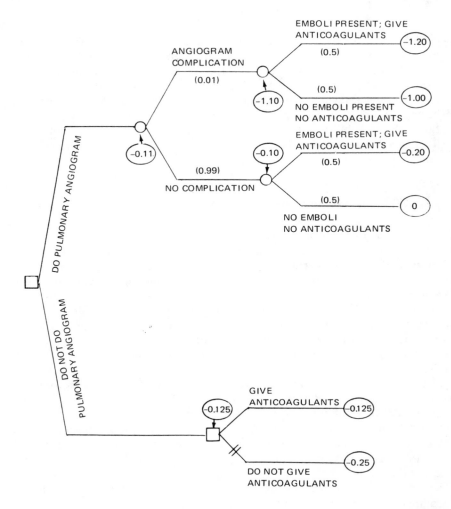

Figure 10-5. Analysis of the Decision Whether or Not to Do a Pulmonary Angiogram

3   A PREGNANT COUPLE

3.1 Case Description

A couple has just learned that the wife is pregnant for the second time. Both parents are lawyers and delayed having a family for many years in order to develop their. careers. The woman is thirty-five years old and the man is thirty-seven. Their first child is a healthy three-year-old boy. Their obstetrician informed them that because the woman was now thirty-five years old and because the incidence of Down's syndrome among newborns increases with maternal age, they should now consider whether or not she should undergo amniocentesis to determine whether her pregnancy is affected by that chromosomal abnormality. They were told that children with Down's syndrome (trisomy 21, "mongolism") can suffer from a variety of medical problems, the major one being moderate to severe mental retardation. The couple was also told that parents are now encouraged to keep children affected by Down's syndrome at home, so state institutionalization may not be an available alternative. Obviously, the attention that such a retarded child would require might interfere with the couple's ability to devote adequate time to their other child and to their careers.

The obstetrician pointed out that if the diagnosis of Down's syndrome could be made prenatally, then the couple would have the option of electing to have a therapeutic abortion and then starting another pregnancy. They are told that the likelihood of having a child affected by Down's syndrome is 1/365 for this pregnancy (maternal age thirty-five) but the likelihood will increase with subsequent pregnancies as the parents get older. (See Table 10-1.) The technique of amniocentesis involves inserting a needle into the pregnant uterus and withdrawing a small amount of the fluid that surrounds the fetus. This fluid contains cells shed by the fetus. These cells can be cultured and then examined. The examination is fairly accurate in detecting Down's syndrome: Affected fetuses are properly labeled 99% of the time, and unaffected fetuses are falsely called "affected" no more than 0.1% of the time. The procedure is, however, not without risk. The major complication of inserting a needle into the uterus is the precipitation of a miscarriage. The obstetrician informs the couple that, in his experience, the risk of miscarriage is approximately one in 200, or 0.5%.

The couple are told that the decision is clearly theirs, although amniocentesis is generally suggested to pregnant women over the age of thirty-five. Should they choose to have the test performed?

3.2 Analysis

Again the first step in reaching a logical decision is to structure the problem. Figure 10-6 presents a decision tree that may be used for this analysis. The upper branch describes the two possible outcomes of declining amniocentesis: having a child affected by Down's syndrome (probability 0.00274 or a 1/365 chance) or having an unaffected child (probability 0.99726). The lower branch of the tree describes the possible consequences

Table 10-1. Incidence of Live-Born Down's Syndrome Children as a
Function of Maternal Age at Delivery*

Maternal Age	Approximate Incidence of Down's Syndrome Per 1,000 Live Births	Fractional Rate
20	0.52	1/1923
21	0.59	1/1695
22	0.65	1/1538
23	0.71	1/1408
24	0.77	1/1299
25	0.83	1/1205
26	0.89	1/1124
27	0.95	1/1053
28	1.01	1/990
29	1.07	1/935
30	1.13	1/885
31	1.21	1/826
32	1.38	1/725
33	1.69	1/592
34	2.15	1/465
35	2.74	1/365
36	3.49	1/287
37	4.45	1/225
38	5.66	1/177
39	7.21	1/139
40	9.19	1/109
41	11.71	1/85
42	14.91	1/67
43	19.00	1/53
44	24.20	1/41
45	30.84	1/32
46	39.28	1/25
47	50.04	1/20
48	63.75	1/16
49	81.21	1/12

*From E.B. Hook and G.M. Chambers, "Estimated rates of Down's Syndrome in live births by one year maternal age intervals for mothers aged 20-49 in a New York State study — Implications of the risk figures for genetic counseling and cost benefit analysis or prenatal diagnosis programs." In D. Bergsma and R.B. Lowry (eds.), *Numerical Taxonomy of Birth Defects and Polygenic Disorders*. Alan R. Liss (New York) for the National Foundation — March of Dimes, Birth Defects: Original Article Series 13 (3A): 123, 1977.

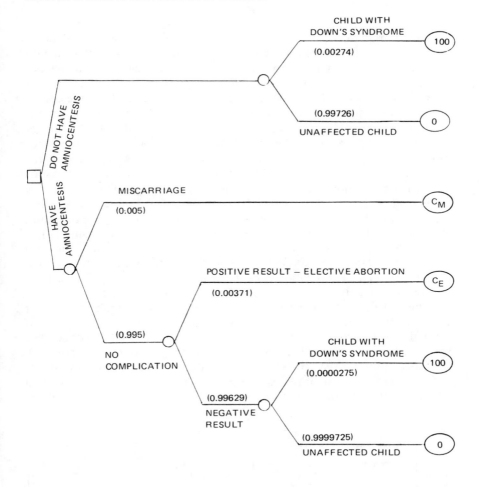

Figure 10-6. Whether or Not to Have an Amniocentesis for the Prenatal Detection of Down's Syndrome in a 35-Year-Old Woman

of amniocentesis. One is a miscarriage (0.5% chance). The likelihood of a positive result is equal to the probability of an affected child times the true positive rate plus the probability of unaffected child times the false positive rate. Thus, the probability of having a positive result is 0.00274 × 0.99 plus 0.99726 × 0.001, or 0.00371. If a positive result is obtained, we presume that the couple will elect to terminate the pregnancy. If a negative result is obtained (probability 0.99629), the pregnancy will go to term and result in an affected (probability 0.0000275) or an unaffected (probability 0.9999725) child. Note that a negative test result decreases the likelihood of an affected child by a factor of 100.

In contrast to the prior example, this decision is largely dependent on the attitudes of the couple toward the burden of having a child affected with Down's syndrome, compared to the burden of miscarriage or of an elective abortion. We therefore chose to establish a negative utility scale (a scale of costs) in which the cost of an affected child is defined as 100 and the cost of an unaffected child is zero. Since attitudes will vary from couple to couple, we shall use symbols to denote the other two costs: C_M denotes the cost of miscarriage and C_E denotes the cost of elective abortion. Since these various costs form a negative utility scale, the preferred option is the one with the *lower* expected cost. Folding back the tree, we see that the expected cost of not having an amniocentesis is 0.274. Similarly, the expected cost of having an amniocentesis is $0.00273 + 0.00369C_E + 0.005C_M$. To keep the solution as general as possible, we shall develop an equation of identity that specifies the relation between C_M and C_E such that the two alternatives (amniocentesis and no amniocentesis) are equally burdensome. Thus, we have $0.274 = 0.00273 + 0.00369C_E + 0.005C_M$. Solving for C_E, we have $C_E = 73.4 - 1.36C_M$. This relation is depicted in the left panel of Figure 10-7. The downsloping diagonal line is specified by the linear equation. Any pair of values for C_E and C_M specifies a unique point on that graph. If the point lies above the identity line, then amniocentesis should not be performed; if the point lies below the line, then amniocentesis should be done. For example, one couple specified values for C_E and C_M of 10 and 10 (point A). For that couple, the costs of miscarriage and elective abortion are sufficiently low that amniocentesis should be done. Another couple specified values of 60 and 30, respectively (point B). For this second couple, the

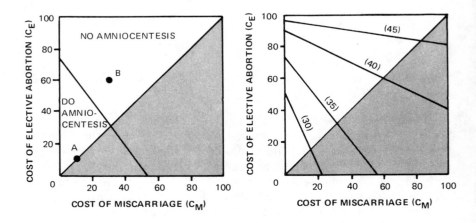

Figure 10-7. Decision Diagrams for Amniocentesis Decision

burden of miscarriage and abortion outweigh the risk of having an affected child, and amniocentesis should be declined. The shaded area of the graph contains points in which C_M exceeds C_E. Many people consider the burden of a therapeutic abortion to be greater than the burden of a miscarriage because abortion involves an active choice. Those people who have no particularly strong feelings about the immorality of abortion view the two outcomes (termination of a pregnancy) as equivalent. We have not, however, identified any couples from whom the burden of elective abortion was less than the burden of miscarriage. Therefore we have shaded the area of the graph corresponding to those points to warn the reader that such values may be in error.

The analysis thus far has assumed that the couples' attitudes toward the various outcomes could be quantified, and that the values of C_E and C_M are known. In the next section, we shall focus on a technique for eliciting these values.

3.3 The Assessment of the Couple's Attitudes

The motivation behind the assignment of utilities is the *principle of substitution*. This principle states that an outcome in a decision tree can be replaced by a chance node involving a π chance of the worst possible outcome and a $(1-\pi)$ chance of the best possible outcome, where the value of π is a measure of the utility of the original outcome that was replaced. One can use a technique called the *basic reference lottery* to assess the appropriate value of π.

In the amniocentesis example, the best possible outcome is "having an unaffected child" and the worst possible outcome is "having a child affected by Down's syndrome." (In fact, some couples might consider abortion to be the worst outcome; for them amniocentesis would obviously be inappropriate and this obviates any further analysis.) Since we have established a scale of costs (and will choose the alternative with the lowest expected cost), we assign 100 to "having an affected child" and zero to "having an unaffected child."

The application of the lottery-substitution technique to this problem is illustrated in Figure 10-8. The upper panel depicts the possible consequences of amniocentesis in a thirty-five-year-old woman. She and her spouse are, in effect, asked to assign relative costs to the outcomes "elective abortion" and "miscarriage." First, consider elective abortion. We might ask the couple to consider a hypothetical situation in which amniocentesis is not available. We then ask them to imagine that their risk of having a child affected by Down's syndrome is 50%. Would they choose to abort the pregnancy? Suppose they answer yes. Now we ask them to consider another pregnancy in which their

risk of having an affected child is only one in a thousand. Would they abort
that pregnancy? Suppose they answer no. We continue to ask similar
questions until we find hypothetical circumstances in which the couple is
indifferent between carrying the pregnancy to term (and risking having an

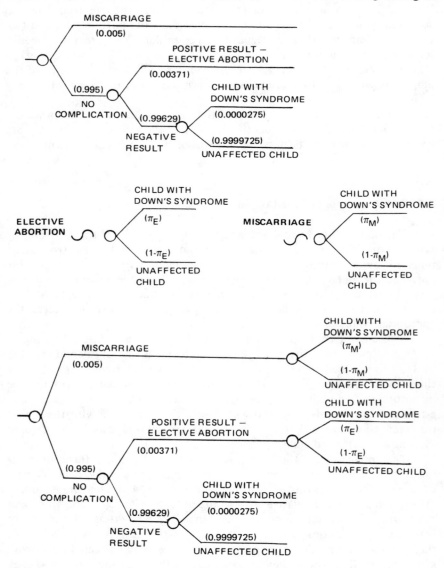

Figure 10-8. The Principle of Substitution and the Lottery

affected child) and electing to abort the pregnancy. The probability of this "indifferent" pregnancy's resulting in a child affected with Down's syndrome is denoted by the symbol π_E. This probability (π_E), expressed as a percent, is a measure of the cost of elective abortion: $100 \pi_E = C_E$.

A similar sequence of questions can be used to find a hypothetical pregnancy for which the risk of having an affected child (π_M) equals the burden of a miscarriage, i.e., $100\pi_M = C_M$. The center panel of Figure 10-8 depicts these two indifference points. As can be seen in the lower panel of this figure, we can then substitute the two basic reference lotteries for the outcomes "elective abortion" and "miscarriage" and thereby convert the original tree into an equivalent tree which contains only two outcomes, "having an affected child" and "having an unaffected child." Having motivated the assessment of utilities by the lottery approach, we can now use the values for C_E ($100\pi_E$) and C_M ($100\pi_M$) in the decision diagram presented in Figure 10-7.

Recall that the indifference line in the left panel of Figure 10-7 was constructed for maternal age of thirty-five years. In the right panel of that figure, we have presented a series of indifference lines for various maternal ages. Since the risk of having an affected child increases with maternal age, the lines become progressively higher and less steep. For example, point B in the left panel (corresponding to C_E of 60 and C_M of 30) would fall in the amniocentesis area (below the indifference line) if the woman were forty years old rather than thirty-five.

The amniocentesis example forms an interesting contrast to the pulmonary embolus case presented earlier. In the former case, the decision was based almost entirely on the relevant probabilities; little attention was given to the issue of utilities and how the young woman's attitudes might affect the decision. In the latter case, the most important factor affecting the decision is the attitudes of the couple toward the various outcomes: the magnitude of the burden of abortion or miscarriage when compared to the life-long burden of having a child affected by Down's syndrome. The decision diagrams in Figure 10-7 can be viewed as a sensitivity analysis of the effect of utilities on the decision.

4   A SCREENING TEST

4.1 Case Description

A fifty-nine-year-old executive has just completed his annual examination, which he takes at his place of employment as a part of his company's health care program. The examination included a chemical test for blood performed on a sample of his stool. The purpose of the test is to screen for cancer of the large bowel since many patients with cancer of that type lose small amounts of blood into their stool while the cancer is still small and potentially curable. The executive is informed that the cancer screening test showed the presence of blood in his stool.

Naturally, he inquired into the meaning of the test and was told that the likelihood of an asymptomatic fifty-nine-year-old man's having cancer of the large bowel was one in a thousand. He inquired into the accuracy of the test and was told that such screening could detect 85% of cases of large bowel cancer and that 2% of patients without cancer nevertheless had a small amount of blood in their stools.

The executive naturally was quite anxious about the test results since the test seemed quite reliable (its sensitivity is 85% and its specificity is 98%) and he assumed that a positive result implied that he more than likely had cancer. Based on the above data, what is the likelihood that this man has cancer of the large bowel?

4.2 Analysis

The likelihood of cancer in this man depends on two factors, the results of the test and the likelihood that he had cancer before the test was performed (the so-called prior probability). These two factors are often combined improperly on an intuitive, informal basis. The formal, explicit approach to the interpretation of such test results is to employ Bayes' Theorem. Rather than present this technique algebraically, we have chosen to utilize a flow diagram for greater clarity. In Figure 10-9 we consider a cohort of one million men. Suppose that each of these men was essentially identical to the executive in our example above, that is, each of these one million men is asymptomatic, each is fifty-nine years old, and each is about to undergo a screening stool examination for the detection of cancer of the large bowel. First, we know that the prior probability (or incidence) of cancer in this cohort is 1/1000. Thus, of the million men, 1000 will have cancer of the large bowel and 999,000 will not. The test is said to detect 85% of patients with large bowel cancer; thus, of the 1000 men with cancer, 850 will have positive test results and 150 will have negative results. Furthermore, the test is said to be falsely positive in only 2% of patients without large bowel cancer; thus, of the 999,000 men free of cancer, 19,980 will have positive results and 979,020 will have negative results.

We can see from the flow diagram that there will be a total of 20,830 positive test results when the entire cohort is tested. Unfortunately, we will not know which of those positive results corresponds to the presence of cancer and which is a false positive result. The best we can do is to estimate the likelihood of large bowel cancer in the subgroup of men with positive

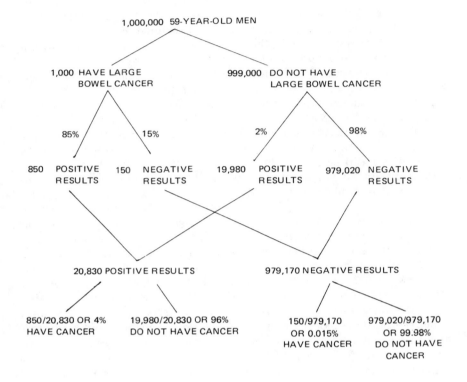

Figure 10-9. The Bayesian Interpretation of a Cancer Screening Test

results. Of the 20,830 men in that group, 850 will actually have cancer. Thus, the likelihood of cancer is 850/20,830, or approximately 4%. Note that we have detected 85% of patients with cancer but the likelihood of cancer is only 4% among men with positive results. Again referring to the graph, we see that we have detected 850 men with cancer, but have also detected almost 20,000 men without cancer.

4.3 Common Errors

Three common situations are very prone to result in erroneous interpretation· of test results if those tests are interpreted on an intuitive rather than an explicit basis. First, consider a test (such as the cancer test) that is quite sensitive and quite specific, and is performed in a setting where the prior probability of disease is low. In such a situation, most positive results come from patients without the disease, that is, they are false positive results. Most physicians will overestimate the likelihood of disease in patients with a positive result because the intuitive reasoning process does not give adequate weight to the prior probability.

Second, consider the occurrence of a negative rest result in a patient very likely to have the disease in question. In this situation, the physician will tend to underestimate the likelihood of the disease, again because inadequate emphasis is given to the prior probability of disease.

Finally, physicians may misinterpret the significance of a negative, or normal, test result. If the physician is considering several diagnostic possibilities and if negative results occur with *different* probabilities in those various diseases, then a negative result should alter the physician's estimate of the relative likelihood of the various diseases. When interpreted intuitively, however, the negative result is often discounted as not providing any differential diagnostic information. It might be useful to consider an everyday example of this error. You are driving home in rush hour traffic and can take a route either over a bridge or through a tunnel. The bridge route is slightly faster if there is no traffic jam, but the tunnel will certainly take less time if a severe traffic jam blocks the bridge but not the tunnel. Based on your past experience, the bridge route is blocked 40% of the time and the tunnel is jammed 20% of the time. Both routes are open 35% of the time, and both are blocked only 5% of the time. Thus, you ordinarily take the tunnel route. You are now approaching the fork where you must decide on your route. The last radio report from the traffic helicopter was five minutes ago and stated that all traffic was moving freely. Which route should you take?

Clearly, you must assess the likelihood that either or both routes are blocked. Again based on your past experience, you assess that the likelihood of such a "normal" report is 90% in the face of good traffic flow, 20% if the bridge is blocked, 40% if the tunnel is blocked, and 10% if both are blocked. The difference in "false negative rates" for the bridge and tunnel routes occurs because the bridge route can be better seen from the air. It should be clear that the negative report will be differentially affected by the likelihood of there being a traffic jam on the bridge and the tunnel, and that Bayes' rule might be used to calculate the revised probabilities. A compact form for the calculation of the revised (or posterior) probabilities is shown in Table 10-2.

Column A presents the four possible states of the world, which obviously must be mutually exclusive. Column B summarizes the prior probabilities of the various traffic situations. Column C provides the conditional probabilities of a negative traffic report in each state of the world. To apply Bayes' Theorem, we simply multiply column B by column C, for each state of the world, and enter the products in column D. The sum

Table 10-2. Application of Bayes' Theorem to the Traffic Problem

A	B	C	D	E
State of World	Prior Probability	Conditional Probability	Product (B x C)	Revised Probability ((B x C) /Sum)
Bridge Blocked	40	20	800	800/4800 = 17%
Tunnel Blocked	20	40	800	800/4800 = 17%
Both Blocked	5	10	50	50/4800 = 1%
No Traffic Jam	35	90	3150	3150/4800 = 65%
			Sum = 4800	

of the products is 4800. Finally, the revised probabilities are calculated in column E by dividing each product by the sum. We can see that the possibility of both routes being blocked is negligible. Before hearing the report, you judged that the bridge was twice as likely to be blocked as the tunnel. After hearing the report, the likelihood of both jams has decreased, but the likelihood of the bridge being blocked is now the same as the likelihood of the tunnel being blocked. In other words, the helicopter's negative report has provided information that changed the relative likelihoods, information you might have ignored if you simply went by your intuitive feeling that the negative report provided little differential information. Based on this information, you might well now choose the bridge route.

5   THE CURRENT ROLE OF DECISION ANALYSIS IN CLINICAL DECISION MAKING

In this chapter we have presented several clinical situations in which the use of formal approaches to decision making might be helpful. Proposals to apply such decision analytic techniques to medical practice have not, so far, received an enthusiastic response. Their use has been criticized on several grounds. The most common objection centers around the lack of good data on the likelihood of alternative outcomes. Many physicians believe that they must have precise and reliable data before they can use quantitative techniques, and that an intuitive process of clinical judgment can by-pass the need for precise data. In fact, little could be further from the truth. Quantitative analysis can be performed on data at any level of accuracy. For example, if one were attempting to estimate how many jellybeans are in a jar, it would be better to estimate the size of a jellybean and the dimensions of the jar than merely make an educated guess. It may be that the results will be true only to one significant figure; however, since the rigor of this approach will help the physician to avoid certain errors of inference, the decisions reached by this approach should make better use of whatever data are available. The intuitive, implicit reasoning process must ultimately rest on the same data, however inadequate they are.

A second type of objection rests on the time-consuming nature of the formal process of analysis. Although one learns to use these tools more efficiently with experience, it will probably always be true that a formal analysis requires more time than an "intuitive leap." We must therefore reserve this approach for those clinical problems which are particularly difficult or unfamiliar or in which diverse opinions, including patient attitudes, must be combined, and where no emergency precludes the time needed for their application. In the future there may come to be a new group of physicians trained in the use of these analytic tools. Other physicians might then call upon these specialists as decision-making consultants, much as radiologists are now called upon to use their skill in interpreting x-ray images and pathologists are called upon to interpret microscopic slides.

One of the most troubling kinds of objection focuses on the dehumanization of the process of medical care, in which it is alleged that formal techniques reduce medical care to a "series of numbers and calculations." The underlying concern of those who make this objection is not that medicine will be dehumanized; it is rather that the physician's role will be demystified. The decision analytic approach forces the clinician to confront his own lack of knowledge in certain situations, the inadequacy of medical data in general, and the frail basis upon which he has to make life and death decisions. Such confrontations can be painful and annoying; they can be avoided by keeping the decision-making process implicit and informal.

Part of the deep distrust of the analytic approach centers on the quantification of the relative merits of potential health outcomes on a utility scale. The creation of such scales is often an arbitrary process, and much research must be done before such quantification can be reliably made. Nevertheless, each attempt at explicit reasoning, no matter how crude, is probably better than the outright neglect of utility considerations altogether. For example, recall the amniocentesis decision. Our analysis demonstrated that the relative burden to the individual couple of having an abortion or having a retarded child is of overriding importance in the decision. Some obstetricians would argue that since the woman is under the magic age of thirty-seven, she should not have an amniocentesis. If the couple then presses the obstetrician further by asking why age thirty-seven constitutes such a breakpoint, they would be told that the risk of amniocentesis (miscarriage occurring at a rate of 1/200 procedures) approximately equals the risk of having an affected child (1/225; see Table 10-1) at that maternal age. Such reasoning tacitly assumes that the cost or burden of a miscarriage is equal to the life-long burden of an affected child. For many couples, these costs are far from equal and a decision-making process that takes this difference into account is probably superior to one that ignores it.

Despite these and other objections to the decision analytic approach, its strengths are impressive. Formal reasoning provides a structure for the problem domain; it enables one to make all assumptions explicit so that they can be examined, utilized, and improved. Decision analysis provides a technique for incorporating diverse opinions into a coherent choice. In classic clinical judgment, the resolution of disagreements (one consultant claiming that surgery should be done while another consultant claims that nonsurgical therapy is better) is often arbitrary and turns on who yells the loudest, or who has the highest academic rank, or to which physician the patient "belongs." In a formal decision analysis each consultant can provide the information (the probabilities) which he knows best and disagreements can be focused on specific likelihoods rather than overall impressions. One consultant rarely considered in the informal decision-making process is the patient himself. Patients are, in fact, experts on their own attitudes and on the potential impact and relative worth to them of various health outcomes. This expertise should not be neglected. The decision analytic mechanism allows this information stream (that is, patient utilities) to be smoothly incorporated into the decision-making process. Current alternatives for increasing patient participation in the process are much less efficient. Either the patient is informed of all potential consequences and then informed what he should do, or the entire decision and all relevant medical data and controversies are dumped into the patient's lap and he is told that the decision is his. Unfortunately, few patients are equipped to retain, comprehend, and utilize such information in arriving at a rational decision. One of the greatest strengths of the decision analytic approach is the ability to perform sensitivity analysis and to determine whether small variations in "soft" and unreliable data might affect the choice of optimal patient management. When decisions are found to be insensitive to such variations, one can have far greater confidence in the correctness of the preferred management strategy.

6   SELECTED BIBLIOGRAPHY

Bunker, J.P., Barnes, B.A. and Mosteller, F. *Costs, Risks and Benefits of Surgery.* New York: Oxford University Press, 1977.

Galen, R.S., and Gambino, S.R. *Beyond Normality.* New York: John Wiley and Sons, 1975.

Gorry, G.A., Pauker, S.G., Schwartz, W.B. "The diagnostic importance of the normal finding." *New England Journal of Medicine,* 298 (1978), pp. 486-489.

Kassirer, J.P. "The principles of medical decision making." *Yale Journal of Biology and Medicine,* 49 (1976), pp. 149-164.

Lusted, L.B. *Introduction to Medical Decision Making.* Springfield, Ill.: Thomas, 1968.

McNeil, B.J., Keeler, E., and Adelstein, S.J. "Primer on certain elements of medical decision making." *New England Journal of Medicine,* 293 (1975), pp. 211 ff.

Pauker, S.G., and Kassirer, J.P. "Therapeutic decision making: A cost-benefit analysis." *New England Journal of Medicine,* 293 (1975), pp. 229-234.

Pauker, S.G. and Kassirer, J.P. "Clinical application of decision analysis: A detailed example." *Seminars Nuclear Medicine,* 8 (1978) pp. 324-335.

Pauker, S.P. and Pauker, S.G. "Prenatal diagnosis: A directive approach to genetic counseling using decision analysis." *Yale Journal of Biology and Medicine,* 50 (1977), pp. 275-289.

Pauker, S.P. and Pauker, S.G. "The amniocentesis decision: An explicit guide for parents." *Annual Review of Birth Defects 1978.* New York: Alan R. Liss, 1979.

Schwartz, W.B., Gorry, G.A., Kassirer, J.P. and Essin, A. "Decision analysis and clinical judgment." *American Journal of Medicine,* 55 (1973), pp. 459-472.

Weinstein, M.C., and Stason, W.B. *Hypertension: A Policy Perspective.* Cambridge, Mass.: Harvard University Press, 1976.

Chapter 11
Linear Programming

1 INTRODUCTION

In today's complex, multifaceted, and multinational world of large private and public organizations, decision makers are often confronted with problems not easily resolved by recourse to trial and error, following one's rivals, or the use of some simple yet arbitrary rule of thumb. Pricing decisions based upon costs plus a fixed percentage mark-up, inventory levels kept equal to one month's sales (or some other fixed period), advertising budgets set to a fixed percentage of sales, are all examples of rules of thumb that can lead to serious problems. Furthermore, they are unlikely to maximize profits or whatever else the decision maker considers important. This is particularly true of the allocation problems of any large organization that manufactures or provides multiple products or services.

The impetus for the use of mathematical models in business decisions dates back to World War II when British and American military intelligence, borrowing heavily from the pioneering work of George B. Dantzig, used linear programming and other mathematical techniques and methods to help make decisions regarding such matters as: the optimum size of a convoy of ships; the most effective strategic bombing runs; patterns of laying sea mines; and the deployment and maneuvering of ships to minimize loss from kamikaze attacks. The term *operations research* (OR), coined during World

Percy H. Hill et al., Making Decisions: A Multidisciplinary Introduction

War II, denotes the application of quantitative methods to the solution of complex decision problems.

Adding further impetus to the use of OR techniques has been the extensive growth of large industries over the last two decades. In part, this growth has been accompanied by an increasing fragmentation of the managerial function and has led to a new class of executive-type problems for which OR is ideally suited. As business firms become so large that department managers develop objectives of their own, there exists the possibility that no matter how well thought out those objectives may be, the company as a whole may suffer. Consider, for example, the behavior of the managers of various departments with respect to a firm's inventory policy. The manager of the production department, concerned about minimizing manufacturing costs, would favor a large supply of raw materials and long uninterrupted production runs of a standard product. The marketing department would rather have a wide variety of finished products with large inventories of each; it would rather work with a production department that could adapt to special orders on short notice with less concern for the higher production costs associated with shorter production runs and costly set-up time. The finance department, in turn, wants to conserve its scarce capital, and would not want to have it tied up idly in inventories of any form. Finally, the personnel manager would like to reduce turnover and to maintain a skilled and stable work force; he might therefore opt for a policy of producing more for inventory during periods of declining sales and less during periods of expanding sales. The conflicts of interest among the various department managers comprise an executive-type problem, in the sense that the best inventory policy is the one that maximizes the objectives of the firm as a whole, not one that maximizes the objective of any single department manager.

2   LINEAR PROGRAMMING

Of all the OR techniques, linear programming is one of the most extensively used. Linear programming is a mathematical technique employed by decision makers to optimize resource allocation when confronted with certain side constraints that limit the range of choices. It is a purely mathematical technique devoid of economic content, but like other branches of mathematics, it has proven to be very useful. The prime virtue of linear programming is that, with the aid of high-speed computers, it provides computational ease to some very complex problems. Its applicability has spread to a wide range of activities. In large multiproduct firms, for example, managers interested in maximizing profits may wish to know how best to allocate their limited supplies of strategic materials, floor space, and skilled labor to the production of their various products so as to achieve the most profitable product mix. Transportation managers want to know the least costly way of routing shipments of various components and finished goods between their many plants and scattered markets. Animal feed manufacturers may need to combine various grains so as to provide the minimum nutrients as promised in their advertisments, at minimum cost. In the context of public policy, linear programming technique has been used to program river systems, taking into account such factors as flood control, power production, irrigation, navigation, and salinity. It has also been used to explore the adequacy of various alternatives to current power sources (oil and gas) in order to meet national demands over the next fifty years.

3   WHEN TO USE LINEAR PROGRAMMING

Certainly not all types of business problems are conducive to linear programming, or for that matter to any OR technique. The criteria for the appropriate use of linear programming may be summarized as follows:

1.   The problem must be sufficiently complex that a simpler or even intuitive approach is unacceptable.
2.   The problem's solution must be rewarding or practical enough so that the added benefits of a linear programming analysis are worth the costs of the extra effort required (we don't need an atomic cannon to shoot fish in a barrel).
3.   It must be possible to describe the problem in quantitative terms.
4.   All the mathematical relationships must be linear.

The goal of this chapter is to familiarize the reader with the nature of linear programming, rather than to teach its mastery as a mathematical technique. Let us therefore examine briefly a simple, illustrative case.

4   AN ILLUSTRATED PROBLEM

Suppose that you, as the manager of a pastry company, wish to determine the profit maximizing quantities of two types of pastries that you make each day. Your accountants inform you that the profits per dozen of fancy pastries is $.80, while for plain pastries the profits are $.60 per dozen.

Your objective (or the objective function, to use the mathematical term) can be stated:

Maximize Z:

$$Z = .8Q_f + .6Q_p$$

where:

Z = total profits
Q_f = quantity (in dozens) of fancy pastries
Q_p = quantity (in dozens) of plain pastries

You learn from your chef that to produce one dozen fancy pastries you need .5 lbs of pastry mix, .3 lbs of fancy topping, and 12.5 minutes of labor time. To produce a dozen plain pastries requires .7 lbs of pastry mix, no fancy topping, and 5.0 minutes of labor time. You have available 350 lbs of pastry mix, 108 lbs of fancy topping, and 5000 minutes of labor time; and while you may use less than these amounts, you cannot use more. Since we know how much of each input is required for each activity, these constraints can be expressed mathematically as:

$$.5Q_f + .7Q_p \leqslant 350$$
$$.3Q_f \qquad\qquad \leqslant 108$$
$$12.5Q_f + 5.0Q_p \leqslant 5000$$

Essentially, these equations say in different terms that the quantities of fancy (Q_f) and plain (Q_p) pastries produced must be such that the amount of each input, say pastry mix, that is used to make both fancy and plain pastries cannot exceed the amount of pastry mix available.

All of the above information can be plotted on a graph. Let us start with the constraints. Temporarily disregard the inequality sign and simply consider the first constraint as an equation in the form $.5Q_f + .7Q_p = 350$. When $Q_p = 0$, $Q_f = 700$, and when $Q_f = 0$, $Q_p = 500$. Other values that satisfy the equation fall on the straight line connecting these two points. If pastry mix were the only constraint, the inequality would mean that all points along and below the line are feasible. By similarly plotting all constraints, we outline an area of technical feasibility beyond which production is impossible (see the shaded area of Figure 11-1).

The objective function can also be plotted on the same graph. However, rather than yielding a single line, it yields a family of parallel lines, with each representing one level of total profits that increase as we move upward and to the right. By specifying a value for Z, say $360, we can solve the objective equation for all those values of Q_f and Q_p that satisfy the equation. These values fall on a straight line, often referred to as an equal or iso-profit line. This line and a few others are plotted in Figure 11-2. The reader should be awaare that there are an infinite number of such lines, each representing a different level of total profits.

Clearly, the objective is to reach the highest iso-profit line without violating the constraints. The optimal choice can readily be seen by combining Figures 11-1 and 11-2. This is done in Figure 11-3. The greatest profit is attained at the circled point where a corner of the feasibility area just touches the iso-profit line that passes through that point. Reading across and down we find that the optimum mix is 280 dozen fancy and 300 dozen plain pastries. Given the profits per dozen of each type of pastry, we can now compute the optimal level of profits, which turns out to be $404.*

Let us stop at this point and examine several of the assumptions employed in linear programming. First, as mentioned earlier, it is assumed that all mathematical relationships are linear. Thus, the objective function assumes that we will continue to make profits of $.80 and $.60 per dozen for each type of pastry, no matter how many dozens are produced. The production processes provided by the chef are also assumed to be linear, such that an $x\%$ increase in all inputs leads to an identical $x\%$ increase in outputs. A second assumption is that if two or more activities are conducted

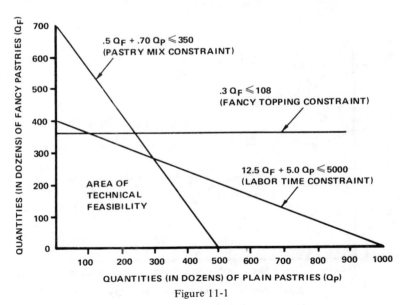

Figure 11-1

---

*Were the illustrative example to contain additional activities and constraints, we would be unable to use the above diagramatic approach. Without the aid of linear programming, an increase in the number of possible combinatons could make the trial and error search method incredibly laborious, if not practically impossible.

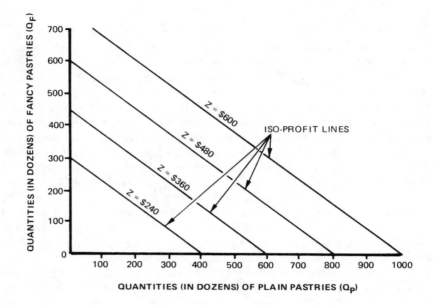

Figure 11-2

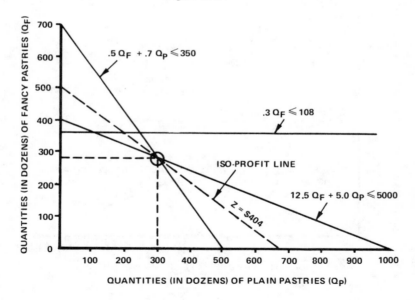

Figure 11-3

simultaneously, their joint output will be the same as would be the case if each were conducted in isolation. In other words, if external economies and diseconomies exist, they cancel each other out.

A challenge to either of these assumptions may be valid at any point. But even where relationships are recognized as nonlinear, linear approximations of the best solutions can serve as valuable guides to our thinking. It could be that within the ranges of values of the variables being considered, the assumption of linearity is not implausible. In any event, linear programming should be thought of as an aid to, rather than a substitute for, effective decision making.

5   THE DUAL

Every linear programming problem has associated with it a counterpart problem called its *dual*, where the original problem is known as the *primal*. The interesting aspect of the dual is that it assigns imputed values or shadow prices to the scarce resources. Without presenting the technique in detail let us simply consider the values that are imputed in the illustrated example and see how these values might be used. The shadow price for pastry mix is $.56, for a minute of labor it is $.0416 (or, $2.496 per hour), and for fancy topping it is zero. The last figure is probably the easiest to understand. A look at Figure 11-3 reveals that at the circled point not all of the fancy topping is used. The zero imputed price indicates that there is nothing to gain by purchasing more of it at a positive price. The reason is not that its market price is zero, but rather that more of it alone would do no good since there already is more than enough. The other two shadow prices indicate what the marginal increase in profits would be if either of them were to be increased by one unit, thus providing a guide as to how much one should be willing to pay for an additional unit of either input.

These shadow prices can also be used to promote a system of decentralized decision making. If we had two bakery divisions in our example, each with its own manager, they could be instructed to try to maximize their own divisional profits. Each time they used one of the resources, however, they would be charged the amounts indicated by the shadow prices. Each would learn, through trial and error or whatever, that the best he could do would be to produce 280 dozen fancy and 300 dozen plain pastries. At the shadow prices given, this would mean that the manager of fancy pastries would incur shadow costs of $224 [i.e., $(.5 \times 280 \times \$.56) + (12.5 \times 280 \times \$.0416)$], and the manager of plain pastries would incur shadow costs of $180 [i.e., $(.7 \times 300 \times \$.56) + (5.0 \times 300 \times \$.0416)$]. Notice that given their unit profits of $.80 and $.60, respectively, each would just break even! The mathematics are such that any other levels of output would produce shadow losses. Such losses, however, would not represent actual losses since indeed profits would be made. Rather these losses would represent the opportunity cost associated with anything less than an optimal allocation of resources.

Consider, for example, a situation where the same resources can be used to make either of two products, a shirt or a blouse. If the profits are $8 and $5 for the shirt and blouse, respectively, then the production of each blouse would result in an opportunity cost (shadow loss) of $3. Thus, both the primal and the dual provide ways of arriving at the optimal solution.

6   CONCLUSION

The example presented above was chosen simply for illustrative purposes. The fact that only two activities were involved allowed us to solve the problem by means of graphical analysis. The same would have been true had the problem contained many activities but only two constraints. In real-world problems that have many activities and many constraints, it is no longer possible to utilize the graphic approach; instead we must turn to the mathematical techniques developed by Dantzig and others. The essence of the problem, however, remains the same. While the manager of the pastry firm could just as easily have reached the optimal product mix via trial and error, it is highly unlikely that the same could be said of the optimal product mix for a firm like Nabisco, General Motors, duPont, or any other large multiproduct firm.

While the use of shadow prices for decentralized decision making in industry is limited, the technique has not been lost on decision makers in centrally planned economies. By solving a somewhat more complex, yet similar system of equations, they can set product and input prices at a level that leads to some desired allocation of resources in the presence of the decentralized market decisions of both consumers and producers.

7   SELECTED BIBLIOGRAPHY

Baumol, W.J. *Economic Theory and Operations Analysis.* 4th ed., Englewood Cliffs, N.J.: Prentice-Hall, 1977.

Charnes, A. and Cooper, W.W. *Management Models and Industrial Applications of Linear Programming,* 2 vols., New York: John Wiley and Sons, Inc., 1961.

Cooper, L., and Steinberg, D. *Methods and Applications of Linear Programming.* Philadelphia, Pa.: W.B. Saunders Co., 1974.

Dantzig, G.B. *Linear Programming and Extensions.* Princeton, N.J.: Princeton University Press, 1963.

Dorfman, R., Samuelson, P., and Solow, R. *Linear Programming and Economic Analysis.* New York: McGraw-Hill, 1958.

Intrilligator, M.D. *Mathematical Optimization and Economic Theory.* Englewood Cliffs, N.J.: Prentice-Hall, 1971.

Chapter 12
Mathematical Models and Forecasting

1   INTRODUCTION

We live in a world that is constantly changing — often it seems the only constant in our environment is change itself. Although change occurs both spontaneously and as the effect of identifiable causes, it is clear that as we continue to learn about the world in which we live, more and more of seemingly spontaneous change can be explained by science.

To gain some historical perspective on the matter, let us consider a phenomenon that has fascinated man for centuries: the motion of celestial bodies. Primitive man could not comprehend what caused the planets to move in the sky, and he therefore quite naturally attributed their motions to the will of the gods. From a scientific point of view, such an explanation explains nothing; it merely replaces one unknown with another. Not surprisingly, however, the mystery persisted until the seventeenth century, when Sir Isaac Newton hypothesized that the motion of the planets merely obey certain physical laws. Planetary motion, he argued, could be precisely determined through the application of mathematics. What emerged were Newton's now famous laws of motion, laws that still form the basis for what is known as classical mechanics. Newton's critics were quick to point out that these laws did not identify the *cause* of gravitational force — to which Newton responded, "I do not deal in metaphysical speculation. I lay down a law, and derive the phenomena from it" (cited in Bronowski, 1973). Even

Percy H. Hill et al., Making Decisions: A Multidisciplinary Introduction

today, we do not yet know the cause of gravitational force. Nevertheless, we have used Newton's laws to determine not only the motion of the planets, but also the motion of projectiles near the surface of the earth. The landing of men on the moon, in fact, was a technological feat made possible through the application of Newton's 300-year-old laws.

We now know that the motion of a physical body is almost completely predictable. And the same appears to be the case for many of the other changes we can observe in our environment. The flow of current along a wire, the production of heat by a boiler, the breaking point of a beam, are all phenomena of change that can be predicted with considerable accuracy. In the physical sciences, the discovery of naturally occurring laws is, by now, highly developed and is undoubtedly the reason why technology has progressed so rapidly in recent history.

In the life and social sciences, the quest for comparable cause-effect or stimulus-response relations has proceeded at a slower pace. It is much more difficult to predict what the Dow Jones average will be tomorrow than it is to determine when a particular spaceship will land on the moon. Nevertheless, there has been a good deal of progress made in the mathematical modeling of biological and social phenomena as well. Biologists know what will happen when they apply a stimulus to a nerve cell; physicians can predict the effect of a particular drug on their patients; manufacturers know what the market for their product is apt to be; and so forth. In fact, were we unable to predict the probable outcomes of such situations, the entire biological and social order would break down, and social life would become quite chaotic indeed.

The shared goal of science is to determine the underlying laws or principles that govern complexity. The classical scientific approach to this task consists of the formulation of hypotheses, the conduct of experiments, and the analysis of resulting data. A striking alternative to this approach has emerged in recent years with the advent of the digital computer. Through computer simulation, one can hypothesize certain laws of system interaction, program these "laws" into the digital computer, and observe whether the simulated response agrees with the real-world phenomenon. Such a method, we might add, more nearly parallels the method used by Newton; he obviously could not perform experiments involving the moon, hence he had to content himself with developing a hypothesis that could be verified through observation alone.

The real world is very complex, so much so that none of us ever really deals with all its aspects. Instead, we formulate simpler models of reality that reduce complexity to more manageable proportions. Newton, for example ignored the color, shape, texture, of a physical body and considered only its mass. We filter out extraneous "noise" and concentrate instead on what we regard as important. What is important to each of us is a function of our role in society. Physicians have more detailed models of the human body than do their patients; lawyers have more detailed models of the legal system than do their clients; television repairmen have a more detailed model of a television set than do their customers. Our environment is thus full of complex systems, which we attempt to understand through the development of models which are of varying complexity. In the following sections, we will see how decision making in the real world may be facilitated through the development and application of simple mathematical models.

2   FORECASTING

We often make decisions based upon what we expect will happen in the future. We regularly put money in a savings account, in the expectation that it will be spent on next year's vacation; we attend college in order to prepare for a future career; we move to the country because we expect urban life to become increasingly hectic and unpleasant. To better anticipate the future, we note certain trends and try to extrapolate their future position. Trends with which we are all familiar include inflation in the economy, population growth, the increase in leisure time, and so forth. Many of these trends are quite consistent, and therefore fairly predictable. We can determine, with a fair degree of accuracy, how much a loaf of bread is likely to cost in ten years, the year in which the nation's population will reach 230 million, or the number of hours per week we will need to work by the year 2000.

Thus, although forecasting is an activity we generally ascribe only to the weatherman, we engage in forecasting almost daily. Let us now turn to those mathematical models that allow the forecast of future trends, thereby helping us to make more effective decisions.

2.1 The No Change Forecast

We often assume that the features of our environment are invariant. We come to expect that our next class will begin on time, that the dining hall will be open when we arrive for dinner, that our favorite television program will be broadcast at the scheduled time. Many of us feel quite comfortable with this orderly, predictable pattern; and in the unlikely event that our schedule is disrupted we may experience various degrees of anxiety.

Over the long term, however, we expect that things will change. Trends occur over the long run that are imperceptible over the short term. Although we know that we grew constantly during our childhood years, the change was not apparent from day to day; it was obvious only when we went visiting aunts and uncles who saw us less frequently. Over the short term, then, a no change forecast may help us to schedule our activities quite effectively. Over the long term, however, most things do change, and an awareness of such trends may often lead us to make better decisions.

2.2   The Constant Rate of Change Forecast

Assume for the moment that you are on the Massachusetts Turnpike (a toll road that runs the length of the state), heading toward Boston. You have stopped at a rest area exactly 25 miles from the New York border to do a bit of calculating. If you maintain an average speed of 55 miles per hour, how long will it take to get to Boston?

To solve this problem, of course, you must know that the Mass. Pike is 135 miles long. Knowing this, you might now reason that since you have already traveled 25 miles, you must be 110 miles from Boston. At a constant speed of 55 miles per hour, it will therefore take two hours to go the 110 miles and reach your destination.

Simple enough. But what if the numbers had not come out so evenly? Would you have solved the problem as readily? An alternative to the above verbal analysis of this problem is depicted in Figure 12-1. In this graph the distance from the New York border has been plotted on the y-axis and the time, starting from this instant, on the x-axis. At this time ($T=0$), you are located 25 miles from the New York border. At the end of the first hour, you will be 55 miles from this point or 80 miles from the New York border; at the end of the second hour, you will be 135 miles from the New York border − or in Boston. Note that the points all lie along a straight line on the distance versus time graph. An obvious advantage of this graphic method of forecasting is that you can predict how long it will take to get to various intermediate points (Springfield, Worcester) as well as to Boston. Springfield is at about the 45-mile mark, and therefore according to the graph, you should be there in about 1/3 of an hour, or 20 minutes. Likewise, you should pass Worcester at the 90-mile mark, in about 1.2 hours, or 1 hour and 12 minutes.

An alternative method of forecasting, and one that is more accurate, is to calculate the distance. To do this we must first determine the rate equation, which also happens to be the equation of the straight line in Figure 12-1.

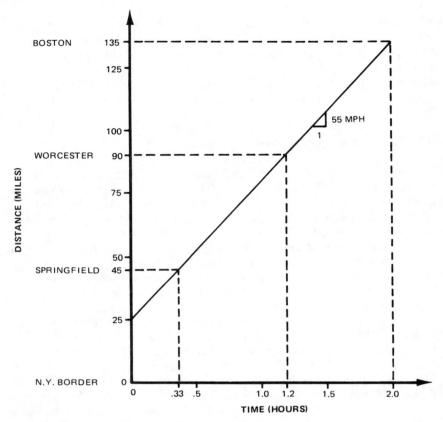

Figure 12-1. Distance Along The Mass. Pike Versus Time, At A Constant
Rate of 55 mph.

The rate equation is:

$$D_T = D_0 + R \times T$$

where:

T	= time from this instant
D_0	= distance along the pike at time zero (25 miles)
D_T	= distance along the pike at time T
R	= rate of speed (55 miles per hour)

The reader can see that this equation is equivalent to the equation of a
straight line on the y versus the x-axis, ($y=mx+b$), where m is the slope, and
b is the y-intercept.
At time zero:

$$D_0 = 25 + 55 \times 0$$
$$D_0 = 25 \text{ miles}$$

At time $T = 2$ hours:

$$
\begin{aligned}
D_2 \quad &= 25 + 55 \times 2 \\
&= 25 + 110 \\
&= 135 \text{ miles}
\end{aligned}
$$

The rate equation can also be used to determine the time at which you will reach a certain distance:

$$
\begin{aligned}
D_T - D_0 &= RT \\
\frac{D_T - D_0}{R} &= T
\end{aligned}
$$

Recall that Springfield was at the 45-mile mark. To calculate how long it takes to reach Springfield, substitute these values into the equation:

$$
\begin{aligned}
\frac{45 - 25}{55} = \frac{20}{55} &= .36 \text{ hrs} \\
&= 21.8 \text{ minutes}
\end{aligned}
$$

Compare this time to the less accurate value of 20 minutes we obtained graphically.

In summary, the values for variables that change at a constant rate can be forecast in a straightforward manner. You can determine how old you will be in the year 2000, how long it will take to fill a swimming pool, even whether to cross the street or not in front of an oncoming car that appears to be traveling at a constant speed. Not all variables, however, can be expected to change at a constant rate. The next section considers another commonly occurring trend, one that exhibits a constantly accelerating rate of change.

2.3 The Constant Percentage Rate of Change Forecast

There are many examples of variables that change, not at a constant rate, but at an increasing rate. For example, we are all vitally aware of the effects of inflation. Inflation occurs because prices seem to change at a constant percentage rate, resulting in the alarming condition known as *exponential growth.* Consider the salary you will earn when you graduate from college. Assume that you graduate from college in 1984, and that you obtain a job paying $15,000 annually. If we also assume that your salary will increase at a fixed rate of 8% per year for the next forty years, then we can determine your salary at the end of this period by the following method. At the end of the first year:

$$S_1 = S_0 + IS_0$$

where:

S_0 = your salary at graduation
S_n = your salary at the end of the nth year
I = the annual percentage increase

For this particular case:

$$
\begin{aligned}
S_1 &= \$15,000 + (.08)(\$15,000) \\
    &= \$15,000 + \$1,200 \\
    &= \$16,200
\end{aligned}
$$

So your salary will have increased by $1,200 to $16,200 at the end of the first year. Note that we can factor the S_0 term in the above expression to obtain:

$$S_1 = (1 + I)S_0$$

Similarly, at the end of the second year, your salary can be calculated by:

$$S_2 = (1 + I)S_1$$

Substituting the expression for S_1:

$$
\begin{aligned}
S_2 &= (1 + I)(1 + I)S_0 \\
    &= (1 + I)^2 S_0
\end{aligned}
$$

At the end of the third year:

$$S_3 = (1 + I)^3 S_0$$

and at the end of the nth year:

$$S_n = (1 + I)^n S_0$$

In this expression, note that n appears as an exponent of $(1 + I)$. This means that your salary undergoes annual exponential growth. So, at the end of the fortieth year:

$$S_{40} = (1 + .08)^{40} \, (\$15,000)$$
$$= 21.725 \times \$15,000$$
$$= \$325,868$$

It may seem difficult to believe, but at the end of forty years, given an annual 8% raise, salary will be almost 22 times as great as it was upon graduation: *almost a third of a million dollars per year!* Unfortunately, a 75-cent loaf of bread today will cost over $16 if food prices also rise at the same 8%. Clearly, then, it is not the actual dollar amount of your salary that is important but its relative buying power. This is particularly disconcerting to those on fixed income.

Using the same formula, we can forecast how much your annual salary will be for each of the intervening years as well. The results are listed in Table 12-1.

Table 12-1. Annual Salary over the Next 40 Years, Assuming A Starting Salary of $15,000, and an Increase of 8% Per Year

Year	Salary	Year	Salary	Year	Salary
0	$15,000	14	$44,058	28	$129,407
1	16,200	15	47,583	29	139,759
2	17,496	16	51,389	30	150,940
3	18,896	17	55,500	31	163,015
4	20,407	18	59,940	32	176,056
5	22,040	19	64,736	33	190,141
6	23,803	20	69,914	34	205,352
7	25,707	21	75,508	35	221,780
8	27,764	22	81,548	36	239,523
9	29,985	23	88,072	37	258,684
10	32,384	24	95,118	38	279,379
11	34,975	25	102,727	39	301,729
12	37,773	26	110,945	40	325,868
13	40,794	27	119,821		

Since it is easier to spot a trend in a graphic portrayal than on the basis of a column of figures, the salary data by time have been plotted in Figure 12-2. Unlike Figure 12-1, whose graph clearly followed a straight line, Figure 12-2 shows that salary increases at a faster and faster rate as time progresses. Notice that salary has nearly doubled in the first nine years, going from

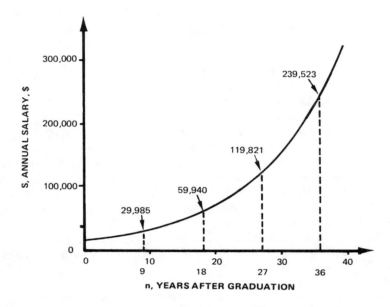

Figure 12-2. Salary Data of Table 12-1 Plotted Versus Time

$15,000 to $29,985. In the same interval of time, from nine to eighteen
years after graduation, we note that salary has nearly doubled again, going
from $29,985 to $59,940. It seems that every nine years, your salary will
double.

What we have just observed is a well-known characteristic of variables
that experience exponential growth: they have a constant doubling time. A
rule of thumb for estimating the doubling time of a variable given its annual
percentage rate of change is:

$$DT = \frac{0.72}{I}$$

where DT = doubling time

The population of the United States has had a doubling time of about thirty
years over the last hundred years which, according to our rule of thumb,
would correspond to an annual percentage increase of 2.4%. It may be
surprising to note that so small a growth percentage would result in this
short doubling time but such is the nature of exponential growth.

Returning to the issue of your escalating salary, we have noted that it is
possible to calculate its size (but not necessarily its value), and that when we

plot it against time it results in a curve with a constantly increasing slope. Unlike the straight-line graph of distance versus time for the car traveling at 55 miles per hour (Figure 12-1), which was easy to draw and therefore quite useful in estimating arrival times, the graph of salary versus time (Figure 12-2) is more difficult to draw and for that reason is less useful in forecasting. Fortunately, if these same data are plotted on a semilogarithmic graph, as shown in Figure 12-3, the data points do lie on a straight line. In a semilogarithmic graph, the scale of the x-axis is linear, as in Figure 12-2; the y-axis, however, is scaled logarithmically. Recall that a logarithmic scale is simply a ratio scale along which equal increments represent equal ratios of the variable. Note that the distance along the y-axis from \$10,000 to \$100,000 is the same as the distance from \$100,000 to \$1,000,000, corresponding to the same ratio of 10 to 1.

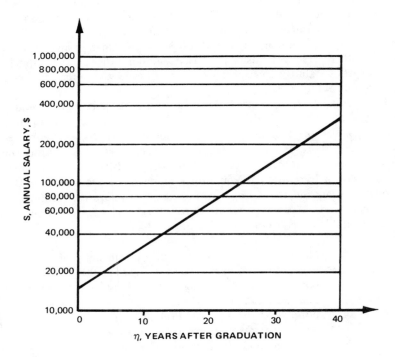

Figure 12-3. Salary Data of Table 12-1 Plotted on Semilogarithmic Coordinates

Forecasters often use semilogarithmic graphs to identify an exponential trend. For instance, assuming that the population of the United States continues to increase exponentially at its past percentage rate, the current population should increase from 220 million to 440 million, by the year

2008! Although such forecasts may be fairly accurate over the short term, they can be far off the mark over the long term. The reason, of course, is that such forecasts do not take into account the many factors that could affect population growth. The next section considers the effects of one such factor.

2.4 Dynamic Forecasting

A variable that experiences a constant rate of change allows us to forecast a linear increase, whereas a variable that experiences a constant percentage rate of change allows us to forecast an exponential increase. The difference between these two forecasts was of great interest to Thomas Robert Malthus. In 1830, he published an essay entitled simply *Population*, which was to become the subject of much discussion even to the present day. In it he wrote ". . . population, when unchecked, increases in a geometrical ratio [exponentially], and subsistence for man in an arithmetical ratio [linearly]." His conclusion was that, sooner or later, the population would surpass its ability to feed itself, at which time widespread famine and disaster would result.

From what we have learned about the extrapolation of such trends, we can easily show that the Malthusian forecast is quite correct, given plausible assumptions. Let us consider an isolated community of 20,000 people, each of whom consumes 0.5 tons of food per year. The community must therefore produce at least 10,000 tons of food per year to survive. Fortunately, our hypothetical community managed to produce 15,000 tons of food this year, and they expect to increase this figure by 1,000 tons per year in the future. Given a population growth rate of 3.5% per year , when will the inevitable crisis occur? To solve this problem let:

FP_T = amount of food produced, in tons, during year T
FP_0 = amount of food produced this year (15,000 tons)
K_1 = constant increase in food production (1000 tons per year)
P_T = population in year T
P_0 = population this year (20,000 people)
K_2 = constant percentage rate of population growth (3.5%)
K_3 = constant food consumption (0.5 tons per person per year)

From the above definitions, it can be determined that the linear forecast in food production is:

$$FP_T = FP_0 + K_1 \times T$$
$$= 15,000 + 1000 \times T, \text{tons}$$

and the exponential forecast of population is:

$$P_T = P_0 (1 + K_2)^T$$
$$= 20,000(1.035)^T \text{ , people}$$

Since each person consumes 0.5 tons of food per year:

$$FR_T = K_3 \times P_T$$
$$= 0.5 \times 20,000(1.035)^T$$
$$= 10,000(1.035)^T, \text{ tons}$$

where FR_T = the amount of food required to feed the population during the year T.

The amount of food produced (FP_T), and the amount of food required (FR_T) have been calculated over the next eighty years; the results are plotted in Figure 12-4. Note that in about the fifty-eighth year, the two trends will cross and a crisis will occur. Before they cross, there is a food surplus (feast); but after they cross there is a food shortage (famine). This was the gloomy Malthusian forecast.

Like Newton, Malthus had many critics. They were quick to point out that although Malthus did demonstrate that the two curves would indeed intersect, the situation he described did not truly represent reality. The critics argued that Malthus' model was too simple. Perhaps its biggest flaw was the omission of any interaction between the two trends – trends that were assumed by Malthus to be unaffected by each until a crisis occurred. Perhaps it would be more realistic to expect that the amount of food produced would have an effect on population growth long before the time of crisis. Malthus was aware of this very possibility:

> Population is always and everywhere, in some measure, pressing against the available food supply. If the means of subsistence should suddenly become abundant, . . . the remaining population, . . . will be apt to marry earlier than otherwise, have more children, and die later. In a short period of time, population will thus have adjusted to the means of subsistence . . . and . . . soon once again be in excess of available food. The oscillation created by the permanent imbalance between food and people is a feature of every country, county, and hamlet in every period of its history. (Malthus, 1960, p. XIX)

According to this argument, even though food production increases at a constant linear rate, population size does not continue to grow exponentially; instead, it oscillates above and below its ability to feed itself. Is it possible to forecast these oscillations? Yes, but not merely by extrapolating trends. The mathematical model must be modified to include the assumed interaction between food production and population size.

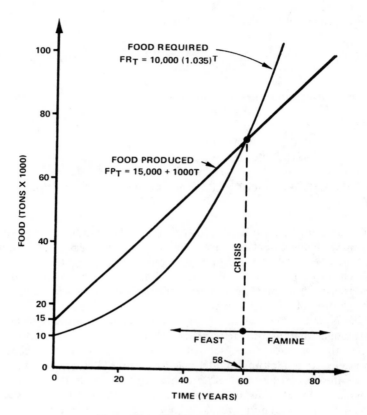

Figure 12-4. The Malthusian Forecast

Consider the *rate* at which the population changes. In the case where no interaction is expected with food supply, the population at the end of the first year is:

$$P_1 \quad = P_0(1 + K_2)^1$$
$$= P_0 + K_2 \times P_0$$

That is, it is equal to the initial population plus a change of $(K_2 \times P_0)$ people. The rate of change of population during that first year is therefore $(K_2 \times P_0)$ people per year. At any time, then, the population growth rate (PGR) is given by:

$$PGR \quad = K_2 \times P, \text{ people per year}$$

That is, for a population of 20,000 people growing at the rate of 3.5% per year, the population will increase at the rate of:

$$PGR \quad = .035 \times 20,000$$
$$= 700 \text{ people per year}$$

Malthus, of course, believed that the population growth rate would also be affected by food supply. The more the available food, the faster the population should grow. Likewise, given a food shortage, the population growth rate should decrease and even become negative. This can be expressed mathematically as:

$$PGR \quad = K_2 \times P + K_4 \times FS$$

where

$FS \quad$ = food supply, in tons
$K_4 \quad$ = a constant, people per year per ton of food supply

The constant K_4 is the key element in this revised mathematical model. If there is a food surplus, then the population growth rate increases by an amount equal to $(K_4 \times FS)$ people per year. Conversely, if there is a food shortage, FS is negative, and the population growth rate decreases by this amount. Assuming an initial food supply of 6000 tons, and a value of K_4 equal to two people per year for each 100 tons of food supply, then:

$$PGR \quad = .035 \times 20,000 + \frac{2}{100} \times 6000$$
$$= 700 + 120$$
$$= 820 \text{ people per year}$$

But what constitutes the food supply? If we assume that in any given year the difference between the amount of food produced and the amount required is added to the amount of food in storage, it is this stored food that constitutes the food supply. The rate at which food is deposited in (or withdrawn from) storage (FSR) is therefore given by:

$$FSR \quad = FP - FR, \text{ tons per year}$$

This assumes, of course, that food can be maintained in storage indefinitely, with no spoilage.

This new interactive Malthusian model can be made even more complex, to reflect reality more adequately. For instance, nothing has yet been included to describe the interaction between the population and the amount of food produced. Similarly, the type of interaction postulated between population and the amount of food in storage is simply additive; a more realistic model might have involved a more complex mathematical function.

A mathematical solution to the system equations for an interactive Malthusian model is beyond the scope of this book. Although these particular system equations may indeed be solved mathematically, even a competent mathematician would have difficulty in solving system equations that are much more complex. It is precisely because of the unavoidable complexity of many mathematical models that investigators often use the digital computer to calculate approximate forecasts.

The interactive Malthusian model described above was programmed on a digital computer. The results of a particular simulation run are shown in Figure 12-5. Compare this forecast with that of the noninteractive

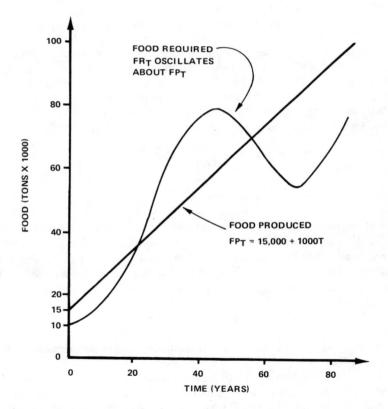

Figure 12-5. Forecast Using The Interactive Malthusian Model (K_4=.02)

Malthusian model of Figure 12-4. All system parameters are the same except that, in the latter case, the population was assumed to increase by an additional two people per year for each 100 tons of food in storage. Notice that this caused the amount of food required (and therefore the population) to oscillate about the constantly increasing forecast of food production — exactly what Malthus had predicted. Changing the parameter values alters the amplitude and frequency of these oscillations but does not alter the oscillatory nature of the response.

This computer simulation does not, of course, prove that the model we derived uniquely represents reality, nor that Malthus was correct. By programming the digital computer, however, it has become possible to develop a representation of an actual system; the model can be manipulated to see what would happen if food were rationed, if birth control were promoted, if agricultural production were increased, and so forth.

Since there appears to be no apparent limit to the amount of information that the digital computer can process, what if one were to formulate a much more complex model of the interaction of population size and food production — a model that included, for example, the arable land area, the populations of animal species, the level of industry, and the pollution level? Armed with such a comprehensive model, might it not be possible to forecast the future state of affairs of the United States, or even of the entire world? Some progress has been made recently in this direction by a small group of researchers who are concerned with the future of mankind. (See Meadows, 1972.) In this model the researchers have recognized that lack of an adequate food supply is only *one* of the possible threats to man's existence; running out of natural resources would be equally devastating. Similarly, the same industrialization that has allowed man to survive in ever larger numbers may eventually envelop us in a sea of pollution and take its toll. Their model includes the interactions among five principal variables: population, food, industrialization, natural resources, and pollution. The interactions are very complex and the forecasts derived from this model are often quite alarming. The results of the world simulation have met with praise from some quarters, and criticism from others. As an exercise in learning to understand the workings of the world system, however, it represents a very significant accomplishment. The digital computer has been used quite effectively in engineering and the sciences to simulate complex systems. Perhaps it can be of similar help to us in the attempt to manage our planet.

3   CONCLUSION

Before man ever set foot on the moon, countless simulations of the trajectory of the space craft were performed on the computer. In a sense, the mission was flown over and over on the ground before the decision was ever made to leave the launching pad. At the other extreme, how many equally important decisions are made by well-meaning government officials, planners, doctors, or businessmen, without the benefit of forecasting methods? It has been shown by Forrester that often such intuitive decisions may result in aggravating rather than solving the perceived problem. The implications are alarming.

Mathematical modeling techniques are now being applied with increasing frequency to the life and social sciences as well as the physical sciences. For example, the circulation of blood through the body has been simulated on the computer and has contributed valuable information to decision makers in the artificial heart program; the continuing deterioration of the inner city, despite massive efforts at urban renewal, was actually forecasted by a computer simulation. If we knew more about human nature, and if computers were available at the time, one might wonder whether we could have forecasted the (counterintuitive?) effects that prohibition would have on the Roaring 20's. Of course, we will never know, but it is interesting to contemplate.

4   SELECTED BIBLIOGRAPHY

Blesser, William B. *A Systems Approach to Biomedicine.* New York: McGraw-Hill, 1969.
Bronowski, J. *The Ascent of Man.* Boston: Little, Brown, 1973. Also available in Spanish edition, *El Ascenso del Hombre.* Bogota, Colombia: Fondo Educativo Interamericano — and Reading, Mass.: Addison-Wesley, General Books Div., 1979.
Forrester, Jay W. *Principles of Systems.* Cambridge, Mass.: Wright-Allen Press, 1968.
Forrester, Jay W. *Urban Dynamics.* Cambridge, Mass.: MIT Press, 1969.
Linstone, Harold A., and Simmonds, W.H. Clive (Eds). *Futures Research,* Reading, Mass.: Addison-Wesley, Advanced Book Program, 1979.
Malthus, T.R. *On Population.* New York: Modern Library, 1960.
Meadows, D. et al. *Towards Global Equilibrium: Collected Papers.* Cambridge, Mass.: Wright-Allen Press, 1973.
Smith, Jon M. *Mathematical Modeling & Digital Simulation for Engineers and Scientists.* New York: Wiley-Interscience, 1977.

Appendix
Case Studies

HOW TO STUDY A CASE

Many textbooks provide exercises either at the end of each chapter or at the end of the book, so that the reader (student) can be drilled on the subject matter. In this section of this book we provide instead a number of case studies. We have found that the case method of instruction is particularly well suited to learning about the decision process. In these pages you will find a collection of case studies in the form of a narrative describing a real-life situation (sometimes fiction, sometimes fact) in which a decision-making situation is characteristically explored. In each case you are asked to take the role of the decision maker. From that vantage point you should then proceed to analyze all of the elements of the case so that you can decide what you would do if you really were in the situation as given.

Each case has been written to present you with the same information available to the decision maker. That does not necessarily mean that *all* of the information is there. On the contrary, you may recommend that the decision maker defer action until more knowledge is obtained. Or you may appropriate further facts when needed as long as they are not implausible or inconsistent with what the narrative provides. Enough is provided in each of the cases to start you on your way, and to enable you to begin the twin tasks of analysis and recommendation.

As you work on the case, develop your evidence and arguments carefully. Be prepared to produce qualitative and quantitative materials to support your conclusions; it is likely that your arguments will be challenged by someone else who sees the case quite differently. Indeed, at their best, case studies are more than mere written assignments; they provide the basis for a lively exchange in the classroom.

The cases stated below should help you to acquire some knowledge about a variety of subjects by dealing selectively and intensively with problems in each of the disciplines. In the process you will come to recognize that there are some underlying regularities in most decision situations. And, as you become increasingly proficient in case analysis, we hope you will also become increasingly proficient at coping with your own personal and professional decisions. Remember, though, learning through the case method is different. Unlike other methods, this one does not teach you the "right" answers. It will help you to learn how to ask the right questions.

Once you become more experienced in the study of cases you will no doubt develop your own preferred style of preparation. In the beginning, however, you might try to follow these steps before composing your final analysis.

1.   Immerse yourself in the case; get to know the details.
2.   Analyze the case; sort out the cast of characters; develop a chronology of events; identify the basic issues (e.g., objectives, problems, risks, opportunities, values, attitudes); consider all the alternatives.
3.   Think of any theoretical material that would be helpful in understanding the case; put it to work in your analysis.
4.   Mull the case over; put yourself in the role of the decision maker; consider how you would see things, and how you would feel, were you required to reach a decision not as a mere exercise but in real life.
5.   Develop one or more recommendations for *each* decision point.
6.   Before you finish your analysis, review it one last time. Use your imagination. Have you analyzed and recommended creatively? Have you gone beyond the initial confines of the case study (if necessary) in order to acquire further information and devise additional alternatives?

CASE STUDIES

Case 004/1

SHOULD FRED TAKE THE JOB OR NOT?*

Fred has just received his Ph.D. in nuclear chemical engineering and finds it difficult to get a job suited to his training and interests. He would like a teaching post at the university, but there are no vacancies. He and his wife have two young children, and she supported them through his graduate training, so their present circumstances put considerable strain on the whole family. Obviously, the situation would be much improved if Fred could get a good job. Fred is not very sturdy, so he is virtually unable to take any job that requires a long daily commute. The family is very attached to the locality where they live and is reluctant to move, even if Fred could get a good job elsewhere. Unfortunately, the economy is in one of its periodic slumps, and no job seems to be in the offing.

One of Fred's former professors says that he would be glad to recommend Fred for a job in a nearby laboratory doing research on power generation by methods of nuclear fission. Fred says that he could not apply for such a post, since he is strongly opposed to the development of nuclear fission power. He believes that the risk of a nuclear accident is too severe to be ignored, and that there is absolutely no solution to the problem of safe disposal of nuclear wastes. The professor admits that he, too, is opposed to nuclear power generation, but reminds Fred that his refusal to take the job will not make it or the research project disappear. What is more, if Fred refuses to apply, another engineer will probably get the job, an ambitious chap not inhibited by moral objections to nuclear power generation, someone who is likely to use all his efforts to accelerate its development – the very reverse of what Fred wants. The professor admits that he would rather see Fred get the job. Fred's wife has no strong objection to his taking the job; frankly, she wishes he would take it so that she could quit hers and spend more time at home with the children.

What should Fred do? What ethical principles should he rely on in making his decision?

---

*Inspired by Bernard Williams, "A Critique of Utilitarianism," in J. J. C. Smart and Bernard Williams, *Utilitarianism For and Against,* Cambridge, Eng.: Cambridge University Press, 1973, pp. 97-98.

Case 004/2

SHOULD THE COMPANY RELOCATE OR NOT?

An electronics firm in Somerville, Massachusetts has decided to move its business to southern New Hampshire, about fifty miles away. Its Somerville plant is in a century-old, inefficient building, expensive to insure, and with access by truck only through congested streets at a considerable distance from major freeway intersections. An entirely new plant, designed according to the company's current and projected needs, has many advantages including easy access by rail and plane as well as by truck. Insurance and the tax climate in rural New Hampshire are much more favorable than in urban Massachusetts.

The chief factor favoring the move is the cheaper labor force across the state line. The company intends not only to move its plant but also to leave most of its current employees behind. About 200 salaried workers will be transferred to the new plant, but 600 wage earners will be laid off and only 250 hired to replace them, a reduction in work force made possible by increased automation and subcontracting at the new plant. This will have considerable economic advantages, because the current labor force is older, under expensive union labor contracts with lots of seniority and substantial pension contributions from the company, whereas in New Hampshire the company can hire younger nonunion workers exclusively. To smooth the transition, the company gave its current work force two weeks notice. It has refused to offer any severance pay for the 600 workers to be laid off (their contract did not call for any), and has announced that it will not rehire any of them even if they are willing to move north with the company.

When the workers learned of the company's plans they were furious. The bulk of the labor force lives within walking distance of the Somerville plant, and faces immediate and probably prolonged (for the older persons, permanent) unemployment unless they relocate; there is no likelihood that existing employers in the vicinity can absorb more than a handful of the unemployed, nor is there any prospect of a comparable business moving into the vacated plant. The workers have organized picket lines around the plant, threatened to strike, and sent a delegation to the governor's office to get help in forcing the company to rescind its move-and-layoff plans. The workers believe they face unfair economic hardship, neighborhood disruption, and domestic distress if the company's plans cannot be stopped. They claim that they at least deserve severance pay — the company can afford it — and active company assistance in finding new jobs, as well as first chance at being rehired in the new location even if at lower wages.

The company's management is concentrated in the hands of its young president, who took over the company three years ago and rescued it from the brink of bankruptcy. For this he was widely hailed throughout the community. During the past fiscal year, the company reported a net profit of $2.3 million on gross sales of $17.6 million. When informed of the workers' protest and demands in reaction to the company's announced move to New Hampshire, the company president called a press conference at which he denounced the narrow views of the employees. "If I hadn't taken over this plant and run it as I did," he said, with a certain trace of bitterness, "they'd have been out of work three years ago because the previous management would have had to close down then. Instead, they've had three years of uninterrupted employment at good wages. But we simply can't continue to meet the competition if we keep our plant here in Somerville and pay the sky-rocketing labor costs under our current contracts. If we don't move now, before you know it we'll be right back where we were three years ago. It's that tough. The workers just don't want to accept the harsh realities of the company's predicament. As for the idea that the workers 'deserve' better from management, that's poppycock. Everything we're proposing to do is perfectly legal. They get paid for their work, and have to take their chances in the marketplace just as management does. Nobody guarantees the company a profit, so the company cannot guarantee the workers a job either. We're not only acting within our rights in making this move now, we're also doing the best thing for everyone concerned, even though the workers don't see it that way — and I suppose can't be expected to."

Both sides in this dispute turn to you, an impartial and ethically sensitive analyst, in the belief that you will vindicate their position. From the moral point of view, what criticisms, if any, would you make of the position taken by management? Of labor?

Case 004/3

WHO SHOULD DIE WHEN NOT ALL CAN LIVE?*

You are among thirty survivors of a shipwreck, crowded into a lifeboat designed for no more than two dozen adults. In the boat with you are two others from the ship's crew, three married couples (one with a baby), three children whose parents went down with the ship, three elderly men and women, six other women, and the rest men, three of whom were very severely injured during the wreck. Already many of the thirty are seasick and most are terrified. It is a dark night, and the weather continues to worsen.

---

*Inspired by *United States v. Holmes,* Circuit Court, Eastern District of Pennsylvania, 1842, 26 Federal Cases 360, #15,383.

The boat is already shipping water at the gunwales; if the sea gets any rougher the boat is sure to swamp and sink. It looks as if the only hope for any to survive is for five or six persons to get out of the boat, leaving the rest to bail and row in the hope that dawn will bring a slackening wind and chance of rescue.

As senior surviving ship's officer, and an experienced seaman, you are looked to for leadership. Having decided that the boat *must* lighten its human load, you ask for volunteers to jump overboard and take their chances in the icy waves. No one responds, even though all sense the danger to the overcrowded boat. You are not surprised at their selfishness, and you quickly review the alternative methods of deciding who shall be the unlucky half dozen.

Voting or a contest of some sort, which might do well enough in another situation, you immediately discard as unworkable here. One method that occurs to you is drawing straws — that seems fair enough — except that it, too, may be unfeasible in the situation. Then you think of a different sort of random selection process, such as designating every fifth person as the unlucky ones. You also consider throwing out the last six people who got into the boat, whoever they turn out to be (*you* are not among them). The thought crosses your mind to calculate the utilities of all possible combinations of twenty-four survivors, and throw overboard the six whose utility is the lowest; but this seems too time-consuming and conjectural under the circumstances. Yet another thought suddenly occurs to you. Perhaps you and the other crewmen have a duty to the passengers to give them safe voyage, and so the three of you must be among the six to abandon the boat however the other three are determined! You are also tempted to dismiss all these vexing ethical considerations and simply grab the weakest and nearest to you and with the help of other able-bodied men throw them overboard as quickly as possible and get it over with. You do not have much time to weigh these alternative methods of decision making — perhaps no more than a few minutes, to judge by the waves and wind, before panic or disaster overtakes all of you.

What method of decision should you choose and why? What result does this method yield, i.e., who goes overboard and who stays?

Case 005/1

WAITING TILL THE SUN SHINES NELLIE

Nellie has just placed a phone call to an airline to make a plane reservation. Her call is intercepted by a tape recording informing her that all phone lines are temporarily busy and that her call will be "handled by the next available salesperson." She has just been put "on hold," and she now begins to wait. Perhaps Nellie does so because, on the basis of her previous experience in similar situations, she believes that her call is likely to be answered within a minute or two — and so she deliberately decides to wait. Perhaps Nellie is not aware of having made any decision at all, and has simply started to wait because it seems like the obvious thing to do.

In any event, she waits for a while. Before long, several minutes have elapsed without any salesperson coming to the phone. Was this a bad time to try to make a plane reservation, Nellie wonders to herself? Perhaps she should hang up and try again — either now, in the hope that she will be lucky enough to get a free line to a salesperson; or later, in the expectation that fewer calls will be coming in then. On the other hand, there's no guarantee that she will be able to make her reservation more quickly if she hangs up and tries again. Moreover, isn't she being just restless and a bit impatient, she wonders to herself. Why not hang on for a few more minutes and accomplish her objective of making a plane reservation? Her call will no doubt be answered soon enough.

And so Nellie waits some more. Now several more minutes elapse, as she twiddles her thumbs and begins to listen carefully for the tiny clicks and buzzes that will signal the impending arrival of the airlines salesperson. Still more time elapses. Finally, Nellie glances at her watch, and finds to her amazement that she's been waiting on the phone for nearly fifteen minutes! Surely there's been some sort of electronic mistake at her expense, and she's become "lost" on hold. Can the airlines personnel possibly really be that busy? It seems unlikely, but how can she know for sure? Probably, Nellie thinks to herself, she should hang up and try again later — she's already wasted fifteen minutes of her valuable time, why waste another moment?

On the other hand, assuming that she has not been lost on hold, the fifteen minutes that Nellie has spent waiting have probably brought her closer to her goal; surely the salesperson will be there to take care of her any second. And anyway, she's got to make her reservation sometime, so she might as well do it now. To quit now will have meant that Nellie wasted all this time for nothing. Why not be patient for a minute or two more?

No, Nellie reasons with grim determination and conviction. She's in a trap. She did the wrong thing in waiting so long, and now she should "cut her losses" and get out of this miserable situation. Even as Nellie is in the act of hanging up the receiver in frustration, however, she finds herself bending over the phone, in the hope and expectation that the salesperson will return at this very moment and allow her to accomplish the objective that brought her to the phone in the first place.

What should Nellie have done in this situation to avoid becoming entrapped in the first place? Having gotten trapped, how would you suggest that Nellie go about getting out? That is, what sort of decision rule(s) might Nellie develop and employ in this situation?

Case 005/2

A BIG NIGHT ON THE TOWN

John Doe lives upcountry on an isolated farm. He has come to the big city for a night on the town. The last Peter Pan bus back home is scheduled to depart in a few hours, and John knows that he must be on this bus. Still, he does have a few hours left in which to have one last fling, an experience made more poignant by John's knowledge that it will be months, perhaps years before he can return to the city.

John quickly decides that he would like nothing better than to go to a movie. But which one should he choose? Thirty feet down the street to his right is a glittering marquee that tempts him with the premiere of an outer-space spectacular, *Expanding Universe*. The film has already received critical acclaim and, judging by the line that has already formed outside the theater, it is clearly going to be a box-office sensation. It stars many of his favorite actors and actresses, and is certain to be a great adventure. The Roxy, where the film is playing, is a first-run movie house, hence a ticket is likely to prove very expensive. Based on past experience, he is absolutely certain that it will be years before *Expanding Universe* comes to his neck of the upcountry woods. Clearly he should go to see this movie, even if it costs a few dollars more than he would like to spend.

Just as John is about to make his move, he glances around the street one last time. Thirty feet down the street to his left is an unprepossessing little art theater that is advertising a devilishly tempting alternative: *Coconut Feathers,* starring the Minx Brothers. *Coconut Feathers* is a comic classic, a film that John last saw when he was too young to really enjoy it, and he has been waiting for years to see it again. Unfortunately, there are no art theaters upcountry, and so the opportunities to see this film have been few and very far between. Judging by the modest appearance of the movie house, it would not cost too much to buy a ticket; moreover, the theater itself is not likely to be very crowded, giving him plenty of room to stretch, squirm, and laugh aloud when he feels like it. Maybe he should simply shelve his plan to see *Expanding Universe* and go to *Coconut Feathers* instead.

John is no fool when it comes to decision making. He has read that renowned Addison-Wesley text, *Making Decisions,* and knows exactly what to do. He writes the words Expanding Universe on the top of one sheet of paper, and the words Coconut Feathers atop another, and proceeds to list the possible advantages (rewards) and disadvantages (costs) of each alternative.

Before reading any further in this case, place yourself in John's shoes and, as carefully and extensively as you can, sort out the several merits and drawbacks associated with each alternative.

To his dismay, John finds that his list making has not really moved him much closer to deciding what to do. All he has to show for his efforts are two pieces of paper and no decision! So, like a good student of decision making, John chooses to flip a coin. "Heads" it's *Expanding Universe,* "tails" it's *Coconut Feathers* — and "tails" it is!! Having decided, once and for all, to go see *Coconut Feathers,* John begins to engage in some fancy cognitive footwork to cover his tracks. As dissonance theory might predict, he finds himself reappraising the potential rewards and costs of each alternative in such a way that he ends up justifying his decision as the correct one.

Again, put yourself in John's shoes and reappraise your own two lists of advantages and disadvantages so as to justify the decision to see *Coconut Feathers.*

Case 006/1

WHO MAY FISH IN THESE WATERS?*

Someone shot at Mrs. Ramona Bennett when she was seven months pregnant. She suspects it was a white fisherman who "tried to blow my head off — our fishermen have been facing this harassment for ninety years." Mrs. Bennett is a Puyallup Indian.

In 1974, a dispute over fishing rights came before Judge George H. Boldt in the federal district court of Tacoma, Washington. He found himself moved, by his reading of the law, to render a civil rights decision that made

---

*This case is based in part on "American Indians: Struggling for Identity and Power," Howell Raines, *The New York Times Magazine,* February 11, 1979.

him a social and political pariah to many whites who had hoped for, and expected, a conservative ruling. After going through every case in our history that pertains to the rights of Indians, Judge Boldt decided in favor of the Puget Sound tribes. On the basis of treaties enacted over a century ago, he concluded that the Indians had the right to take half of the fish in an annual salmon catch now worth $200 million a year.

White reaction was one of anger. State fishery officials refused to enforce Judge Boldt's ruling. The judge, in turn, took over regulation of the fishing industry. The level of outrage increased. Judge Boldt's critics claimed to have raised $100,000 to finance an impeachment campaign; he was said to have an Indian mistress; bumper stickers proliferated that said, "Let's Give 50 Percent of Judge Boldt to the Indians."

Judge Boldt's decision was upheld by the Ninth Circuit Court of Appeals and the Supreme Court refused to review it. But white protest grew still louder. Eventually it was heard all the way back in Washington, D.C., a company town highly sensitive to all manner of political noise. In response to pressure from the white community, the solicitor general of the United States finally agreed to join with white fishermen and Washington state officials in asking the Supreme Court to reconsider its earlier refusal to hear the case. The Bureau of Indian Affairs opposed the effort on the part of the Justice Department to get the case back before the court, but it was overruled.

The nine members of the Supreme Court must now issue a ruling. They must decide between the historically and legally justified claim of an Indian minority, and the current and future demands of a much larger and more powerful white majority that feels itself suddenly threatened by the twin scourges of decreasing resources and increasing inflation.

How should the Court decide and why?

Case 006/2

DECIDING WHERE THE GRASS IS GREENEST

Louise Weil is up for reelection in the Thirteenth Congressional District of a large midwestern state. Unlike almost three-fourths of her colleagues in the House, she is marginal, that is, her seat, far from being safe, is up for grabs by either party each time there is a new election. More than most, therefore, she attends to her constituency, trying to please its different groups by the services she renders and the positions she takes. But like all representatives, Weil must contend with competing demands. First, there are her own interests; it is her immediate goal to be reelected by as wide a margin as possible. Second, she must reckon with her peers in the House, fellow legislators with whom she should get on well if she is to maximize her impact.* And third, there are the folks at home, a heterogeneous constituency that complicates matters considerably. Yet trying to please these various persons and groups, however difficult, is nonetheless easier than trying to find the happy medium between what Weil believes to be right and what is politically expedient. Not infrequently, conscience and politics are in conflict, and Weil finds herself then hunting for the fine line between the ideal and the practical. She has her principles but, as an up and coming lawyer and politician, she does not want her political career to founder because of needless scruples on her part.

Weil is a liberal Republican from a district that has "three worlds." One is a city that has won a national reputation as an urban disaster area. Another is composed of fast growing suburbs that provide homes, and sometimes work, for a high percentage of the political activists in the Thirteenth District. The rest is farmland, a flat, fertile area with a long tradition of support for any and all Republican candidates — and a "world" slower than the others to accept deviation from tradition. The congresswoman's liberal Republicanism has worn well. In the city, it is an advantage to be outside the mainstream of the Grand Old Party. In the suburbs, many identify with her careful mix of respect for the old and support for the new. And rural denizens are willing to accept as valid her Republican credentials as long as she does not push them too far to the left. In short, liberals, conservatives, and those in the middle think they can see parts of themselves mirrored in Weil.

As it happens, Weil's easy-going manner encourages that impression. Perhaps because of her marginal seat, or her marginal position in the party, or her marginal status among House liberals, or her marginal gender, her

---

*Weil must pay particular attention to colleagues to whom she is closest: e.g., those in her party; those from her state; and those on the same committees (i.e., responsible for the same issue areas).

public persona seemed designed to smooth ruffled feathers. Weil had grown up in the district's largest city (before it fell prey to the worst of urban ills), graduated from a good liberal arts college outside the state, studied law in a well-respected state school, and at about the same time began to become active in local Republican politics. Success in the party came quickly. It was a time when to be young, female, and liberal had advantages in state politics, and the Republicans opened their ranks. Weil became something of a darling in higher party circles and by the time she was thirty-one she had enough support to secure the nomination for Representative from the Thirteenth District. She got along well with everyone. Never verbose, when asked questions she replied candidly; not one to seek out controversial issues, when asked to take a position, she did so decisively; neither too liberal nor too conservative, when pushed she found a middle road apparently leading somewhere. She was also seen as a hard worker who had won early respect from colleagues in Washington without neglecting her diverse constituency back home. She was ambitious, clearly, but as long as she continued to do a good job, no one seemed to mind. If Louise Weil was not exactly beloved, she certainly was very well liked.

Despite her good reputation, Weil could by no means count on reelection. In addition to the marginality of her seat, it was an "off year," so presidential candidates provided no strong indicators. As for the times, well, they were strange. It was said, and the polls seemed to prove it, that people were becoming more conservative on a whole host of issues. In particular, anti-tax programs were gathering considerable support from unexpected quarters around the country. At first glance, this appeared to be a move to the right; at the least, lower taxes meant less funding for a variety of social programs. But the public response seemed to indicate it was more complicated than that. Liberals were joining with conservatives, and Democrats with Republicans in a series of shifting alliances that made reading the public mood a risky business indeed.

As if to confirm the unpredictability of the times, Weil's Democratic opponent was a conservative and a political outsider whose claim to fame and knowledge was a strikingly successful insurance business. William Anthony Coppolla, 50, silver haired and tongued, was finding political gold in a Democratic family tradition that went back two generations, in a political career that went back two months, and in an ideology said to be new because it was so firmly entrenched in the old. Unlike Weil, Coppolla *did* ruffle feathers, and he was "proud of it." Verbose, issue oriented, and straight as a Republican, Coppolla attracted wide and loud attention as a "new Democrat." With strong financial backing from old friends and newly interested groups, and a telegenic style, he received early and wide television exposure. Before Weil knew what had hit her, Coppolla had pulled even. Polls conducted by the largest newspaper in the state showed that one month before the election, Weil and Coppolla were expected to have a photo finish.

So far, the campaign had been routine. There was the usual arguing among the voters about which candidate had more charisma, and the usual position taking and hedging by the candidates on unavoidable national, state, and local issues. But on October 10 an event took place that changed the nature of the Weil-Coppolla contest. A mass rally was held on the greens and avenues of Washington, D.C. by NORML, The National Organization for Reform of Marijuana Laws, to drum up support for the legalization of pot. Ordinarily, such a demonstration would barely come to the attention of those in the Thirteenth District. But the times were not quite ordinary, and so a fresh academic year and a heated debate in the state legislature on the decriminalization of marijuana coincided with the noisy events in Washington to make the drug issue *the* issue during the remaining month of the Weil-Coppolla campaign.

Of course, neither Weil nor even the more loquacious Coppolla had any interest in making the marijuana laws the basis for any voter's decision. But in an "off" election year, devoid also of any searing issues such as busing, Vietnam, or Watergate, the public was ready to have each candidate's stand on a lesser (albeit salient) issue symbolize their position on a wide range of other sociopolitical policy problems. Bearded "freaks" on the tube and campus activists searching for a controversy locked horns with state legislators, and their clamor filled the political vacuum. For better or worse, how Weil and Coppolla handled the marijuana issue might well dictate the results of the election.

Coppolla's response was prompt. He used an article from the *New York Times* to establish the case for the harmfulness of drug abuse:

> Scientific studies worldwide have shown that chronic marijuana use causes inhibition of cellular growth, reduction in sperm production, development of abnormal sperm cells, interference with synthesis of important genetic material in cells, interference with immune systems, destruction of chromosomes and, above all, brain damage.

Quote in hand, he concluded that to prevent a further increase in the more than 11 million regular smokers, strict measures such as those in New York State* should be put on the local statute books.

Typically, Weil was slower to take a position. She had never thought much about marijuana, either as part of her public or private life, and she had certainly never imagined that it would play any kind of a role in her political future. Weil had smoked a few times, mostly when she was a law

---

*These laws permit first time offenders to be punished with a hefty fine and a jail sentence.

student. Since then, her exposure to marijuana was infrequent, and she had never bothered to buy it herself. Weil had few preconceived notions about whether or not marijuana was "bad for your health." Even if it was, she had no thoughts about how government should respond. As a liberal, she had, of course, tolerated smoking in others, and in general opposed paternalistic interventions by the law. She never quite understood what it was about marijuana that made some people so anxious that they lumped it together with hard drugs.

A face-to-face television debate between Weil and Coppolla had long been scheduled to take place on October 27, ten days before the election. Now, the week preceding the debate turned into one big brouhaha over the legal future of marijuana. Interest groups including campus chapters of NORML, medical associations, and church groups entered the fray. Knowing that she would be called on to take a clear position on the subject at some point during the televised encounter, Weil resolved to investigate the medical and legal aspects of marijuana as best she could before that public test.

The law with regard to marijuana was relatively easier to master than the science. Weil found that in nine states it was already decriminalized: Alaska, California, Colorado, Maine, Mississippi, Minnesota, Ohio, Oregon, and South Dakota. These states made possession of a small amount a civil offense, like a traffic violation. At the other extreme were states like Arizona and Nevada, where mere possession could be prosecuted as a felony. The other states fell somewhere in between, with a dazzling array of variations. Oregon in 1973 had been the first to decriminalize. There was no apparent increase in use the following two years, but there was a rise in 1976. What effect, if any, the statutory change had on this increase was not known. There were, however, early indications that appreciable dollar savings are realized in any state that penalizes most offenders with fines rather than incarceration. Among costs that might be reduced are those associated with arrest, sentencing, confinement in prison, probation and parole. On the federal level, there was also an increasing trend toward decriminalization. As of 1977 it was, in fact, presidential policy to recommend decriminalization as far as the federal government is concerned.

Weil's staff did the best it could in the short time available to obtain the latest medical literature on the controversial drug. What they found came as a surprise to Weil who had heretofore thought that the medical profession, like herself, had a tolerant attitude. In fact, it appeared that although physicians and researchers differed on what stance the government should take toward marijuana, there was increasing agreement that its effects could well be harmful. There had definitely been a recent shift in professional opinion. In 1972, when the typical marijuana available in this country was comparatively weak and the number of users comparatively few, no one was much concerned. Now that both of these conditions had been turned around, that is, "higher grades" of the drug were being used more extensively by more people, the medical profession had become much more conservative.

There was evidence that moderate and heavy users became psychologically dependent, sometimes demonstrating "amotivational syndrome" and, after prolonged use, a loss of libido. In addition, there were tentative indications of physical insult: pulmonary effects, brain damage, psychomotor impairment, lowered sperm count, and chromosomal change. The issue, however, was complicated by more than the shift in opinion. Medical researchers also appeared to believe that there were situations when marijuana showed considerable potential as a therapeutic agent. A recent editorial in the *New York Times* noted the probable benefits:

> It eases pressure within the eyes of glaucoma victims. It reduces or eliminates the nausea, vomiting and loss of appetite in some cancer patients undergoing chemotherapy. It appears to help the breathing of asthmatics. It may also be useful against elipepsy, alcoholism and multiple sclerosis, and as a sedative or antidepressant.

Although the *Times* came out firmly against the legalization of marijuana, it did push for accelerated research to explore its medical value.

As Weil, with the help of a staff that had itself become newly curious, went over the legal and medical literature in short order, she concluded that she had three options:

1. Support the enactment of stiff (criminal) penalties as Coppolla had done.
2. Support a measure to decriminalize, to make the possession of marijuana a civil offense.
3. Support a law that would make possession and private use entirely legal.

These choices and the supporting materials fell into place only on October 26, a day before the debate. Contemplating her divergent constituencies, her desire to beat her opponent by as wide a margin as possible, the legal and medical confusion over pot (and Coppolla, who in his decisive conservatism had garnered some important new support), Weil knew, perhaps for the first time, the agony of decision. She had just about ruled out alternative (3) but she was in a quandary over the choice between the other two alternatives.

What should she decide and why?

Case 008/1

CHOICE OF A MAJOR COLLEGE PROGRAM

Each college student must decide, usually at the end of the freshman or sophomore year, on the field in which he or she will concentrate (or major). This choice can be a difficult one to make. Lucky the student who comes to college with his mind already made up! The great majority of students are undecided, however, and begin to panic when the choice of major deadline approaches. Their natural plan of attack is to talk with upperclassmen, and friendly faculty, hoping someone will suggest a choice that "seems right," and that in due course sufficient reasons for that choice will emerge. However, decisions made on this basis often leave the student uncertain and unhappy with the resulting program of study.

This anxiety over the choice of a major is brought on through parental pressure, the need to concentrate on a subject that holds out some career potential, and the difficulty of the work in one department when compared with that in others. Probably the overriding factor that makes the choice so difficult is the lack of experience on the part of the student in deciding what he wants to do with the rest of his life. What he studies now will in all probability affect the job he will take two to three years hence, establish his income level, set his living location, determine his friends and associates, and thus affect his entire lifestyle. It is unfortunate that the student cannot study what he enjoys and postpone choice of a major until he has received the B.A. or B.S. degree. Some do, but the high cost of an education makes it more and more difficult.

Assume that you are a college student faced with the selection of a major, or that you are an upperclassman who is assisting a friend in the choice of a major. Put yourself in either situation. Follow clearly the Decision Making Process (Chapter 3), and proceed step by step to make this decision. Use the decision matrix (Chapter 8) as an aid in the selection of alternatives. Document each step in the process through a fairly detailed description, and include this in your final report. The report (about 1000 words) should be written in such a way that the informed reader will have no difficulty understanding the rationale behind the decision that was ultimately made.

Case 008/2

WHAT TO DO AFTER GRADUATION

Increasing numbers of students have difficulty in deciding what to do after they graduate. Should they get a job and begin to pursue a career? Or should they enter graduate school in order to enhance their chances of employment at a position with greater responsibility, or should they take a year off, travel, and see what turns up? Will a given job pay you at a higher rate if you hold a graduate degree? Will the cost of tuition and loss of income during graduate education offset what can be earned with a graduate degree? Will a graduate degree open up opportunities not available to those with only a baccalaureate degree? These are among the many questions now being asked by juniors and seniors as they approach graduation. Their problem is compounded by a relatively good job market and increased openings in many graduate programs.

Assume that you are a college student faced with this kind of decision. Follow closely the decision-making process (Chapter 3) and proceed through each of its steps. Use the decision matrix (Chapter 8) as an aid in the selection of alternatives. Document each step in the process through a detailed description and include it in the final case report. The report (about 1000 words) should be written in such a way that the informed reader will have no difficulty understanding the rationale behind the decision that was ultimately made.

Case 008/3

THE PURCHASING AGENT

Ten years have passed since you graduated from college and you have advanced rather rapidly. The experience you have gained in your last three positions has been invaluable to you in securing your new job. You have moved from sales to personnel to assistant buyer and now find yourself purchasing agent for the Acme Printing Company. Acme's business is industrial printing, including college bulletins, advertising literature for large industrial companies, and service and instruction equipment manuals. It is one of the largest commercial printing establishments in the greater Boston area.

One of your first assignments as purchasing agent is to sign a one-year contract with a local auto rental agency (car dealer) for a fleet of 25 salesmen's cars. Previous rentals had been made with a Ford agency, but your company has recently acquired a GM account to print advertising brochures, so you feel that you must switch to a GM rental agency. After a visit to several agencies in the general neighborhood of your plant, you decide on the following cars as possibilities for rental: Buick Regal, Pontiac Grand Prix, Oldsmobile Cutlass, Chevrolet Monte Carlo.

These cars are all popular American models. Their sticker prices range from $6,300 to $7,000; they rent from $120 to $160 per month. The rental fee includes full service and adequate liability insurance coverage. All dealers will allow purchase of cars at a discount by salesmen at the end of the rental year. In your investigation and interviews with dealers you find that there is little basis for choice among them. The advantages and disadvantages among the dealers seem to balance out, so the final selection must be based on the merits of the car for the job.

Based on the limited information provided in this case, you are at liberty to make any further assumptions, provided you explain the rationale behind them. After some basic research on your part to attain some knowledge about each of the four cars listed, make a recommendation as to the choice of vehicle based on the decision matrix (Chapter 8) technique. Explain each step in the process of making your decision. (A written narrative explaining the appropriate charts would be the best way to present an analysis of this case.)

Case 009/1

COSMESTICS, INC. (1972)*

Beauty Aids Inc. is a parent cosmetics company that distributes its products throughout the United States and Canada. Beauty Aids started in 1963; its gross sales have gone from $350,000 in 1963 to $8,900,000 in 1972. In 1970, Beauty Aids was listed as an over-the-counter stock. Beauty Aids, Inc. actually consists of many separate distribution companies. Peter James owns one of these companies, Cosmestics Inc.

Cosmestics Inc. was purchased as a franchise for $40,000 in 1964, and authorized to distribute in only five states. By 1972, its yearly gross sales

*The authors would like to acknowledge Mark Feigenbaum for much of the background material in this case study.

reached $930,000. Under an agreement with the parent company, Cosmestics Inc. must buy its products only from Beauty Aids. These products are sold to Cosmestics Inc. at 33% of the suggested retail prices established by the parent company. In accord with the franchise agreement, James in turn sells the products to his sales managers, who buy them for 45% of the retail price.

James enjoyed owning his own company and he was pleased to be doing more than 10% of the Beauty Aid total volume. However, by 1972 the economics of his situation troubled him seriously. According to the franchise agreement, James was obligated to supply each of his sales managers with a company car. Also, other annual costs (e.g., accountants, secretaries, shipping costs) now amounted to nearly $65,000. Thus, despite the fact that Cosmestics Inc. had more than 10% of the Beauty Aid gross sales, the company showed virtually no profit, and James' annual income was about $20,000. James felt this modest income was not commensurate with his educational level (he had a M.B.A.), his years of experience, and his responsibility as an owner of a company. He was caught in the middle of a profit squeeze.

In 1972, James went to David Emerson, the president of Beauty Aids Inc. After explaining the problem, he found Emerson unsympathetic. Emerson said that James should be happy with the current arrangement. Emerson hinted that there might be even more of a profit squeeze in the future since Beauty Aids was considering decreasing the costs of its product to the sales managers to 43%. This reduction might be a useful incentive to promote greater sales, and thus would increase the value of Beauty Aids stock. James wanted to change the franchise agreement to enable him to buy for less and distribute over a larger geographic area. Emerson refused, and stated that if Cosmestics Inc. violated the 1964 agreement, then Beauty Aids Inc. would legally enforce the agreement through the courts.

James came away from his meeting with nothing changed. He still wanted to own his company, and he was not willing to work as an employee in another company. However, he was concerned; the future of Cosmestics Inc. would be gloomy if it did not show greater profits. He focused on two possible courses of action open to him: (1) stay with Beauty Aids as the parent corporation, or (2) form his own "parent" company, i.e., buy directly from other cosmetic suppliers. If he chose the first alternative, then he would be certain of his income and he could maintain employment for his staff, but the growth of Cosmestics Inc. would be limited.

The second alternative at first did not seem legally possible. His attorney asserted that, in his opinion, the franchise agreement between the companies was a violation of the Sherman Antitrust Act and the Clayton Act. The attorney assured James that the case against Beauty Aids was excellent and it had better than an 85% chance of winning. However, to fight Beauty Aids would take time and a considerable amount of money, perhaps as much as $125,000 in legal fees.

James then talked to bankers and suppliers of cosmetic products. He obtained a promise of a $70,000 loan from a bank if he needed it. The loan would be enough to start the company with considerable inventory. He also found suppliers. James figured that the total cost of products and transportation plus interest charges would amount to 20% of the retail price. He also figured he could sell to sales managers for as low as 40% of the retail cost if the managers' sales volume was high. This would provide an excellent incentive for increased sales. Also, James could distribute to a larger geographic area. He thought he had about a 70% chance of good gross retail sales (i.e., $1,000,000), about a 20% chance of fair retail sales (i.e., not less than $600,000), and about 10% chance of poor sales (i.e., not less than $300,000).

James felt a responsibility to his growing family, and a responsibility to provide employment to his staff. What action should he take and why?

Case 009/2

FARMER JIM

Jim Fowler, a farmer, is trying to decide how to plant one of his fields. He is considering three crops for this field: melons, tomatoes, or beans. The rainfall during the growing season will certainly affect the anticipated profits. All of these crops will do their best with a moderate rainfall of 3 to 5 inches per month. Jim anticipates that with moderate rainfall the profit this year for planting only melons would be $21,000, whereas for planting only tomatoes it would be $26,000; for beans it would be $25,000. Beans and tomatoes have the advantage over melons that they can be harvested twice, the first harvest in July and the second in September. Melons have only one harvest, in August.

With a wet summer (more than 5 inches of rainfall per month), Jim expects that the profit would be $20,000 for melons, and $15,000 for either tomatoes or beans. The melons like the rain but they also require a lot of sunshine. Consequently, the reduction in sunshine that usually accompanies a more heavy rainfall also decreases their yield and profitability. With a heavier rainfall, tomatoes tend to split and the split tomatoes cannot be sold to commercial markets; and beans tend to develop various fungus diseases.

With a dry summer (less than 3 inches of rain per month), all the crops would need some irrigation; this would increase costs and reduce profits.

Melons would require the greatest amount of irrigation, beans the least. Under these conditions, Jim believes he would make $12,000 profit for melons, $14,000 for tomatoes, and $18,000 for beans.

The rainfall averages for the past twenty years are:

Year	Average rainfall per month from May to Sept.
1979	1.53
1978	7.22
1977	3.96
1976	3.21
1975	4.72
1974	4.87
1973	4.17
1972	5.25
1971	0.87
1970	3.85
1969	8.38
1968	4.28
1967	6.57
1966	2.38
1965	5.67
1964	3.59
1963	4.45
1962	3.78
1961	3.11
1960	1.12

What crop or combination of crops should Jim plant this year?

Case 010/1

WHEN HEMOPHILIA RUNS IN THE FAMILY

John and Sarah Smith have been married for two years and are now considering starting a family. Their decision is made difficult, however, because hemophilia has affected several of Sarah's male relatives (two uncles and one brother). Hemophilia is caused by an inadequate level of one of the body's clotting factors and results in a marked tendency to hemorrhage. Persons with this disease develop severe deformities in their joints because of repeated episodes of bleeding, and many eventually become crippled. Because any bodily injury can induce a major hemorrhage, people affected with hemophilia must severely limit their lifestyles. Bleeding episodes can be treated with intravenous infusions of blood or blood products, but it is expensive, painful, and takes a great psychological toll. Obviously, such patients have shortened life expectancies.

Hemophilia is inherited as an X-linked, recessive disorder, i.e., mainly males are affected. Males pass the abnormal X chromosome to their daughters but not to their sons. A woman with a single affected X chromosome is a carrier; she is not herself affected, but she can pass the defect on to her children. Male children of a carrier female have a 50% chance of having hemophilia; female children of a carrier have a 50% chance of being a carrier. An affected male will pass his X chromosome to all his daughters (who will be carriers) but not to his sons (who receive only his Y chromosome).

Based on the family history, Sarah's mother must be a carrier. Therefore there is a 50% chance that Sarah carries the abnormal gene. If she is a carrier, then half her male children will have hemophilia. Sarah and John have seen the burden of this disease in Sarah's family and would prefer to adopt children rather than have an affected son. They have just learned, however, of the technique of amniocentesis through which the sex of an unborn child can be determined. They could elect to have amniocentesis and abort the pregnancy if the fetus were male. They are told that amniocentesis has a 0.5% risk of causing the pregnancy to miscarry. They are also told occasional errors occur in sex typing: male fetuses are correctly identified as male 98% of the time; female fetuses are correctly identified as female 99% of the time.

Should they arrange for Sarah to have amniocentesis?

Their decision is complicated by the fact that a new test is available for determining whether a woman is a carrier of hemophilia. The test involves analysis of a small amount of the woman's blood and is without risk. The test correctly identifies 80% of carriers, but it also falsely labels as carriers 12% of women who are not carriers. If Sarah undergoes the test and if it is positive (i.e., she appears to be a carrier), should they then plan to have an amniocentesis? If the test result is negative, should she still have any amniocentesis?

One further complication arises. A new, experimental procedure has been announced for sampling the blood of a fetus in the uterus and then testing that sample to see if the fetus will be affected by hemophilia. Presumably, the test would only be done on male fetuses of presumed carrier females. The test is not successful in obtaining a blood sample 5% of the time, but if a sample is obtained, the test results are always correct. The test is not without risk; 5% of pregnancies subjected to fetal blood sampling miscarry. Should Sarah and John plan to have this test performed, if amniocentesis shows that a pregnancy is male? How would their decision be affected by the results of the carrier detection test? (N.B. In order to assign utilities where needed in this example, consult your own attitudes.)

Case 010/2

COPING WITH CANCER OF THE LEG

Until two months ago you have been quite well. At that time your right leg developed a dull ache that has increased in severity. Over the past two weeks you have also noticed a swelling of your thigh and decided to visit a doctor. She examined you, took an x-ray and a biopsy of your leg, and found a growth. The biopsy showed that the growth was a malignant tumor.

Your doctor tells you that there are two alternative ways to treat your tumor: either radiation and drugs, in an attempt to poison the tumor cells without poisoning the normal cells in your body *or* amputation of the diseased limb. Experience has shown that patients who undergo amputation survive somewhat longer than do patients who receive only radiation and chemotherapy. If your leg is amputated, there is every reason to expect that you could be fitted with a prosthesis (artificial leg) that would allow you to walk. Radiation and chemotherapy will almost certainly cause side effects of severe nausea, fatigue, bleeding problems, and alopecia (loss of hair).

Your prognosis depends in large part on whether or not the tumor has spread. If the tumor is localized, then amputation should cure the problem. If the tumor has spread, then other tumors will appear and you will have to receive further radiation and chemotherapy. Unfortunately, there is no way to tell whether the tumor has spread. The best your doctor can do is tell you that the likelihood of widespread tumor is 30%. If so, there is a 70% chance that amputation would cure you. If you receive primary radiation and chemotherapy and if the tumor has not spread, there is a 50% chance that you will live five years. If the tumor has spread, then your chance at five-year survival is only 10%; there is a 50% chance that you will die in the next eighteen months.

Your doctor tells you that she does not know what to do — the decision is really yours to make. Do you want to undergo amputation with the prospect that you might be cured, or do you want to keep your leg and almost certainly resign yourself to a shorter life span?

Case 011/1

DREAM HOUSE

While they were college students, Bill and Julie Wilson always had money problems. Having a child did not make things easier. But, buoyed by the belief that eventually conditions would change for the better, they emerged from the ordeal with their college degrees in hand, healthy, in good spirits, and they looked forward to the future and never wanted to see another plate of spaghetti again. The next two years seemed to fly by. Bill was employed as a financial management trainee in a large bank, and Julie still somewhat restricted to child care found part-time work as a dental hygenist. They had also moved out of their cramped student quarters into a modest four-room apartment in another part of town. The amenities were considerably better: more room, quieter neighborhood, parking facilities, even a lawn. Yet both looked forward to the day when they would own a home of their own. Amassing the savings for a downpayment would take a number of years, but given their age and expected upward income mobility, they confidently looked forward to a day in the not too distant future when they would be able to buy their dream house.

Three years and another child later, Bill and Julie, romantically clinging to their dream, are now seriously doubting whether they will ever be able to realize it. Saving has not been easy. To date they have put aside $5,000. Inflation, especially in the housing sector, has pushed many homes beyond their reach. Indeed, their dream has undergone some remodeling. However, there are still several neighborhoods with attractive housing of the style and quality that the Wilsons desire. Housing prices in those neighborhoods have doubled in the last six years and there is no telling when or whether they will ever stabilize. One home has recently come on the market for a firm $75,000, i.e., the seller will not take less. It is not their dream house, but as they have done so often in the past the Wilsons went to inspect the property knowing full well that even if they liked it there was no way that they could buy it since a conventional mortgage would require a minimum 20% downpayment, or $15,000.

Just when things were looking their bleakest, Bill's father offered to make them a loan of $10,000. He would accept an unsecured personal note with annual interest set at 7% of the outstanding balance. The principal could be repaid at any time, in any amounts, or not at all. In the latter event interest payments would continue until his father's death at which time the debt would be forgiven. Bill's father is currently 58 years old. It was an offer that could not be refused. Or was it? The loan would enable them to buy the house, but could they afford it? In any event it was worth going over the figures one more time.

Bill and Julie estimated their current annual income, expenses, and savings to be as follows:

Income

Bill	$23,000
Julie (part-time)	7,000
Total Income	$30,000

Expenses

Taxes (Fed., State, Soc. Sec.)	$8,100
Rent ($300/mo.)	3,600
Utilities (heat, light, phone)	1,100
Food ($100/wk.)	5,200
Medical (incl. insurance)	2,300
Clothes	1,800
Transportation (2 used cars)	2,200
Personal & household supplies	1,200
Babysitters	1,800
Entertainment & recreation	1,000
Miscellaneous	800
Total Expenses	$29,100

Savings $900

From their discussions with local bankers, the Wilsons learned that there were several different forms of mortgage finance available. With a downpayment of $15,000 they could borrow $60,000 for a term of 30 years at an annual rate of 9%. However, the monthly payments varied depending upon the form of mortgage chosen. The predominant and traditional form is the fixed-payment mortgage, in which the borrower agrees to make fixed dollar payments each month for the life of the loan.

A new form of mortgage that has become popular recently is the graduate-payment mortgage. It allows for lower payments in the early years of the mortgage, but the payments would increase each year at a stipulated rate for a specific number of years and then become permanent for the remainder of the term of the mortgage. Two such plans are compared with the traditional fixed-payment mortgage.

MONTHLY PAYMENTS (loan: $60,000; term: 30 yrs. rate 9%)

Year	Fixed-Payment	Graduated-Payment (Grad. period: 5 yrs.) (Grad. rate: 7-1/2%/yr.)	Graduated-Payment (Grad. period: 10 yrs.) (Grad. rate: 3%/yr.)
1	$483	$365	$401
2	483	392	413
3	483	422	425
4	483	453	438
5	483	487	451
6	483	524	465
7	483	524	479
8	483	524	493
9	483	524	508
10	483	524	523
11	483	524	539
.	.	.	.
.	.	.	.
.	.	.	.
30	483	524	539

The higher the rate of graduation and/or the longer the graduation period, the lower the initial payment, and the higher the total interest payments over the life of the loan. In the two graduated plans shown above total interest payments are approximately $11,000 more than those under the fixed-payment plan. The lower initial payments, however, do make it possible for families with expected upward income mobility to match their payments with their ability to pay. Of course, these plans pose a risk to anyone whose income fails to keep pace with the scheduled payment increases. On the other hand, the fixed-payment plan, with its much larger early costs, gradually becomes less burdensome as a family's income grows.

A third option available is the variable-rate mortgage. Under this plan interest rates are initially set 1/2% lower than the rate on fixed-payment mortgages, but the rate is subject to change every six months, as determined by a formula that links it to the rates on U.S. Government Bonds. While there is no minimum rate, the bank has set a maximum of 2-1/2% above the initial rate. Thus, in our example, if the Wilsons opt for this type of mortgage the interest rate would be 8-1/2%, with monthly payments of $461. At worst (i.e., at 11%) they would have to pay $571 per month. Of course, rates could just as well go down; they are currently at or near their historic highs. Unlike the other plans the variable-rate mortgage carries no prepayment penalties.

In addition to mortgage payments, Bill and Julie noted that they would have to consider other annual expenses as well as some possible savings, such as:

Expenses

Mortgage closing costs (one-time expense)	$ 300
Property taxes	2,250
Homeowners' insurance	400
Minor repairs and maintenance	300
Additional utility costs	400
Interest on personal note	700

Savings

Income tax savings (the result of itemization with substantial deductions of interest and property taxes and other allowed items as compared to the standard deductions taken in prior years)	2,750
Rental savings	3,600

They also noted that the roof needed to be retiled. It is possible to let it go for another year; beyond that there would be risk of serious damage in the event of heavy snow and frost. Retiling would cost $2,000, which could be financed through a home improvement loan at 11% for five years with fixed monthly payments of $43.50. Since they would now have seven rooms as opposed to four, they further recognized the less urgent need to buy more furniture.

While Julie's earnings are still a matter of uncertainty, Bill's current salary is considerably above the $12,000 at which he started some five years ago. His average annual increase has been roughly 14%.

After a lengthy discussion they agreed that they liked the house, did not particularly like paying rent to build somebody else's equity, and decided, at last, to turn to you for a final judgment. What do you advise them to do? Be as specific as possible.

Case 012/1

SHANGRI-LA*

The Tibetan Plateau is a vast, cold, and largely unexplored region of the world. The climate is terribly severe, and a numbing grit-laden wind blows continually. Nestled within this forbidding wilderness, however, lies a beautiful valley called Shangri-La. Shielding the valley on the north is a huge snow covered peak called Mount Karakal. Were it not for this natural barrier, the whole valley would be a lake nourished continually from the glacial heights around it. Another remarkable feature of Shangri-La is that in a vertical descent of a few thousand feet, one experiences a change in climate from temperate to tropical. The valley floor is a virtual paradise. It is here that most of the inhabitants reside, farming the exceptionally fertile land.

Clinging to Mount Karakal, and overlooking the valley is the lamasery, a huge monastery that houses the governing body of Shangri-La. The white lamasery walls are pierced by row upon row of windows; above them can be seen the red Phodang-marpo, the palace of the High Lama. The lamas are benevolent dictators who spend their days in prayer, in learning, and in the management of the affairs of Shangri-La. Completely isolated from the outside world, this self-sufficient community has existed for centuries in an idyllic state free from the stresses of modern society.

All of this may be about to change, however, for the population of Shangri-La has been growing recently at an unprecedented rate. This situation is of great concern to the High Lama who fears that he must act very quickly to alter this trend, or he may not be able to feed all of his people. He recently convened a planning committee to investigate the situation and advise him regarding a proper course of action. The interim report of this planning committee to the High Lama follows.

---

*Based on the novel by James Hilton, Wm. Morrow & Co., 1934.

INTERIM REPORT TO
HIS EXCELLENCY, THE HIGH LAMA OF SHANGRI-LA
Regarding
THE BALANCE OF FOOD AND POPULATION

At your request, we have investigated the many factors that affect the food supply and the population in our valley. Our findings to date are summarized below. We trust that you will consider this matter of highest priority so that we may ward off the impending crisis facing our people.

To evaluate the recent past, we consulted the bureau of records and determined that the population *has* increased significantly, whereas the level of food production has increased only moderately. Most alarmingly, the food stores have been decreasing *rapidly* in recent years. (See Table 1.) It would appear from these data that there is certainly cause for alarm. Based upon an agricultural yield of 1.5 tons per acre, we estimate that our valley can potentially feed a population of 40,000, and no more.

We have attempted to determine the major causes for the current state of affairs. It seems that, all things being equal, the more people there are in Shangri-La, the faster the population grows. This is an explosive situation if population continues to grow without bound. Of course, this is ridiculous in the extreme because it does not take into account the fact that the survival of the population depends upon an adequate food supply. If there is an abundant food supply, the population seems to grow faster than if the food supply is merely adequate. A food shortage, on the other hand, would result in a famine and thus slow the population growth rate. In extreme conditions, the population would actually decrease, and we might face extinction.

We feel that it may be possible to avoid these devastating possibilities only if action is taken immediately. Among the policies which we suggest for your consideration are: increase the rate of food production; ration the available food supply; lower the birthrate. Although we do not know exactly what the effects of such policies will be, we believe that if one or more of them is enacted, the situation will improve, and we may save our civilization. To assist you in formulating these policies, we have prepared the following computer simulation.

for the committee,

Lama Chang, Chairman

Table 1. Recent Statistics on Food and Population in Shangri-La

Year	Population	Annual Food Production (tons)	Food in Storage (tons)
1948	2136	1520	941
1950	2272	1698	1503
1952	2468	1876	2145
1954	2732	2045	2833
1956	3070	2232	3530
1958	3484	2410	4198
1960	3974	2588	4799
1962	4533	2766	5299
1964	5154	2944	5666
1966	5823	3122	5876
1968	6527	3300	5913
1970	7249	3478	5766
1972	7971	3656	5437
1974	8674	3834	4934
1976	9341	4012	4276
1978	9955	4190	3488

```
EX SHANLA
FORTRAN: SHANLA
MAIN.
LINK:   Loading
[LNKXCT SHANLA Execution]
```

THIS PROGRAM FORECASTS THE FUTURE OF SHANGRI-LA

YOU HAVE THE OPTION OF IMPLEMENTING ONE OR MORE OF THE FOLLOWING
POLICIES TO ATTEMPT TO BALANCE THE POPULATION AND FOOD SUPPLY.

A) INCREASE FOOD PRODUCTION....
FOOD PRODUCTION IS EXPECTED TO INCREASE AT A CONSTANT ANNUAL
RATE OF 89 TONS PER YEAR. WITH A CONCERTED EFFORT, HOWEVER,
THIS FIGURE CAN BE INCREASED UP TO A MAXIMUM OF 250 TONS PER
YEAR UNTIL ALL THE ARABLE LAND IS CULTIVATED.

B) RATION THE FOOD SUPPLY....
THE RESIDENTS OF SHANGRI-LA CURRENTLY CONSUME
AN AVERAGE OF 0.5 TONS OF FOOD PER PERSON PER YEAR.
THROUGH GOVERNMENT RATIONING, THIS FIGURE CAN
BE REDUCED TO 0.3 TONS PER PERSON PER YEAR WITH
NO ADVERSE EFFECTS ON THE HEALTH OF THE POPULATION.

C) CONTROL OF POPULATION GROWTHRATE....
THE POPULATION GROWTHRATE IS DEPENDENT UPON THE SIZE OF
THE POPULATION AND THE AMOUNT OF FOOD IN STORAGE.
   1. THE POPULATION WILL GROW AT THE RATE OF 5% PER YEAR
   EVEN IF THERE IS NO FOOD IN STORAGE. BY   GRANTING
   POSITIVE INCENTIVES, THE RESIDENTS CAN BE MADE TO REDUCE
   THIS FIGURE TO 0.5%.
   2. FOR EVERY 100 TONS OF FOOD IN STORAGE, THE POPULATION
   WILL GROW BY AN ADDITIONAL 20 PEOPLE PER YEAR. BY INFORMING THE
   RESIDENTS OF THE DANGERS OF THIS PRACTICE, THIS FIGURE CAN
   BE REDUCED TO A MINIMUM OF 3 PEOPLE PER YEAR PER 100 TONS OF FOOD
   IN STORAGE.
   (NOTE THAT A FOOD SHORTAGE WILL RESULT IN A FAMINE.)

IN 1978, THE POPULATION IS 9955., FOOD PRODUCED IS 4190. TONS,
AND THE FOOD IN STORAGE IS 3488. TONS.

DO YOU WANT TO INCREASE FOOD PRODUCTION?
?NO

DO YOU WANT TO RATION THE FOOD SUPPLY?
?YES

HOW MANY TONS OF FOOD PER PERSON PER YEAR?
?.4

DO YOU WANT TO REDUCE THE POPULATION GROWTH RATE?
?NO

FOOD PRODUCTION TO INCREASE BY 89. TONS PER YEAR.

FOOD CONSUMPTION TO BE .40 TONS PER PERSON PER YEAR.
POPULATION TOINCREASE BY 20. PEOPLE PER YEAR FOR EACH 100 TONS OF STORED FOOD.
POPULATION TOINCREASE BY 5.00% FOR NO STORED FOOD.

ARE YOU SATISFIED WITH THESE POLICIES?
  ?YES

                              FORECAST

YEAR	POPULATION	CONSUMED	PRODUCED	SURPLUS/SHORTAGE
1978.	9955.	3982.	4190.	3488.
1980.	12369.	4948.	4368.	2727.
1982.	14564.	5826.	4546.	491.
1984.	14100.	5640.	4724.	-1946.
1986.	8462.	3385.	4902.	19.
1988.	9625.	3850.	5080.	2684.
1990.	11894.	4758.	5258.	4097.
1992.	14797.	5919.	5436.	3637.
1994.	17609.	7044.	5614.	1227.
1996.	18543.	7417.	5792.	-2190.
1998.	11156.	4462.	5970.	-837.
2000.	10782.	4313.	6148.	3041.
2002.	13427.	5371.	6326.	5462.
2004.	17111.	6844.	6504.	5460.
2006.	20897.	8359.	6682.	2753.
2008.	23723.	9489.	6860.	-2102.
2010.	14871.	5948.	7038.	-2345.
2012.	11553.	4621.	7216.	3007.
2014.	14412.	5765.	7394.	6849.
2016.	18874.	7550.	7572.	7753.
2018.	23810.	9524.	7750.	5093.
2020.	27825.	11130.	7928.	-678.
2022.	21644.	8658.	8106.	-4357.
2024.	11180.	4472.	8284.	2045.
2026.	13867.	5547.	8462.	8474.
2028.	19173.	7669.	8640.	11494.
2030.	25802.	10321.	8818.	9748.
2032.	31901.	12760.	8996.	3274.
2034.	33255.	13302.	9174.	-5430.
2036.	13681.	5472.	9352.	-1911.
2038.	11734.	4694.	9530.	8149.
2040.	17085.	6834.	9708.	15062.
2042.	25295.	10118.	9886.	16246.
2044.	34159.	13664.	10064.	10697.
2046.	41037.	16415.	10242.	-525.
2048.	30122.	12049.	10420.	-8638.
2050.	7330.	2932.	10598.	3796.

DO YOU WANT TO TRY AGAIN?
  ?NO

END OF EXECUTION
CPU TIME: 0.52 ELAPSED TIME: 3:37.88
EXIT

```
.TYPE SHANLA
00100              WRITE(5,10)
00200      10      FORMAT(///,10X,'THIS PROGRAM FORECASTS THE
00300              1 FUTURE OF SHANGRI-LA'///)
00400              WRITE(5,11)
00500      11      FORMAT(5X,'YOU HAVE THE OPTION OF IMPLEMENTING
00600              1 ONE OR MORE OF THE FOLLOWING ',/,' POLICIES TO ATTEMPT
00700              2TO BALANCE THE POPULATION AND FOOD SUPPLY.'/)
00800              WRITE(5,12)
00900      12      FORMAT(5X,'A) INCREASE FOOD PRODUCTION.... ',/,5X,'
01000              1FOOD PRODUCTION IS EXPECTED TO INCREASE AT A CONSTANT
01100              2ANNUAL',/,5X,'RATE OF 89 TONS PER YEAR.  WITH A
01200              3CONCERTED EFFORT, HOWEVER,',/,5X,'THIS FIGURE CAN BE
01300              4INCREASED UP TO A MAXIMUM OF  250 TONS PER',/,5X,
01400              5'YEAR UNTIL ALL THE ARABLE LAND IS CULTIVATED.'/)
01500              WRITE(5,13)
01600      13      FORMAT(5X,'B) RATION THE FOOD SUPPLY.... ',/,5X,'
01700              1THE RESIDENTS OF SHANGRI-LA CURRENTLY CONSUME
01800              2 '/,5X,'AN AVERAGE OF 0.5 TONS OF FOOD PER PERSON
01900              3PER YEAR.'/,5X,'THROUGH GOVERNMENT RATIONING, THIS
02000              4FIGURE CAN'/,5X,'BE REDUCED TO 0.3 TONS PER PERSON PER
02100              5YEAR WITH'/,5X,'NO ADVERSE EFFECTS ON THE HEALTH OF THE
02200              6 POPULATION.'/)
02300              WRITE(5,14)
02400      14      FORMAT(5X,'C) CONTROL OF POPULATION GROWTHRATE....'
02500              1,/,5X,'THE POPULATION GROWTHRATE IS DEPENDENT UPON THE
02600              2 SIZE OF'/,5X,'THE POPULATION AND THE AMOUNT
02700              3 OF FOOD IN STORAGE.  '/,8X,'1. THE POPULATION
02800              4 WILL GROW AT THE RATE OF 5% PER YEAR'/,8X,'
02900              5EVEN IF THERE IS NO FOOD IN STORAGE.  BY
03000              6GRANTING '/,8X,'POSITIVE INCENTIVES, THE RESIDENTS
03100              7 CAN BE MADE TO REDUCE'/,8X,'THIS FIGURE TO 0.5%.
03200              8'/,8X,'2.  FOR EVERY 100 TONS OF FOOD IN STORAGE, THE
03300              9POPULATION'/,8X,'WILL GROW BY AN ADDITIONAL 20 PEO
03400              1PLE PER YEAR.  BY INFORMING THE'/,8X,'RESIDENTS OF THE DANGERS
03500              1 OF THIS PRACTICE, THIS FIGURE CAN '/,8X,'
03600              2BE REDUCED TO A MINIMUM OF 3 PEOPLE PER YEAR PER 100
03700              3 TONS OF FOOD'/,8X,'IN STORAGE.'/,8X,'
03800              4( NOTE THAT A FOOD SHORTAGE WILL RESULT IN
03900              5 A FAMINE.)'////)
04000              WRITE(5,300)
04100      300     FORMAT(2X,'IN 1978, THE POPULATION IS 9955.,
04200              1 FOOD PRODUCED IS 4190. TONS,'/,2X,' AND THE FOOD
04300              2 IN STORAGE IS 3488. TONS.'///)
04400      18      WRITE(5,20)
04500      20      FORMAT(1X,'DO YOU WANT TO INCREASE FOOD PRODUCTION?')
04600              READ(5,21)J
04700      21      FORMAT(1A1)
04800              IF(J.EQ.'N')GO TO 30
04900      19      WRITE(5,22)
05000      22      FORMAT(1X,'HOW MANY ADDITIONAL TONS OF FOOD TO BE PROD
05050              1UCED PER YEAR?')
05100              READ(5,23)C2
05200      23      FORMAT(F5.0)
05300              IF(C2.GT.250.)GO TO 100
05350              IF(C2.LT.89.)GO TO 100
05360              GO TO 139
05375      30      C2=89.
05400      139     WRITE(5,31)
05500      31      FORMAT(1X,'DO YOU WANT TO RATION THE FOOD SUPPLY?')
05600              READ(5,32)R
05700      32      FORMAT(1A1)
05800              IF(R.EQ.'N')GO TO 40
```

```
05900    29      WRITE(5,33)
06000    33      FORMAT(1X,'HOW MANY TONS OF FOOD PER PERSON PER YEAR?')
06100            READ(5,34)C5
06200    34      FORMAT(F4.2)
06300            IF(C5.GT.0.5)GO TO 105
06350            IF(C5.LT.0.3)GOSQ TO 105
06360            GO TO 138
06375    40      C5=0.5
0640SQ0  138     WRITE(5,41)
06500    41      FORMAT(1X,'DO YOU WANT TO REDUCE THE POPULATION
06600            1 GROWTH RATE?')
06700            READ(5,42)P
06800    42      FORMAT(1A1)
06900            IF(P.EQ.'N')GO TO 159
07000            WRITE(5,44)
07100    44      FORMAT(1X,'BY MAKING IT LESS SENSITIVE TO THE
07200            1 FOOD SUPPLY?')
07300            READ(5,42)S
07400            IF(S.EQ.'N')GO TO 47
07500    39      WRITE(5,45)
07600    45      FORMAT(1X,'HOW MANY ADDITIONAL PEOPLE PER YEAR
07700            1PER 100 TONS OF FOOD IN STORAGE?')
07800            READ(5,46)C3
07900    46      FORMAT(F5.0)
08000            IF(C3.GT.20.)GO TO 110
08050            IF(C3.LT.3.)GO TO 110
08060            GO TO 149
08075    47      C3=20.
08100    149     WRITE(5,48)
08200    48      FORMAT(1X,'FOR NO FOOD SURPLUS, WHAT % POPULATION
08300            1GROWTH RATE DO YOU DESIRE?')
08400            READ(5,49)C1
08500    49      FORMAT(F2.0)
08600            IF(C1.GT.5)GO TO 115
08650            IF(C1.LT.0.5)GO TO 115
08655            GO TO 50
08660    159     C3=20.
08670            C1=5.
08700    50      DT=1.
08800            T=0.
08900            Y=1978.+T
09000            P=9955.
09100            FC=C5*P
09200            FP=4190.
09300            FS=3488.
09400            WRITE(5,25)C2,C5,C3,C1
09500    25      FORMAT(1X,'FOOD PRODUCTION TO INCREASE BY',
09600            1F5.0,' TONS PER YEAR.',/1X,'FOOD CONSUMPTION TO BE',
09700            2F4.2,' TONS PER PERSON PER YEAR.',/1X,'POPULATION TO
09800            3INCREASE BY ',F3.0,' PEOPLE PER YEAR FOR
09900            4EACH 100 TONS OF STORED FOOD.',/1X,'POPULATION TO
10000            5INCREASE BY ',F4.2,'% FOR NO STORED FOOD.'//)
10100            WRITE(5,63)
10200    63      FORMAT(1X,'ARE YOU SATISFIED WITH THESE POLICIES?')
10300            READ(5,64)L
10400    64      FORMAT(1A1)
10500            IF(L.EQ.N)GO TO 18
10510            WRITE(5,81)
10520    81      FORMAT(///25X,'FORECAST')
10600            WRITE(5,82)
```

```
10700   82      FORMAT(////1x,4X,'YEAR',4X,'POPULATION',4X,'CONSUMED',
10800           14X,'PRODUCED',4X,'SURPLUS/SHORTAGE'/)
10900           WRITE(5,230)Y,P,FC,FP,FS
11000   83      DO 250 I=1,36
11100           DO 150 K=1,2
11200           IF(FS.GT.0)GO TO 85
11300           PGR=(C1*P+200*FS)/100.
11400           GO TO 90
11500   85      PGR=(C1*P+C3*FS)/100.
11600   90      FPR=C2
11700           P=P+PGR*DT
11750           IF(P.LT.0.)GO TO 135
11800           FC=C5*P
11900           FP=FP+FPR*DT
11950           IF(FP.LT.12000.)GO TO 95
11975           FP=12000.
12000   95      FSR=FP-FC
12100           FS=FS+FSR*DT
12200           T=T+DT
12300           Y=1978+T
12400   150     CONTINUE
12500   200     WRITE(5,230)Y,P,FC,FP,FS
12600   230     FORMAT(4X,F6.0,3F12.0,6X,F12.0)
12700   250     CONTINUE
12800           GO TO 96
12900   100     WRITE(5,121)
12950   121     FORMAT(1X,'MUST BE BETWEEN 89. AND 250.')
13000           GO TO 19
13100   105     WRITE(5,122)
13150   122     FORMAT(1X,'MUST BE BETWEEN 0.30 AND 0.50')
13200           GO TO 29
13300   110     WRITE(5,123)
13350   123     FORMAT(1X,'MUST BE BETWEEN 3. AND 20.')
13400           GO TO39
13500   115     WRITE(5,124)
13550   124     FORMAT(1X,'MUST BE BETWEEN 0.50 AND 5.00')
13600           GO TO 47
13650   135     WRITE(5,140)
13675   140     FORMAT(///1X,'SHANGRI-LA IS NO MORE. ALL HAVE PERISHED'///)
13700   96      WRITE(5,125)
13800   125     FORMAT(///1X,'DO YOU WANT TO TRY AGAIN?')
13900           READ(5,126)S
14000   126     FORMAT(1A1)
14100           IF(S.EQ.'Y')GO TO 18
14500   160     CALL EXIT
14600           END
```

Case 012/2

ADMISSIONS POLICY, HARRISON UNIVERSITY

Each year the Admissions Office of Harrison University must select enough qualified applicants to matriculate a freshman class of the desired size. Predicting the yield (the percentage of students who will accept Harrison's offer of admission) involves the gathering and weighing of information from many sources.

In the past, these projects have usually been accurate to within plus or minus 60 to 100 students out of about 4000 total enrollment, and have presented no particular problem. In the event that the entering class is slightly less than the projected figure, the difference can usually be made up from the waiting list; if the entering class is slightly larger than the projected figure, this difference can be absorbed into the normal operation of the university. If, however, the class size deviates either way by large amount, action is required.

From May to December, 1980, the staff of the Admissions Office was involved in the recruiting of desirable applicants for September 1981. Applications from prospective students began arriving in October 1980 until the deadline date, February 1, 1981. At the final count, these applications totaled 7164, an increase of 14.6% (913) over the previous year.

The Admissions Office, working with the Office of the Dean of Students, attempts to admit a class of the desired size. As the year progresses, this desired class tends to change its size due to student drop-outs, transfers, early graduations, etc. The previous year, for instance, the size initially desired for the class entering in September, 1980 was 900. This was later increased by the Dean of Students to 1100; in April it reached 1175. The number that actually matriculated was 1225. This had been the pattern for many of the previous years: the desired class size increased as the year went on. This year, however, the desired class size was first set at 1075. It fluctuated up and down slightly during the year, and ended up again at 1075. (This target figure was rounded upward to 1100 by the Admissions Office.)

Before April 12, 1980, 290 early-decision applicants were admitted, and after that date, 2613 additional letters of acceptance were sent. Last year the yield for non-early-decision applicants was 31%, whereas this year it increased to 42%, or 1110 students.

The freshman class entering Harrison University in September 1980 numbered 1400, which was 300 more than the Admissions Office projected. This excess has been attributed to a variety of possible causes, including that Harrison's new president projects a dynamic image that attracts more students; the Admissions Office, under new leadership, has been more aggressive at recruiting new students; and there is a 5% increase in applications nationally. Regardless of the cause, the situation required that the universtiy make several important decisions. Additional housing? More staff? Increase the size of the next entering class, or compensate for this year's overage by a reduction in the size of the next entering class? What is the projected size for next year's entering class? As an administrator of Harrison University, you are to formulate a plan of action that will result in a stable student population in an atmosphere of academic excellence.

Index

241